'An indispensable book for understanding a practice that has moved as an undercurrent through art for nearly a century, challenging artists and critics to reconsider the enduring, urgent question: what is art for?'

Tania Bruguera, artist and activist

'With concrete examples and grounded Liverpudlian wit, John Byrne presents a clear, accessible and timely case for why the concept of Useful Art can provide an antidote to, and a way out of, the systems that envelop us.'

Alistair Hudson, Chairman, ZKM | Center for Art and Media Karlsruhe

'An articulate and generous guide to art's potential in a world of exploitative value-capture, illustrated by detailed descriptions of a network of transnational art projects initiated within the spaces prised open by artists and co-workers in order to imagine and practise quotidian acts of utopian transformation.'

Andrea Phillips, Professor, Northumbria University & BALTIC Centre for Contemporary Art

'John Byrne offers us a highly engaging and accessible insider's view of the Useful Art movement. An elucidating and enriching read.'

Giles Smith, Assemble

'With his stacks of convincing stories-as-arguments, John Byrne's Useful Art might be the closest attempt from the English-speaking world to date to capture the original understanding of seni (Indonesian for art), which is neither autonomous nor binary. Reading this book will convince you that we have not lost everything. Yet.'

Farid Rakun, ruangrupa

'Culture, resistance, community: Byrne has written an essential wayfinder that shows us how Useful Art can challenge the neoliberal occupation of our lives, drawing on global ideas to "dig where you stand" for change.'

Owen Griffiths, artist

Useful Art

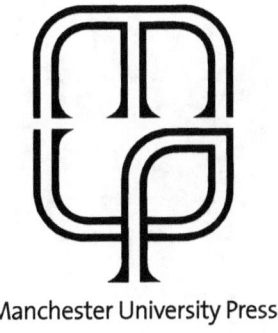

Manchester University Press

Useful Art

How activist artists can change the world

John Byrne

MANCHESTER UNIVERSITY PRESS

Published by Manchester University Press
Oxford Road, Manchester, M13 9PL

www.manchesteruniversitypress.co.uk

British Library Cataloguing-in-Publication Data
A catalogue record for this book is available from the British Library

ISBN   978 1 5261 8154 1   hardback
ISBN   978 1 5261 8157 2   paperback

First published 2026

EU authorised representative for GPSR:
Easy Access System Europe, Mustamäe tee 50, 10621 Tallinn, Estonia
gpsr.requests@easproject.com

Typeset
by New Best-set Typesetters Ltd

To Rosena, my pole star

Contents

Figures

List of figures

Acknowledgements

I'd like to thank Emma Brennan of Manchester University Press for believing in, editing and driving this project with such wit, engagement and collaboration. I'd also like to thank Alun Richards, again of Manchester University Press, for all his post-production care and attention.

Over the last twenty years or so, I've also had the privilege of working alongside, collaborating with and being continually inspired by all those artists, curators, thinkers, doers, makers and activists who have, in one way or another, helped me to think otherwise and who, in turn, have made this book and its ideas possible: Alistair Hudson, Adam Sutherland, Karen Guthrie, Paul Sullivan, Charles Esche, Annie Fletcher, Stephen Wright, Steven ten Thije, Tania Bruguera, Franco Berardi, Alessandra Saviotti, Gemma Medina Estupiñán, Nick Aikens, Jonas Staal Renzo Martens, Kuba Szreder, Elinor Morgan, November Paynter, Aida Sánchez de Serdio Martín, Adela Železnik, Owen Griffiths, Jo Marsh, Barto Bartolomeus, Keina Konno, Kartika Menon, Keijiro Suzuki, Satoshi Ikeda, Farid Rakun, Angga Wijaya, Suzanne Lacy, Valiana Aguilar, Tom Murphy, Brit Jurgensen and Samantha Jones. Also, I'd like to thank

Acknowledgements

Liverpool John Moores University for providing me with the sabbatical that gave me the time to write this book, and to my colleagues and students whose creativity and curiosity have always inspired me to think beyond the current limitations of art and design.

Introduction: is it art, and are they artists?

I'm standing in a queue waiting for a pie. To be more precise, I'm waiting in a queue for a 'vegan scouse' pie, from Homebaked.[1] It's a match night. As a Liverpool Football Club supporter and long-term season-ticket holder, this visit to Homebaked has become part of my pre-match routine. There are several reasons why I choose to queue for my pre-match pie at Homebaked, which may seem so far to have little or nothing to do with art. First is proximity. Homebaked sits across the road from the famous Kop end of Anfield stadium, where I have my seat. Second, Homebaked do a very good (award-winning) pie. Third, my match-day visit to Homebaked is a time and a place (both physically and mentally) when I can think through some of the complex intersections between my life, my identity, my job (my own work and/or labour), my location and their relationship to broader issues of politics, economics, environment and art – and all of this through the lens of Useful Art.

If this sounds a little grand, and even fanciful, allow me to explain. Homebaked, whose website states their aim of regenerating the locality 'brick by brick and loaf by loaf', is a Community Land Trust which sits on the boundary between Everton and

Liverpool (the council wards, that is, not just the football teams) in the north-west of England. It started its life in 2010 as the project '2up2down', a Liverpool Biennial Commission for the artist Jeanne van Heeswijk.[2] Initially, Heeswijk rented the property as a space in which to invite residents to think through the future of their community on their own terms. This was at a time when much of the local area, including the former bakery that Heeswijk was renting for the site of the '2up2down' project, was condemned for demolition.

During 2up2down's use of the site – as a hub for public discussion and planning – people began to pop in and ask if they could still buy bread. This, in turn, led to the reimagining of the '2up2down' project as both a community-led bakery and also as a ground-up strategy for redeveloping and revitalising the street that '2up2down' (now Homebaked) is on, as a multi-use business, education and affordable housing project.

Based on the belief that 'we all deserve to live well',[3] Homebaked now provides food and employment in an area previously identified as a 'market failure' and which had, in 2002, been designated as a Housing Market Renewal area by the UK government. As an example of Heeswijk's conviction that 'art can create "fields of interaction" that build relationships and trigger debates that can assist people to shape their surroundings', the project continues to have multiple and interesting effects on those who use it.[4] So as well as being a place to buy pies on a match night – and a place to think of the complex relationships between art, locality, community and economy – I have also used Homebaked as a supplier of pies for a range of art-based events.

I have also frequently used Homebaked as an example of Useful Art, when talking to undergraduate and postgraduate

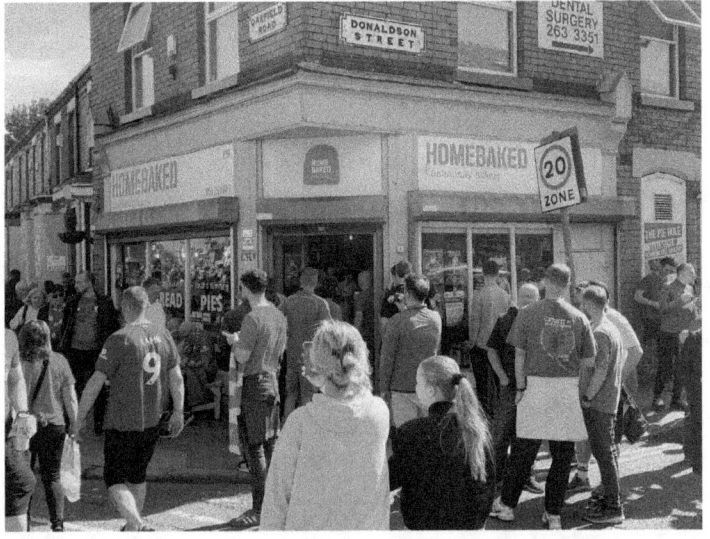

0.1 Homebaked on match day, 27 April 2025. Image courtesy of the author

students as part of my role as Professor of Useful Art at Liverpool John Moores University. And of course, I'm using Homebaked again now as the first example of Useful Art in the Introduction to this book. This is for two key reasons. First, Homebaked offers a clear example of how Useful Art operates, or what it might 'look' like. It operates on a '1:1 scale', that is, as a working bakery that functions in the real world. Second, Homebaked does not use the conventions which would normally allow us to recognise it as an artwork in a museum or civic space. As can be seen, Homebaked illustrates the kinds of ways that Useful Art questions and problematises some of our fundamental common-sense understandings of what art is or might become.

3

Because of this, spending a little time at the beginning of this book confronting the elephant in the room – the question of whether or not Useful Art is art at all – might allow us to clear some of the issues which stand in the way of thinking through Useful Art as an activist tool of social, economic and political change. In doing so, we will also be able to approach the question of Useful Art in a more open, flexible and nuanced way. So I'll begin by asking three questions – which I've developed over the years through numerous seminars, workshops and conversations with artists, colleagues, collaborators and students – that allow us to begin to understand the possibilities of Useful Art in ways that escape the gravitational pull of clichéd art thinking.

Is Useful Art art?

'Is Useful Art art?' is the key question and the best place to start thinking about Useful Art. It challenges us to rethink what art, as we know it or knew it to be, can become. The inescapable binarism (art or not art) of this question is the biggest clue here. And the best way to start thinking beyond outmoded notions of genius artists, who produce unique artworks, is to question where we came across these ideas in the first place.

On reflection, there is a lot about 'art' that we just accept without really thinking much about it. If you spend some time scratching away at this you will eventually find that most of the 'truths' about art that we hold so dear are quite vague and historically specific (emerging from the eighteenth century onwards) and simply have not been shared by all people throughout the ages. As has been true throughout human history, the boundaries of what art is are up for negotiation and change. Thinking this way is to see art as a live and active process that you can have a say in. And if it is just as creative an act to instigate social change as it is to make a picture or a sculpture, then Useful Art also allows for a wider definition of what art can do.

What can Useful Art do?

Thinking of what art can do usually depends on the idea that for something to be 'art' some manifestation of the creative act must be left behind – captured in an object or specific happening, such as a painting, sculpture or performance. More often than not, this is an aesthetic quality which is extracted by audiences or spectators who view the original artwork in appropriate surroundings (usually a derivative of the museum or gallery). But if Useful Art is about initiating and co-producing real-world projects – as opposed to symbolic representations and objects of art – it can also be a tool of real-world social empowerment.

Of course, terms like real-world social empowerment can often seem like they are referring to large-scale social, political and economic change – but what if Useful Art could help us to begin making those changes on a more manageable and incremental scale? Among other things, Useful Art has the potential to help us make changes which positively affect our health and mental well-being – enabling us to take back some control of individual and social lives which seem lost within the condition of neoliberal occupation. The act of making and doing together, or of living a life more artfully, can (some might say) be enough of an impactful act to begin reclaiming some level of agency over our lives. And if this is so, then Useful Art also allows for a wider and more flexible definition of who or what artists, participants and users can be.

Who can be a Useful Artist?

Continuing the theme of superficial assumptions about art, a closer inspection of the role and function of artists soon reveals a set of shared, vague and often outmoded clichés and ideas about who artists are, what they do and why. We are all familiar with the romantic idea of the struggling artist, rejecting society and money, ridiculed for their work (which is almost always 'ahead of its time') and recognised only after their untimely death. Again, these underpinning ideals are both vague and historically specific (and some people within the multi-billion-dollar globalised art industry do make lots of money as artists.) But if Useful Art is the instigation of social projects or processes that are intended to change real-world conditions for the better, and which are made, propagated and contributed to by many users across time, then the simple distinction between artist and audience begins to erode – artists become users and users become artists. And, if this is the case, then the idea that we can all be artists doesn't necessarily mean that we all have to make the equivalents of paintings or sculptures. Instead, artists and/or users can reappropriate, reactivate and remake Useful Art as shared tools of activism and resistance from within the condition of neoliberal occupation.

Homebaked, as an example of Useful Art, doesn't follow the protocols of presentation or re-presentation that allow us to understand that it is supposed to be art. It is not a painting, a drawing, a print, a photograph, an installation, a performance or a concept. It is, straightforwardly, a bakery and a social enterprise: a local business and a place for experimenting with how we might use art as a means for developing and enacting forms of ground-up social activism. It is 'Useful' Art because it does not 'represent' anything other than itself. It does not represent or re-present a person or thing in the real world, nor does it use the currently established protocols of art to represent, re-present or propose an idea of how that real world could be different.

Homebaked, for instance, doesn't need to be seen in a museum or gallery for us to understand it as art. It doesn't have a certificate of ownership or authentication. Nor does it need to be seen solely as the work of the artist Jeanne van Heeswijk. Because of this, Homebaked escapes the framing and capture mechanisms of the art world (or at least the framing and capture mechanisms of the art world as we currently know it or knew it to be). It exists and operates as Useful Art on a 1:1 scale. Or, to put this another way, as Useful Art Homebaked does not have to fulfil any other function than being itself – it does not have to belong to a museum or gallery, nor does it have to sit accessibly in a designated civic space. So Homebaked flags up some of the key assumptions that we have in the Global North about what art actually is, or what kind of thing it is that art should do. Clearly, making sense of something like Homebaked can't be done by simply stretching our current understanding of art beyond the gallery space and into the environment of a working bakery.

So how, we might ask, is it possible to encounter, think about, make or share Useful Art projects such as Homebaked if it is impossible to 'see' them in the way we might conventionally understand art to be? Answering this question is, in a sense, one of the purposes of this book. By asking how activist artists can change the world, we are also asking how Useful Art can become both a toolkit and a process for making those changes happen. In doing so, we are also asking how we might begin to renegotiate our relationships to what art now is, or to what it might become.

Useful Art

One way of beginning this process has already been offered by the artist Tania Bruguera via her collaborative project 'The Association of Arte Útil'. Growing out of a series of workshops at the Queens Museum of Art in New York in 2010, and developed over the following years via a series of instigations, installations, workshops and exhibitions (such as 'The Museum of Arte Útil' at the Van Abbemuseum in 2013, which we will look at more closely in Chapter 3), the Association of Arte Útil has developed eight criteria which should be taken into account for either initiating or evaluating Useful Art projects. According to these criteria, an Arte Útil or Useful Art project should:

1 Propose new uses for art within society
2 Use artistic thinking to challenge the field within which it operates
3 Respond to current urgencies
4 Operate on a 1:1 scale
5 Replace authors with initiators and spectators with users
6 Have practical, beneficial outcomes for its users
7 Pursue sustainability
8 Re-establish aesthetics as a system of transformation

Seen like this, Useful Art provides us with a way of changing the world together, a means by which we can think and make our way out of, or through, our current condition of neoliberal occupation. I believe that Useful Art can enable us to grasp a very different way of looking at how and why we might want to use art as an active tool of social change. After all, if we consider inverting the usual revolutionary cry that everybody can be an artist and, instead, say that everyone can use and share art as an open-source toolkit for instigating and activating real-world change, then things might begin to subtly shift.

This book contains five chapters, each of which is organised into a series of related sections. Each of these five chapters (and indeed some of the corresponding sections) can be read on their own, or in an alternative order. Overall, the aim of this book is to provide a step-by-step guide by which the reader might more clearly understand, and thereby be able to actively deploy Useful Art as a tool for participation within the struggle that now faces us all.

The first chapter, 'Counter-neoliberalism: Useful Art and social change', delves into that struggle, seeking to put Useful Art within the context of the recent history of money and globalisation, and the way these things have affected the art world in particular and our lives in general. Beginning with the example of the architecture group Assemble winning the Turner Prize in 2015, my key argument in this section is that we now live within the condition of a globalised neoliberal occupation, and that the abiding logic of this occupation – the financialisaton of all activities, both work and leisure, into measurable and interchangeable/exchangeable commodities – is the condition that we must resist and subvert.

I'm also going to argue that there is no longer an 'other' space to occupy – a kind of alterity, represented by art and museum or gallery spaces – in which we can simply imagine an alternative. Instead, I'm going to argue that we must begin to use art, museums and galleries as tools and sites of activist encounter, and begin to build real alternatives to our condition of neoliberal occupation on both a local and a global scale. In doing so, I will look at the shifting role of art as we knew it to be (as a form of symbolic representation), and suggest that Useful

Art can offer us a shared resource for using art otherwise – as a means to disrupt the flows and circuits of the all-encompassing and pervasive forms of global networked neoliberalism that currently occupy the very limits of our possibility and imagination. In order to do this, I will spend some time looking at how certain key historical, social, political and economic shifts which have taken place over the last fifty years or so have led us to the situation of cultural impasse where we now find ourselves.

Chapter 2, 'Remapping the network: 1:1 Scale Practice and artistic activism', begins by looking at ways in which the metaphor of mapping itself, and particularly 1:1 Scale Mapping, may give us some clues as to how we might deploy Useful Art as a tool. Beginning with philosopher Steven Wright's account of what 1:1 Scale Art Practice might be – in which he reuses the Lewis Carroll story of a map so big it would cover the earth – I will look at two other uses of similar metaphors/stories (by Martin Heidegger and Jean Baudrillard, respectively) to give a theoretical backdrop to how we might think differently about our own social needs and desires.

I will then follow this with a brief overview of 1:1 Scale Art Practice as it began to emerge from the 1970s onwards, through the examples of Suzanne Lacy, Jeanne van Heeswijk and Theaster Gates, to show successful models for the radical rethinking of the role, function and purpose of art as a form of collective and activist resistance. I will also explore some of the recent work being developed by the Welsh artist and community activist Owen Griffiths, whose work with gardens, pottery and citizen-led urban design is linking up with the gallery space Tŷ Pawb in Wrexham (via the development of a community garden and micro-business) as a means to illustrate how activations of 1:1 Scale Useful Art Practice address specific local needs (or 'urgencies') by co-creating solution-focused community and collaboration. In doing so I will also unpack two reusable conceptual toolkits, 'Digging Where You Stand' and 'Taking it to Market', which offer ways that anyone can explore the radical possibility of 1:1 Scale Useful Art Practice.

Chapter 3, 'Useful Art and the Useful Museum', will examine some of the ideals, principles and implications of the Association of Arte Útil. This is a growing global network of artists and activists (or 'artivists'), instigated by the artist Tania Bruguera as a result of her long-term project 'Immigrant Movement International'.[5] More specifically, this section will begin to examine the legacy of 'The Museum of Art Útil' project, which subsequently took place as a collaboration between Bruguera and the Van Abbemuseum (from December 2013 to March 2014) and which set out to reimagine what a museum of the future might be like if it were to focus on the instigation, rather than simply the display, of Useful Art projects.

Then, I will outline some of the key themes and issues that arose from this project surrounding the existing relationship between museums, galleries, art and use (or usership), and explain how this exhibition eventually led to the idea of 'The Constituent Museum' – a new form of collaborative museum that would both act as a site for the development and instigation of activist solutions to real-world problems, and would set out to collect relationships rather than objects. Key to this will be an introduction to and analysis of 'The Association of Arte Útil Archive', which acts as both an online and offline resource of 1:1 Scale Useful Art Projects which can be reused and repurposed as tools for useful change.

Chapter 4, 'Useful Art and use value', uses the example of Grizedale Arts and the complex of projects they have instigated over the past twenty-four years to examine the historical precedents for developing a use value-based theory of Useful Art. Introducing some of the critical and theoretical resources that were offered by Jacques Rancière and Franco Berardi during the 'Autonomy' project (which ran at the Van Abbemuseum from 2008 to 2012), I will argue for the development of an activist Useful Art Practice that would need to be evaluated in terms of its use value as opposed to its aesthetic value.

The key example in this chapter will be 'The Farmers Arms' – a project in which a disused village pub is being repurposed and reimagined as a way of bringing re-employment and reconnection back to the village of Lowick Green in Ulverston. Rather than simply describing this project, this chapter will seek to establish how this example of Useful Art Practice (a crowd-funded hub, resulting in the collaboration of craftspeople, designers, artists, local businesspeople and volunteers) can be 'read' and evaluated as an example of Useful Art. I will then go on to develop the argument that the activation of Useful Art also demands a corresponding theory and practice (or praxis) of Useful Art that can only be fully understood as use value rather than aesthetic value.

Finally, Chapter 5, 'Useful Art and the power of the local', will argue that Western/ Global North cultural institutions should look towards non-Western/Global South forms of collaborative politics (such as the 'Democratic Confederalism' of Abdullah Öcalan) as a means to rethink their relationships to Useful Art and decolonisation. Useful Art offers us a means to rethink and recalibrate our traditional relationships to art, artwork and use, and such rethinking and redoing would also offer us the opportunity to begin developing longer-term strategies to learn our way out of our current condition of neoliberal occupation.

Introduction: is it art, and are they artists?

Beginning with the example of documenta fifteen, and ruangrupa's use of the *lumbung* as a new type of open-source production and curation platform, this chapter will go on to examine other key examples of Useful Art praxis that challenge us to renegotiate our current and local relationships to art and activism. These will be the long-term work undertaken by Renzo Martins in his collaboration with the Congolese Plantation Workers Art League, 'The New World Summit' (in which the artist Jonas Staal used 1:1 Scale Art Practice to open a 'People's Parliament of Rojova' as a new form of assembly) and the 'Speculative Library' project, instigated by Barto Bartolomeus at the Yamaguchi Centre for Arts and Media (YCAM), Japan, which combines and collides a range of Useful Art strategies and tactics to activate forms of rethinking and remaking in the city of Yamaguchi and beyond. This chapter also seeks to understand how the open-source praxis of Useful Art can be used to challenge and counteract existing notions that would reduce the idea of localism to nationalism and globalisation to neoliberal occupation.

In the concluding chapter, I look again at how we can activate Useful Art as a tool for change. Taking the example of Suumil Móokt'aan, a Mexican farmers' collective which has used its traditional skills and knowledge bases to evolve an intergenerational learning space, I end with a series of suggestions that readers might consider in the instigation of Useful Art projects in their own communities.

I've written this book very much in the first person, and from my experience of spending twenty years involved in the development of Useful Art. This mode of writing was first suggested to me in a conversation at the Van Abbemuseum with the activist academic Rolando Vázquez of Utrecht University. As one of the instigators and drivers of the annual Decolonial Summer School at the Van Abbemuseum, Rolando proposed that the objective 'we' or beloved academic 'third person' tended to ring with the hollow certitude of colonialism. And that, instead, I should consider a more everyday decolonial strategy – owning my point of view, as one among many, that could be argued with as part of an ongoing conversation. I can claim both knowledge, and often a working experience of the key examples I introduce here, which, I hope, I acknowledge clearly and use as a positive contribution to an evolving and ongoing debate. I also realise that this means that I display, on more than one occasion, a critical bias towards the good they can do within what I argue to be a new and unfolding set of possibilities for the way we use and think about art.

1

Counter-neoliberalism: Useful Art and social change

On 7 December 2015 I was invited by members of the Granby 4 Streets Community to watch the Turner Prize award ceremony with them at Liverpool's Small Cinema. When Assemble were announced as winners, it was like being at a football match when your side scores the winning goal. With a roar, everybody who was there leapt from their chairs, danced, jumped about, hugged each other, punched the air and shouted, 'We've won, we've won.' I have never before or since been to an 'art event' – and certainly not a prizegiving – like it. It wasn't only the refreshing break with art-world protocols – manners, decorum, etiquette – that was so revitalising: it was the collective feeling of participation and ownership that was, frankly, overwhelming. It is an experience that has stuck in my mind, and has also shaped my thoughts, ideas and attitudes to what art is, can be or can become.

Let me explain a little more about this, and perhaps put it, and my response to it, in perspective. First of all, and certainly over the last three decades or so, there has been a shift in the contemporary art world towards the development of long-term and sustainable community-based projects. This shift, or 'Social

Turn', as the art critic and theorist Claire Bishop has framed it, has not been without its problems.[1] For every sensitive, long-term, integrated and impactful project developed between artists and communities across the globe, there have been instances in which artists have been parachuted into communities. Often these communities have been in fashionably 'deprived' areas, and artists have been asked to make short-term projects with them as part of biennials or festivals. Equally often, these art projects have left those participating communities feeling stranded and alienated once their usefulness to the world of contemporary art is done.

Also, and perhaps more difficult to contend with, there has been a growing suspicion that socially engaged art practices are being used, and funded, through changing governmental arts policies, as a form of health and well-being placebo – that is, as a way to make citizens and communities feel better about their predicament without having to implement or support real, systemic or long-term social change. This latter concern – regarding governments, large-scale corporations and businesses who rebrand themselves though their visible support of the arts – has led to the understandable suspicion that 'big society' is using art to do 'the dirty work of neoliberalism' on its behalf.

Alongside this is the suspicion that anybody interested in using art as a radical tool for enabling long-term, ground-up social change to take place might also be complicit with 'centralised government' and the agendas of global corporate capitalism. This has led to recent accusations that 'useful' art is somehow morally, ethically and aesthetically bankrupt, and that those involved in it are complicit in the misuse of art as a utilitarian tool of suppression, coercion and control.

Useful Art and social change

This accusation, of course, misses the possibility that not all uses of art as a radical tool for social change might be the same. Nor might they be undertaken for similar motivations or reasons. Perhaps more tellingly, such an overly simplistic accusation quickly leads to the conclusion that Useful Art is bad and that 'useless' art is good: as if the same governments and global neoliberal corporations had not somehow realised that their support for, and influence over, an increasingly commercialised and privatised contemporary art world would not yield equally favourable results.

The idea that useless art is good and that Useful Art is bad also depends on a shared belief that useless art somehow offers a kind of social, political and economic 'safe haven' that allows us, as a community, to represent ourselves to ourselves and each other with a kind of unregulated critical impunity. Such a view also ignores how successfully the art world has been colonised by the regulatory frameworks of centralised government and its dependence upon neoliberal commercialism – primarily, but by no means exclusively, through sponsorship. It also ignores how the rhetorics of corporate capitalism – that we are all free, flexible and creative individuals, able to make our way successfully in the world if only we work hard enough – have successfully hijacked and weaponised the languages of the radical left (autonomy, equality, self-determination) for their own financialised purposes. So, by default, I would argue that a naïve belief in the idea that useless art is somehow good, and that Useful Art is somehow bad can just as easily lead to an uncritical complicity with those who would seek to misuse art as tool of social control rather than as a tool of emancipation.

Useful Art v. useless art

Take our case in hand – the Granby 4 Streets Community celebrating 'their' win of the 2015 Turner Prize and some of the responses that appeared in the mainstream art press in relation to their collaboration with Assemble.

Granby 4 Streets Community Land Trust (CLT) in Liverpool evolved out of a twenty-year struggle by residents against attempts by local and national government to depopulate and demolish their local community and its infrastructure. At one point, around 2007, when only five houses on one street (Cairn Street) remained occupied, a group of female residents began to develop forms of everyday resistance and activism by moving their lives onto the street: planting flowers, sitting at tables, redecorating boarded-up buildings and, above all, developing a shared knowledge of housing and property law. The Granby 4 Streets CLT was itself formed in 2011 as a not-for-profit community-interest company. Emerging, as they did, from a two-decade-long grass-roots struggle, the CLT successfully lobbied and secured assets from the local authority for redevelopment. As part of this process the CLT also engaged Assemble, a London-based art, architecture and design collective with a proven track record of working closely with communities on long-term projects, to help them develop a vision for regenerating the area.

During this collaboration, in which Assemble worked in partnership with local residents and the CLT to repurpose derelict homes into affordable housing, new projects for developing social spaces, local training and employment opportunities also began to emerge. This included the setting-up of the Granby Workshop, which used local skills and labour, as well as local waste materials – such as rubble from derelict houses – to make products for the new homes that were being built: ceramic tiles, wooden door handles, printed textiles and the signature 'Granby fireplace'. When Assemble were nominated for the Turner Prize in 2015 they took the opportunity, in consultation and collaboration with the community, to build a full-scale replica of the Granby Workshop in Glasgow's Tramway Gallery. Rather than simply being a work of art that would represent the project and the community for visitors to the Turner Prize, Assemble used the opportunity of the exhibition to sell these products to the public on a pre-order basis. This strategy proved

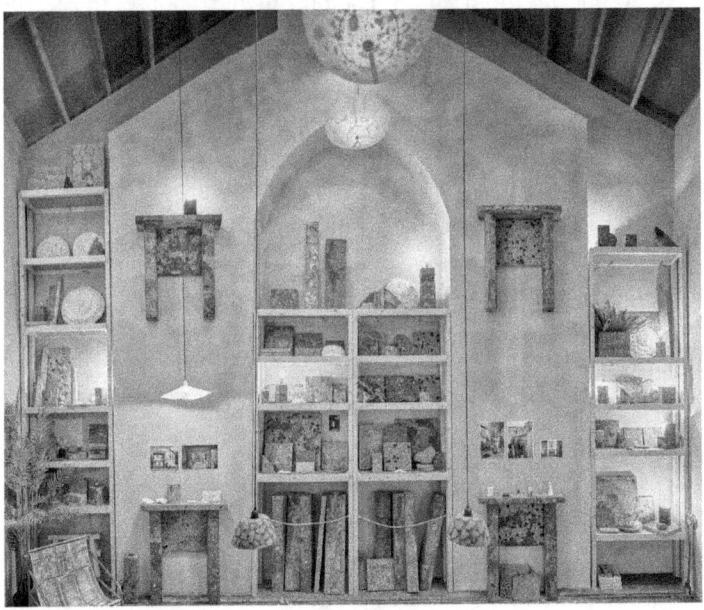

1.1 Assemble's Turner Prize-winning installation at Glasgow's Tramway Gallery, 2015. Image courtesy of Assemble

so successful that, by the beginning of 2016, enough orders had been placed to establish the Granby Workshop as an independent company.

So far so good, but Assemble's winning the 2015 Turner Prize also underscored some of the complex anxieties that are re-emerging within the art world regarding the relationship between Useful Art, utility and use. More specifically, critical reception to Assemble's Turner Prize win highlighted the idea that art's preferred role and function, if it is to remain a critical tool for understanding and rethinking our current condition, is to remain radically useless – thereby resisting neoliberal occupation in a society that is otherwise dominated by exploitation, profit and loss. To put this more simply, Establishment responses to Assemble's Turner Prize win largely claimed that, because it was useful, it could not be art.

This position was clearly illustrated some three days after the Turner Prize announcement, when Morgan Quaintance, one of the two Channel 4 hosts of the televised event, published a post in the *e-flux* journal conversation forum with the title 'Teleology and the Turner Prize or: Utility, the New Conservativism'.[2] In this article, Quaintance, who describes himself as a London-based artist, writer and curator, was chiefly concerned that the award of the prize to an architecture group, and not an artist's collective, was 'about the new conservatism of utility' rather than the question of whether the project was art or not. Instead of looking at more recognisable forms of art-led socially engaged practice, or awarding the Prize to Granby 4 Streets CLT, Quaintance argued that the Turner Prize judges had seemingly made a hollow, tokenistic gesture of pseudo-radical intent, instrumentalising a depoliticised architectural collective in order to drive home a point about Useful Art.[3]

Useful Art and social change

There appear to be two key causes for Quaintance's concern here. First, the possibility of a shift away from the critical concerns of contemporary art practice as he sees it. Second, and simultaneously, a parallel shift towards the idea of Useful Art and the Useful Museum. Epitomising both of these positions was, for Quaintance, the participation of Alistair Hudson as a member of the 2015 Turner Prize jury. Hudson, who had taken over as Director of the Middlesbrough Institute of Modern Art (MIMA) in 2014, is an advocate of both Useful Art and the Useful Museum. For Hudson, the Useful Museum, or Museum 3.0 (both of which I will look at in detail in Chapter 3), would be a place where museum and art alike were made available as shared tools and resources for rethinking and remaking our relationship to society.

As I know Hudson personally and have worked closely with him on the development and implantation of some of these ideas for close on twenty years, I have to declare an interest. But I also know that the intention of Hudson, and of Useful Art and the Useful Museum, is not to simply make people happier with their current lot. Instead, it is to provide a toolkit with which both individuals and communities can take some control back of their lives on a local scale and, in doing so, provide real alternatives to the financialisaton of their lives and relationships by centralised government and capitalism more generally.

However, in Quaintance's hands, this ambition to use art as tool for enacting radical and real-world social change – in which the museum is repurposed as a useful and active site within which diverse communities can collaborate – is doomed to be a politically vacuous failure. Instead, he argues that such a Useful Museum would simply appear 'like a huge, tool filled, multi-floor hardware shop' whose only role would be to present visitors with 'an array of objects whose sole purpose is to perform some utilitarian function'.[4] While it seems that Quaintance would be OK with the Useful Art approach if it were left as the curatorial imperative of a single museum director (in this case Hudson) – as a means of 'selling audiences short to increase footfall and broaden audience reach' – he is much more concerned by the detrimental influence, as he sees it, that such ideas may have had upon the Turner Prize jury during their selection of Assemble as winners.[5]

For Quaintance, the award was not only 'a decision that saw non-artists instrumentalised to introduce and legitimise the "useful" ideology'; it was also 'a decision that could have seriously detrimental ramifications for British contemporary art'.[6] This is because he believes only the trained artist, working from a position of critical distance, and not an architectural practice or its equivalent, is capable of exercising useless non-compliance. To put this another way, he maintains an alternative ideology of uselessness, diametrically opposed to that of Hudson, one in which it is only the artist – as someone who is uniquely able to adopt a position and perspective that is separate from the non-art world of utility and financialisation – who can effectively show us how to resist:

> contemporary art is a critically engaged field that, for the most part, produces critically engaged actors who are uncomfortable with state power and its various methods of citizen subjection – this is nowhere more prevalent, diligently observed or else thoroughly critiqued than in socially engaged practice. Because Assemble are not and do not claim to come from this discipline, because they are not critically engaged, and because they are a firm of architects employed to creatively fulfil a design brief,

however open, theirs is an acritical almost completely depoliticised response to a highly politicised social situation.[7]

While I would completely agree with Quaintance, in so far as most contemporary artists are critically engaged and uncomfortable with state power, I have difficulties with the overly simplistic claim that other practitioners, in this case Assemble, are not. Nor am I convinced by the implicit suggestion that only politicised artists could successfully work with a community like Granby 4 Streets CLT to produce radical alternatives to the political, social and economic status quo. However, I would concede that there are far more important things than personal differences of opinion at stake here. What Quaintance's anxieties understandably illustrate is a concern that art itself is becoming instrumentalised and that, as a consequence, it will lose its critical role and function in the face of a predatory and aggressive globalised economy – one which is increasingly capable of capturing, repackaging and reselling radicality as if it were any other desirable commodity on the shelf.

In the light of this, as I have also argued, it is little wonder that forms of Useful Art practice, such as Assemble's multi-purpose and open-ended collaboration with Granby 4 Streets CLT, pose such difficulties to an art world that can only see or read the symbolic, rather than the operational, as art. In fact, trying to 'stretch over' the existing classificatory logics of what is or isn't art, or what art should or should not do, beyond the conventional confines of the museum or gallery and into the real world, does little more than highlight the key preoccupation now facing the art world – that of maintaining a grip on what it sees as its traditional role of offering a clear-sighted, untarnished and critically autonomous perspective on the world beyond its own confines.

The fact that projects such as Assemble's collaboration with Granby 4 Streets CLT need to be repackaged as 'installations' by 'artists' in order to win awards like the Turner Prize shows up the incapacity of the current art world to contend with the complexities of the real world that it purports to represent. There is an uncomfortable contradiction at play here. On one hand, there is the idea that critical art, by its very nature, should somehow adopt a position away from, or outside, the current social, political and economic milieu. On the other, there is the simultaneous idea that art's role and function is to critically present or re-present this other, outside world.

This contradiction allows Quaintance to caricature Assemble's reconstruction of their Granby Street workshop for the Turner Prize exhibition as 'a showroom for the display of bespoke, domestic product design, with no reference to the political or social situation that led to their employment by the Granby Community Land Trust (CLT)'. In fact, I would argue, it is precisely because of this residual requirement, for art to always manifest itself in a museum or gallery setting, that Assemble had to install a full-scale re-presentation of their practice in the first place. And this is the point, I would suggest, at which we begin to develop one of the key arguments for this book – that Useful Art poses such a profound challenge to our current systems for understanding what art is or could be become that only a fundamental overhaul of those systems will make them capable of understanding the radical potential of Useful Art. Further to this, I'd also suggest that such an overhaul would need to begin by fundamentally rethinking art's complex and co-dependent relationship to neoliberalism.

Useful Art and social change

Useful Art and neoliberalism

In his 2009 article 'Self-Design and Aesthetic Responsibility', Boris Groys points to a key contradiction that lies at the heart of our relationships to, and understanding of contemporary art.[8] On one hand, he argues that most people would agree that the idea of art as a separate and autonomous category – governed entirely by its own rules and logic, and removed from everyday life – is over. However, Groys also argues that when contemporary art attempts to become political, it finds that the political field has already become aestheticised – our contemporary world understands itself, and represents itself, through and across a constant flux and circulation of images and text.

While this has been the case for more than a century now, it has accelerated over recent decades through the increased availability of social media platforms and handheld/connected devices capable of dealing with high-resolution imagery and film. These devices can make and distribute images and text as well as receive them, and Groys argues that artists now find that their previous historical role – as the image-makers of political and sovereign power – has been usurped. As a result of this, any artist who wants to intervene in the world of contemporary politics has to contend with, and inevitably contribute to this exponentially growing circulation of information.

Astutely, Groys then points towards the mixed feelings that accompany this realisation. On one hand he argues that we applaud ethically motivated attempts by artists who try to escape the traditional confines of the art system (as he calls it), and whose work has had a palpable impact on the world beyond art. On the other, we deplore such attempts when they fail to transcend the aesthetic sphere – 'instead of changing the world,'

Groys contends, 'art only makes it look better'.[9] As a result, Groys suggests, the contemporary art world seems to be in an almost bipolar state of flux, oscillating 'back and forth between hopes to intervene in the world beyond art and disappointment (even despair) due to the impossibility of achieving such a goal'.[10]

Faced with this dilemma, Groys argues that the contemporary artist is forced to choose between two options: either compete head-on with celebrity culture – where the artist, or the image of the artist, becomes at least (if not more) important than the art they actually make – or, on the other, to opt for an alternative – where the artist attempts to 'socially engage' with communities by co-producing artworks with them.

By framing these two alternatives for re-engaging art with the world beyond the art system in this way – either through an attempt to retain the traditional role of the artist in a world of digital celebrity or by foregoing guarantees of artistic authorship in deference to the political potential of collaboration – Groys usefully maps out the key terms and conditions of engagement that underpin any attempts to reconcile the useful/useless art divide. More specifically, the second of these approaches, which has been a curatorial staple for museums and biennials alike since the last decade of the twentieth century, became contentious for its alleged complicity with the financially driven political logic of neoliberalism. And, as we have already seen through my brief examples of 'Homebaked' and Assemble's Turner Prize-winning collaboration with Granby 4 Streets CLT in Liverpool, this concern tends to manifest in the accusation that forms of Useful Art – and by proxy the idea of Useful Art and the Useful Museum – are more public workshop than aesthetic display: utilitarian at best and dangerously apolitical at worst.

Useful Art and social change

As is clear from other reactions to Assemble's 2015 Turner Prize win, the equally oversimplistic alternative to this would be the idea that Useful Art is somehow a critical, politically engaged and financially incorruptible form of alternative to art as we know it or knew it to be. However, as Groys's observations have underlined, there is perhaps something more complex going on here – something that can't be pinned down by the either/ or of Useful Art versus useless art, or the in–out categorisation of non-art or art. And this complexity, I will argue, is less to do with the ability of art to be political or not, and more to do with global neoliberalism itself.

Although the condition of neoliberalism can be hard to clearly define, the idea of Useful Art and the Useful Museum can help us identify neoliberalism more clearly and challenge it. In this process, we will find that there is no longer simply an 'outside' to which the art world can point, or an 'inside' that provides us with the sanctuary of an alternative. It is my belief that our current neoliberal condition is not only the context for the development of Useful Art practice, but that Useful Art practice has developed as one of the only means by which art can be used as an effective tool of counter-neoliberal activism. So, instead of simply thinking from the inside out – of the critical artist stepping outside the art world (only to find that the political field has been aestheticised by digital social media and celebrity) – or from the outside in – of the critical artist bringing instances of the real world into the art system as a means to analyse them more clearly in the laboratory of aesthetic privilege – I would argue that we also have to begin thinking asymmetrically: the previously autonomous art world has already been captured and occupied by a neoliberal logic that thrives on the instru- mentalisation of work or labour.

Useful Art and asymmetric occupation

We have to begin thinking asymmetrically about Useful Art because, within the current condition of global networked neoliberalism, we find ourselves in an age that is dominated by digital commodity exchange – an age in which art, as we know it or knew it to be, is complicit. This is an increasingly online landscape in which objects – whether they be sweaters, retro CDs or vinyl, paintings, footballs, apps, fast-food deliveries, digital downloads, chatbots, AIs or whatever – only have meaning in so far as they can function, at least temporarily, as signs of value within a vertiginous kaleidoscope of endless economic exchange. This is a world of PayPal, internet banking and premium delivery. A world in which online market giants such as Amazon seem to offer us everything right now, at the touch of a screen, with interest-free-credit options already arranged.

This is also a world of the gig economy and the zero-hours contract, a world in which the once romanticised avant-garde dream of the itinerant, jobless, drifting-but-free artist has become the harsh reality of a disenfranchised, fractalised and flexible global labour force. It is also a world in which the once allegedly separate arenas of art and life have been combined together as dystopian nightmare rather than emancipatory dream.[11] Everybody's life, it seems, is dictated by their own continual branding exercise carried out across linked social media platforms which, in turn, reward us with ever-more-targeted advertising and algorithmically induced recommendations to read increasingly short-sighted political rants.[12] It has become a world in which the once-firm distinctions of truth and fiction, reality and lie have become so intermingled it is virtually impossible to take a reasonable stand any more. Yet it is also a world in which climate crisis, energy crisis, rising unemployment and corresponding physical and mental health issues abound. It is a world in which the wealthiest one per cent now reportedly own more than half the world's wealth. It is also a world in which, it seems, everyone now has their own 'aesthetic'.

Without doubt we now find ourselves within a world in which financial instrumentalisation has become a baked-in part of our social, cultural and political (as well, of course, as our economic) DNA. And because of this, it seems almost impossible sometimes to imagine a way of navigating through or out of this morass either together or as individuals. But it is also here that I would argue that art, or more specifically Useful Art, can help, by providing ways in which we can build concrete alternatives.

Before we look at how this might begin to happen in more detail, I would argue that it is also worthwhile reminding ourselves of how, and how quickly, this new historical epoch of neoliberalism has manifested itself. Rather than something we can step outside, I'm also going to argue that this moment of crisis is best understood as our current condition of neoliberal occupation. While some may find this term overly dramatic, I would argue that understanding global neoliberalism as a condition of occupation allows us to begin coming to terms with the complexity and asymmetry of the problems we face.

Neoliberal occupation is not something we can simply step aside from or evade capture by. Nor should we surrender to it. And if Useful Art provides us with a series of toolkits for instigating anti-neoliberal challenge and change, it is perhaps worth reminding ourselves that our current conditions are only about fifty years old. It is only by reminding ourselves of this that we can begin imagining ways in which those conditions could be made otherwise. And it is also at this point that I feel it necessary to clarify another key point of this book – that Useful Art is neither a consequence nor a function of these conditions. Instead, I'm going to argue that Useful Art provides us with a toolkit for resisting or subverting neoliberal occupation, whereas useless art has become so co-opted into the current mechanisms that it no longer offers any real alternative.

The condition of neoliberal occupation

Our current condition of neoliberal occupation can often appear as a vague and abstract shibboleth – something simply too big to imagine, comprehend or think through.[13] Because of this it can be tempting to dismiss it as an oversimplification and a convenient barrier – a shorthand for debates and circumstances we might find uncomfortable and undesirable and a way to bracket off big business, big pharma, big government, the one per cent, and so on as being something palpably different from us. It can also be tempting to see it as simply a historical development of, or extension to, earlier identifiable epochs of capitalism. This, in turn, can lead to the easy assumption that our condition of neoliberal occupation is, or was, just inevitable.

However, I would argue that there are four key reasons, linked closely to developments that have taken place over the last half a century, that are essential for developing an understanding of what Useful Art is and, also, how activist artists might use it to effect real-world change. First, our current neoliberal occupation provides the social, political and economic context for how the contemporary art world – or 'art system', as Groys defines it – has evolved since the end of the Cold War into a global industry of tourism and leisure. Second, this same condition has become a means by which many define contemporary art in relation to neoliberalism: the idea that art is pure creativity and simply the opposite of capitalism. This in turn gives rise to the naïve idea that the contemporary art system offers a kind of unsullied sanctuary from our condition of neoliberal occupation, from which effective critical oppositions can be launched in the form of useless art.

Third, this way of defining neoliberalism as non-art also offers a means to identify Useful Art as anything that might be complicit with neoliberalism per se. As we have already seen via Morgan Quaintance's response to Assemble winning the Turner Prize, the crude generalisation that Useful Art equates with neoliberalism, and that useless art does not, caricatures the complex and asymmetric conditions of neoliberal occupation. Fourth, and most importantly, an understanding of our current condition of neoliberal occupation also provides the context in which activist artists are developing strategies of Useful Art to challenge neoliberalism on and within its own asymmetrical territories of occupation, capture and control.

In developing this understanding, we can see how Useful Art offers us a way to move beyond the historical legacies of binary thinking around art that have plagued us since the Enlightenment – inside/outside, art/life, useful/useless. This will help us to find more appropriate ways of thinking how Useful Art might be deployed to disrupt, redirect and remake the flows of financialised and instrumentalised logic.

The rise of neoliberal logic in the 1970s and 1980s

I can remember, as a child in the 1970s, a global oil crisis and, in the UK, a seemingly endless era of industrial action, strikes and economic decline. In fairness I can also remember this being the backdrop to incredible music (especially the punk/ DIY revolution of 1976) and a feeling that the world could finally change for the better.[14] So what happened and what went wrong? Perhaps the most simple answer is that, during the late 1960s and early 1970s, a post-Second World War economic boom (in the Western world at least – as the Global North used to call itself), driven largely by the success of the US economy, began to grind to a halt.[15] As a result, the once powerful 'free world' or 'first world' – which modelled itself in social, economic and political opposition to the Communist 'second world' (everywhere else was referred to by the now often misunderstood collective noun 'third world') – began to lose faith in its own narrative of endless technological progress and boundless consumption.

Perhaps the clearest sign of this economic shift was President Nixon's scrapping of the Gold Standard in 1971. This removal of the value of the dollar from its literal equivalent value in gold triggered three main consequences that still affect us today. First, the US was able to begin pump-priming its flagging economy through a process of quantitative easing – this is where a government literally prints more money and uses this to buy stocks, shares and bonds from big banks and the stock market with the aim of stimulating a flagging economy. This was made possible because, after the Gold Standard had been removed, there was no longer a finite limit to government spending based on the physical amount of gold residing in the US reserve.

Second, as the regulated economy became free from the impediment of the 'real' material world – as the value of the dollar was no longer directly linked to the value of the finite base metal, gold – it began its journey towards becoming the abstract and deregulated economy that we know today – one that is governed by the continual fluctuations of purely numerical and digital exchange of stocks and shares. As a result of this the dollar became, and remains, a free-floating currency measured only in relation to the value of other world currencies.

Third, the uncoupling of the dollar's value to the value of gold had the immediate effect of increasing the value of gold and decreasing the value of the dollar which, in turn, hit the oil-producing countries of OPEC (Organization of the Petroleum Exporting Countries) as the dollar was (and remains) the standard currency by which oil is valued by the barrel. In response to this the OPEC countries raised their benchmark oil prices by 70 per cent while agreeing among themselves to reduce oil production. Oil prices quadrupled and an unprecedented global recession ensued, triggering high inflation, high unemployment and the loss of traditional industries.

In the UK, this shift in the world economy led to growing inflation and a demand for increased wages from unionised workers, particularly in the coal and rail industries, which had been nationalised in the UK after the Second World War. These actions, and the corresponding power cuts that followed, led to the implementation of a 'three-day week' in 1973, as Prime Minister Edward Heath sought radical ways to conserve the UK's energy. Less than five years later, simmering tensions between unions belonging to the TUC (Trades Union Congress) and the then Labour government – who had sought to bring in legislation curbing the right of unions to take unofficial action and to reach unofficial local agreements in wage disputes in the early 1970s – led to an unprecedented series of strikes and industrial action.

In the run-up to the 'Winter of Discontent', from 1978 to 1979, another series of inflation-related wage demands, which far exceeded the 5 per cent limit imposed by the Labour government of James Callaghan, saw strike action correspond with one of the coldest winters since records had begun. Car workers, lorry drivers, NHS ancillary staff, refuse collectors and public-sector workers all took action over increased wage demands. In my home city of Liverpool this led to a famous unofficial strike by council-employed gravediggers.

Margaret Thatcher, then leader of the Conservative Party in opposition, took the opportunity to demand that a state of emergency be called by Labour, and that new laws to prevent striking and picketing be implemented. Coupled with a ground-breaking media assault, as the advertising company Saatchi & Saatchi were employed to develop the now famous 'Labour isn't working' campaign, a vote of no confidence in the Labour government led to a snap election in 1979 and a new Conservative government. Once in power, Margaret Thatcher made a clear point of ditching the post-war consensus of industrial nationalisation, trade-union bargaining, government regulation of markets and finance, high tax policies and the maintenance of a strong welfare-state support system which had come to be seen, by many on the left, as an inalienable human right.

The 1980s and the rise of Thatcherism and Reaganomics

If the 1970s was the decade in which the post-Second World War economic boom began to go bust, then the 1980s was the decade in which the foundations for neoliberalism's global dominance were laid. Beginning with the USSR's invasion of Afghanistan and ending in the fall of the Berlin Wall, the decade saw an easing of cold-war tensions between East and West. At the same time, both the Reagan government in the US and the

Thatcher government in the UK implemented radical economic policies aimed at removing government control and legal obligation over business.[16]

The era of Thatcherism and Reaganomics, as it became to be known, was driven by the theoretical belief (and it is worth remembering that neoliberalism began as one theoretical belief among others) that a low-tax economy, coupled with the systematic removal of centralised financial regulation, would encourage entrepreneurship and financial growth.[17] In order to make this happen, it would be the responsibility of government to systematically undo any social reliance on the provision of state welfare and to erode any labour laws that might stand in the way of a cheap and unprotected workforce. Against a background of growing unemployment and continued social unrest, this reinvention of a liberal and laissez-faire economic approach, often pitted against the alleged 'socialism' of the Eastern Bloc countries, played itself out as an aggressive dismantling of trade-union power coupled with the privatisation of previously nationalised industries. In the UK this saw British Steel, British Gas and British Telecom become private companies, floated on the stock market, with a raft of small stakeholder shares made available for public purchase.

The 1980s also saw an aggressive rebranding of individualism and economic autonomy, as both an ethical choice and an aspiration, encouraging a climate of self-interested wealth accumulation and a negative view of any reliance on the State or society. In the UK, the Secretary of State for Employment, Norman Tebbit, famously suggested that the unemployed should get on their bikes and look for work. Similarly, Margaret Thatcher claimed that there was no such thing as community.[18] The results of such upheavals were brutal and divisive. In the early 1980s the spread of racial as well as economic inequality and division saw a wave of riots engulf the UK – in Toxteth, Liverpool, Brixton in London, Handsworth in Birmingham, Chapeltown in Leeds and Moss Side in Manchester. The wholesale upheaval of previously accepted norms, epitomised by the 1984 miners' strike, saw traditional and state-funded industries disappear, and with them, the support networks of community and class identity that had grown around them over previous generations. As manufacturing in the West became too expensive to sustain, cheaper goods began to be imported from newly emerging 'global supply chains'. At the same time, major industries began relocating their sites of production to countries where low labour and material costs could be guaranteed. As a result, unemployment figures peaked, and standards of living fell for many.

As supply-chain economies began to maximise cheap labour forces and newly emerging markets from around the world, many towns and cities, which had established themselves during the Industrial Revolution, began to witness severe economic decline. As an example, in Liverpool the global shift to shipping containerisation led to a sharp decline in its dockside economy which, in turn, led to high unemployment and corresponding social discontent. As a result of this decline, and publicly prompted by the scale of the Toxteth riots of 1981, the UK government was forced to provide an economic redevelopment package to the city and its region. However, instead of this funding being directed to the source of the social unrest, and being used to improve housing and living standards – such as those in Toxteth where, some forty years later, Granby 4 Streets CLT and Assemble would win the Turner Prize for their regeneration initiatives – it was earmarked to be spent on an International Garden Festival and the redevelopment of the Albert Dock complex.

Useful Art and social change

When the Albert Dock first opened in 1846 it was the first brick-built and fireproof warehousing in the world – cutting the unloading and loading of shipping time in half. The fall of these buildings into dereliction during the 1970s provided a symbol of Liverpool's economic decline. Their subsequent repurposing into a visitor and retail destination – reopening to the public in 1984 and attracting the first regional Tate art gallery to locate there in 1988 – was held up by the UK government as an example of the necessary shift from traditional industrial economy to the service industries of tourism and leisure. In turn, this acts as a key example of how post-industrial cities across the world were beginning to reinvent and reposition themselves as cultural hubs within a growing network of global economies.

The shift towards globalised neoliberalism

This shift towards decentralised and deregulated international supply-chain economies, which began in the 1980s, became a truly global network of internationally agreed economic policy after the disintegration of the former Eastern Bloc of Soviet countries. The impact of the collapse of Communism, which was symbolically broadcast around the world in 1989 with the fall of the Berlin Wall, was seismic. Suddenly, a large part of the world's raw materials, agriculture and labour force became available to the West which, in turn, represented itself as the financial victor in the Cold War against Communism. In 1991 this led President Bush to proclaim the optimism of a 'new world order' – a realignment of global trade and financial laws that would ease international economic expansion and make the world a better place.[19] In 1995, the World Trade Organization (WTO) emerged as a transnational mechanism that would help to facilitate and fund global trade realignments that would encourage former Eastern Bloc countries, as well as those of the developing Latin American, Asian and African nations, to adopt business-friendly policies. This was backed up with direct financial aid from the International Monetary Fund (IMF) and World Bank (WB), long-established sister institutions to the newly formed WTO.

Through a series of bond and bailout programmes, the WTO began to send out a clear global neoliberal message: if countries undertook economic reforms in alignment with WTO regulations, then they would receive direct financial help and support. In turn, those countries that wished to join and benefit from WTO membership and regulation had to do so by undertaking financial reforms, based on privatisation, deregulation and subsequent legal reform, that would lead in turn to the expansion of property rights.

On the surface, the idea of the WTO was that neoliberal economic reform would make struggling countries more attractive to foreign investment. The deeper rationale behind these developments was a growing belief that a peaceful new world order would be achieved if these countries adopted the explicitly Western values of liberal economics. So the systematic globalisation and instrumentalisation of neoliberal policies and beliefs began to be implemented as a 'one size fits all' requirement for any country or nation that wanted to trade on favourable terms.

Neoliberalism and the rise of networked culture

If the economic belief which underpinned the 'new world order' provided one of the key pillars of an emerging global neoliberalism, the other was provided by the expansion of global digital networks for the exchange, movement and circulation of money. As early as 1986 the London Stock Exchange had begun to shift the buying and selling of stocks from the physical trading floor to digital brokerage systems. By 1987 this meant that as many digital transactions were taking place per month as had previously happened in a year of face-to-face trading. The acceleration was accompanied by an increase in the speed that stocks and shares could lose their value (as evidenced by 'Black Monday' in 1987, when the London Stock Exchange lost 26 per cent of its value in a single day). During the 1990s, the growth of the internet, or World Wide Web, as it was known at the time (which coincidentally began to materialise in the same year as the collapse of the Berlin Wall) also meant that trading floors around the world could be digitally linked.[20]

In 1989, the English scientist Tim Berners-Lee, who was working at the European Centre for Nuclear Research (CERN), developed a series of now familiar digital protocols (HTML, HTTP and the use of URLs) to link up computers and share knowledge across the world in ways that had previously been unimaginable. Subsequently, the growth of the World Wide Web, and with it access to digital networks which had previously demanded a knowledge of coding protocols, became exponential. The first web page, as would be recognised today, was launched in 1991 by Berners-Lee and contained open-source information about how to write and publish subsequent web pages. By 1992 there were ten websites. By 1996, the year Google launched, there were over two million.

The shift of international trading in stocks and shares to digital platforms and the exponential growth of the internet had the perhaps inevitable effect of paving the way for the availability of online payment and credit. Credit cards had become available to individual consumers as early as the 1960s, and a global network of digital pay points and ATMs began to facilitate the use of both debit and credit cards in the 1980s and 1990s. But it was a global relaxation in national and international credit laws during this period that saw card payments – and a growing culture of buying on credit – begin to replace bank-regulated savings and loan schemes. During the 1990s it also became increasingly possible to use credit cards and bank details to make encrypted purchases directly through the internet to emerging companies such as Amazon (who began trading as an online bookshop in 1995) and eBay (the ubiquitous online auction platform which launched online in the same year). What had started out as an open-source and free digital library of information exchange rapidly became the go-to global mechanism by which companies traded and advertised.

The post '89 emergence of a global art system

After the disintegration of the former Soviet Union in 1991 there seemed, to many, no viable alternative to the advance of global neoliberal economic policies. However, one of the political consequences of post-Soviet globalisation was a growing confla-tion between the post-Second World War dream of an inter-national liberal democracy and the hard-edge policies of neoliberal economics. As Francis Fukuyama famously argued in his 1989 article 'The End of History', the abrupt end of the Cold War had triggered an ideological evolution which signalled a new era: one in which Western forms of liberal democracy would become the world's default governmental system.[21]

At the same time, a loss of faith in the linear narratives and institutional promises of Western modernity – endless progress, seamless advance, equality for all – morphed into the asymmetrical phenomena of a rootless and eclectic postmodern culture. Suddenly all histories, traditions, images and artefacts were a resource to be recycled, mixed, matched and montaged at will. As radical artistic activity had been traditionally sympathetic towards the left, or at least associated with the left by the indignant intolerance of those on the right, Western avant-garde art practice suddenly found itself without any automatic claim to offer a cultural alternative. Instead of providing a signpost to the future, avant-garde tactics of shock and dissent became part of a new lexicon for design, advertising and commercial market capture.

For example, as the knitwear producer Benetton became a global brand, the photographer and designer Oliviero Toscani famously caused a media scandal by reappropriating and colourising a deathbed image of the HIV/AIDS activist David Kirby as part of its 1992 'United Colours of Benetton' campaign. Within this new cultural milieu, the inherited certainty by which artists and art institutions alike had been able to claim a left-wing moral and ethical high ground began to crumble.

The 1990s was also the decade in which a growing and complex contemporary art market became an identifiable component of this neoliberal global economy. The absorption of avant-garde strategies of dissent into the sphere of global image culture during the 1980s and 1990s only exacerbated the rapid absorption and dispersal of contemporary art across the expanding territories of the global network. For example, in the work of ex-Wall Street trader Jeff Koons, commodity and kitsch began to combine into slick sculptures of oversized shiny balloon dogs, larger-than-life ceramic sculptures of Michael Jackson and his pet chimpanzee Bubbles and hardcore paintings of Koons coupling with his porn-star wife Ilona Staller (aka Cicciolina). In a nod to Andy

Warhol's famous 'Factory' production studio, Koons also made a virtue out of paying other artists and craftspeople to make his work for him.

In the work of Takashi Murakami, which he himself describes as 'superflat', the traditional dividing lines between art and everyday life were subverted, as opposed to bridged, through a series of initiatives that combined traditional Japanese painting techniques, manga, digital technologies and mass-production/distribution techniques. As well as producing paintings for major exhibition venues around the world, Murakami worked closely with the Louis Vuitton fashion house (designing their signature bag logo) and the musician Kanye West (designing the cover for his 2007 album *Graduation* and directing the music video 'Good Morning', which was released in the same year).

As art historian Hans Belting argues, art on a global scale meant that there was no longer any inherent aesthetic or particular quality that could be identified in art, nor was there any single concept available of what that art might be.[22] Unlike modern art, with its self-appointed notions of universalism, Belting suggests that the new forms of contemporary art that began to emerge after the collapse of the Soviet Bloc were global in the same way that the World Wide Web was global. Like the internet, contemporary art was becoming ubiquitous; and like the internet, it could never carry a singular message or a common form of content. For Belting, this led to a global art that has become difficult for existing Western paradigms of art criticism and theory to accept. Instead, contemporary global art now simply exceeds familiar categorisations and resists the constraints of established institutions.

At the same time as the tradition of avant-garde European art was giving way to global art, and as developing forms international contemporary art were becoming clearly distinguishable from their modern predecessors, the growth of a new global art market was beginning to challenge the ways in which contemporary art was produced, distributed and consumed. During the 1990s and the 2000s contemporary art began to play an integral part in the remarketing of new national identities and their attendant urban regeneration programmes, which had begun during the 1980s. Major and secondary cities all over the world began to reframe their aspirational transitions from sites of industrial entropy to global economic hubs in the language of cultural renaissance.

Initiatives such as the Tate Modern in London and the Guggenheim in Bilbao saw intricate mutual relationships develop around contemporary art. These kinds of relationships were frequently formed between a diverse mixture of contradictory stakeholders – such as central government, local government, private enterprise and the burgeoning tourism and leisure industries – who found common ground through the complex economic repositioning of culture. For example, the Guggenheim Bilbao was designed by the world-renowned architect Frank Gehry and built in partnership with Spanish and regional Basque funding. Opening in 1997, the manifest intention of the Guggenheim Bilbao was to regenerate the economy of a declining post-industrial area through the global draw of contemporary art and the Guggenheim brand.

Art was no longer simply the ideological window-dressing of state and nationhood; it had become a real contributor to the new global economies. This, in turn, had a direct impact on the kinds of roles that contemporary art was supposed to play within the cultural industries and society as a whole. In an attempt to distinguish itself from other forms of globalised culture, a growing global art industry now had to deploy a variety of means to secure a discrete position in an increasingly competitive market place. Ironically, this led to much art-industry production in the 1990s and 2000s redeploying the shock tactics of earlier avant-garde movements – particularly those of the futurists, Dadaists and surrealists – in order to stand out from the crowd. This more desperate recycling of earlier avant-garde strategies, which were already being absorbed into popular culture and dispersed across the global art network, more often than not resulted in slick-looking, media-friendly art – art that momentarily grabbed attention but which frequently lacked any depth of content.[23]

In the UK artists such as Damien Hirst – known for his 'shark in a tank' or, to give it its full name, *The Physical Impossibility of Death in the Mind of Someone Living* of 1991 – and Tracey Emin – equally famous for her *My Bed* of 1998 – became tabloid-media sensations as art, pop and reality TV began to seamlessly elide. The manufactured phenomenon of the Young British Artists, or YBAs, by advertising mogul Charles Saatchi – of which Hirst and Emin were luminaries – was coupled with the reinvention of London as a centre for the world contemporary art market.

This heady cocktail of art, media and celebrity was further strengthened when, after the New Labour landside election 1997, the new Prime Minister Tony Blair held a drinks reception for artists, musicians, sports personalities, actors and creatives of all stripes at Number Ten Downing Street. Seen at the time as marking a new era of 'Cool Britannia', and capitalising on the widespread popularity of the Britpop phenomenon and bands such as Oasis and Blur, the imbrication of art, creativity, economics, politics and celebrity seemed to be accepted as a new form of mutually beneficial brand building.[24] At the same time, artists began to see themselves as being able to achieve wealth, celebrity status and fame during their early careers while accompanying ideals of rootless, globe-trotting artistic 'nomadism' became the norm.

In 1999 my home city of Liverpool hosted its first Contemporary Art Biennial under the title 'Trace'. A year later, as the new millennium dawned, this trend towards art-based economic and urban regeneration was confirmed when the new Tate Modern was opened in a long-disused power station on the banks of the River Thames in London. As well as being one of the most visited contemporary art museums in the world, Tate Modern was also manifestly supported by its corporate partners and exhibition-associated merchandising. Nicolas Serota, who masterminded the development, and with it the expanding portfolio of the Tate brand, was also careful to product-place key works of art by YBAs as part of a themed permanent display – making sure that Britain's most recent generation of economically viable celebrity artists began to be seen, quite literally, in the company of other modernist greats.

The global occupation of neoliberal logic

Unfortunately, the 2000s began with a violent disruption to George Bush's dream of an economic 'new world order'. On 11 September 2001, terrorists flew two planes into the Twin Towers in New York. Against the backdrop of a return to the 'us and them' rhetoric of the Cold War, when newly elected President George Bush, Jr branded large parts of the world as 'evildoers', the continual deregulation of markets and loosening of financial rules around credit and debt led, in 2007, to the worst global economic crisis since the Great Depression of the late 1920s. By coincidence, 2007 also saw the release of the first-generation iPhone, marking the point at which forms of everyday connection began to resemble the network of digital exchange that we know today.

Offering a touchscreen combination of previous devices (digital music player, phone and handheld computer), the iPhone and its many derivatives allowed us to begin constructing our parallel world of social media profiles and identities, as newly formed platforms such as Facebook (launched in 2004), YouTube (2005) and Twitter (2006) began to be used by celebrities and politicians alike. Barack Obama's use of social media during his 2008 presidential campaign is regarded as the first manifestations/ use of this new media to engage and mobilise a general public online.

The 2000s also began to see the more directed use of art, especially emerging forms of socially engaged practice, by governments, such as New Labour in the UK, who wished to see any publicly funded art institutions become more socially accessible.[25] As an example, under UK Secretary of State Chris Smith, the British government sought to identify, reimagine and repackage effective forms of alternative production and distribution (often utilising developments in digital and new-media technologies) into the 'Creative Industries Mapping Document'.[26] This not only allowed New Labour to identify itself with the media hype of 'Cool Britannia';[27] it also allowed for the implementation of cohesive political strategies which sought to professionalise the previously liberating effects of creative work. In this way 'immaterial labour', to use a term coined by the Italian *Autonomia* movement, was turned into a corporate tool for implementing new patterns of work and managing new forms of consumer desire.[28] As philosopher Brian Holmes has argued:

> The imaginary of rebellion and liberation, the quest for individual authenticity, the ideal of self-management, the anti-hierarchical social form of the network/rhizome, all have been appropriated as rhetorical and organizational devices that respond to broad aspirations of emancipation, but deliberately channel those aspirations so as to reinstate exploitation and alienation under another guise.[29]

At an institutional level, this shift towards the corporatisation of cultural management tended to play out via new requirements from funding bodies such as Arts Council UK, which demanded that art museums and galleries begin to provide 'measurable outcomes' in exchange for support. Usually, this requirement aligned with the New Labour ethos that funded institutions must evidence increased engagement with community sectors who do not usually attend art galleries and museums. While this form of centralised instrumentalisation – the insistence that only measurable outcomes would be funded – was rightly seen as a dangerous shift towards the neoliberalisation of art, the response that art, as we know it or knew it to be, should somehow remain politically autonomous from its own manifest collusion with global neoliberal economics seemed contradictory to its core.

As we know, Boris Groys had argued as early as 2009 that there was no simple exterior or interior beyond the reach of the market.[30] This new and difficult situation was exacerbated further by the adoption of previously identifiable left-wing and art-world terminology by global networked neoliberalism as 'management speak' – as those without access to regular work, or regular income, were encouraged to be creative, use initiative, move from one project to another and find solutions to problems that were not of their own making. As the artist Liam Gillick put it in his 2010 article 'The Good of Work':

> The accusation … is that artists are at best the ultimate freelance knowledge workers and at worst barely capable of distinguishing themselves from the consuming desire to work at all times, neurotic people who deploy a series of practices that coincide quite neatly with the requirements of neoliberal, predatory, continuingly mutating capitalism of the every moment [*sic*]. Artists are people who behave, communicate and innovate in the same manner as those who spend their days trying to capitalise every moment and exchange of daily life. They offer no alternative.[31]

If Gillick is right, then we find ourselves at a difficult and complex cultural impasse. On the one hand, it becomes increasingly challenging to resist the condition of neoliberal occupation through any kind of recognisable artistic gesture – material or otherwise – without falling into the trap of an already commodified and commercialised art industry. On the other, it is similarly impossible to step outside the framework of the art industry – as a recognisable form of radical gesture or resistance – when any attempt to do so runs the risk of direct complicity with the deregulatory logic of capital. What was once seen to be the pursuit of an alternative artistic lifestyle, the refusal to 'fit in' or to follow the patterns and rhythms of a nine-to-five job, is now the new standard of precarious labour. Any symbolic value in this form of alterity has already been commodified and re-consumed as neoliberal forms of autonomous 'self-management'.[32]

Perhaps the biggest contradiction here, I would argue, is that the growing condition of neoliberal occupation – and its accompanying ideology of creative and artistic self-management – began to play out against the backdrop of a post-2007 shift towards austerity as the solution to global economic collapse and the sclerotic fixity of global decline.[33] As ideas of 'zero-hour contracts' (where legally unprotected workers agree to contractually binding terms and conditions for work and pay without any guarantee of regular income) and the 'gig economy' (where workers sustain a hand-to-mouth living, often in the service-sector industries, by moving from one small paid job to the next instead of earning an hourly wage) became the norm, new forms of social media-driven nationalism and racism began to emerge.

In the UK, the newly elected prime minister, David Cameron's, ideal of a 'big society' (where devolved forms of governmental and legal control, regulated by strict adherence to neoliberal financial policy, promised a sham of self-directed autonomy) led almost inevitably to the debacle of Brexit in 2016. In the US, the continuing disenfranchisement of rust-belt communities, who increasingly felt that they were being demographically overlooked in favour of other and more amenable voting groups, led to the election of Donald Trump in the same year. In both cases, a manifest use of online manipulation, lies, fraud, impossible promises and retrofitted myths of national empowerment have subsequently led to the growth of Alt-Right identities, such as America First and the Proud Boys, with an upsurge and adoption of anti-liberal and anti-left-wing political agendas across the globe.

Counter-neoliberalism: emerging alternatives to the logic of 'no alternative'

It is worth mentioning at this point in our analysis of Useful Art that the triumphal rise of a post-Eastern Bloc 'new world order' – based on the free flow of unregulated capital and trade and the concomitant Thatcherite idea that 'there is no alternative' to global networked neoliberalism – did not go without its detractors. It is also worth remembering that some of these forms of resistance and counter-culture can also provide some of the toolkits by which we can help to rethink Useful Arts as a viable form of activist social change.

For example, in 1994 (on the same day that the North American Free Trade Agreement, or NAFTA, came into force) a small group of Mexican revolutionaries took over the southern Mexican city of San Cristóbal de Las Casas for twelve days. Taking their name from the early twentieth-century revolutionary Emiliano Zapata, the aim of the Zapatista Army of National Liberation (EZLN, or Zapatistas, as they came to be known) was not to occupy territory or to seize power and control in the traditional sense of a political coup. Instead, the Zapatistas wished to draw attention and give voice to a global struggle of the oppressed and powerless – those whose traditional ways of life were being threatened by the multinational corporations who were taking their land, exploiting their labour and stealing their raw materials.

Using the possibilities afforded them by the early internet, the Zapatistas sought to address a global audience with a call for transnational solidarity and unity among those 'left behind' in the economic and social shift towards President Bush's 'new world order'.[34] According to Subcomandante Marcos, the name adopted by the Mexican insurgent and spokesperson for the EZLN, Rafael Sebastián Guillén Vicente (the name was also used to refer to the organisational infrastructure of the Zapatistas), the growth of neoliberalism signalled both a new kind of religion – through which Western forms of territorial capture played out – and also the beginning of 'The Fourth World War' (as the Cold War, from the perspective of the Global South, marked a Third World War which more often than not played out over their territories and natural resources). For Marcos:

> The Fourth World War is destroying humanity as globalization is universalizing the market, and everything human which opposes the logic of the market is an enemy and must be destroyed. In this sense, we are all the enemy to be vanquished: indigenous, non-indigenous, human rights observers, teachers, intellectuals, artists. Anyone who believes themselves to be free and is not.[35]

By the turn of the century what had started as an informal organisation of worldwide opposition to the consequences of neoliberal financial deregulation had turned into the large-scale and often carnivalesque 'alter-globalisation' movement. Highly visible protests began to be held outside meetings of the WTO, the IMF, the G7 and the newly formed G20.[36] The growing opposition to global networked neoliberalism tended to manifest itself in an inchoate network of overlapping interest and resistance groups. What they had in common was not anti-globalisation but rather alter-globalisation. Instead of proposing nationalist rejections of globalisation, the alter-globalisation movement presented local, regional, national and international proposals for thinking and making the world otherwise. With the slogan 'Another World is Possible', the alter-globalisation coalition sought to challenge the economic imperative of major global organisations and corporations with calls for climate and environmental justice, protection of workers' rights, civil liberties and the rights of indigenous peoples to lay claim on their natural resources.

After the economic crisis of 2007/8, groups who were increasingly concerned with the growing financial inequality between rich and poor, and a breakdown in social and economic justice, deploying the strategies and tactics of the alter-globalisation demonstrations – and particularly the playbook of Reclaim the

Streets, a movement which began as a series of protests to return public spaces back to common people – took to the Streets as the 'Occupy' movement. Beginning with an occupation of Wall Street in New York in September 2011, this led to similar protests taking place in over 950 cities across the world by the following month. Similarly to the Arab Spring movement of the previous year, the Occupy movement, which organises around the slogan 'We are the 99%', used online platforms and the hashtag #Occupy to motivate and organise protests and raise awareness of what participants saw as the morally and ethically bankrupt behaviour of global finance, corporations, market investors and governments. Similarly, the anti-austerity 'Indignados Movement' in Spain, which also began in 2011, and the rise of the left-wing and oppositional Syriza movement in Greece (which saw their leader Aléxis Tsípras elected as Prime Minister from 2015 to 2019), marked a shift away from the acceptance of global networked neoliberalism as offering the only plausible solution.

Activist art as neoliberal alternative

During this period many artists and art-led groups began to use forms of activism, direct protest, culture jamming and media hijack to draw attention to global injustice and effect change.[37] Often these forms of art-led dissent used the tools and mechanisms of neoliberal globalisation against itself, using available digital media, online platforms and social distribution systems to challenge the effects of instrumentalising logic on its own terms. For example, during the 2000s and 2010s 'The Yes Men' developed satirical websites that could be mistaken for those of major companies such as the World Trade Organization, Dow

Chemical and McDonald's, Shell Oil and Exxon Mobil. Through their hoax web presence The Yes Men would often be mistaken for the 'real' companies and subsequently asked to present and discuss their spurious claims on major news channels and at international conferences.[38]

In another example, the activist group 'Liberate Tate' undertook a series of high-profile and unsanctioned performances in various Tate Gallery locations in order to force Tate into disclosing its funding agreement with the multinational oil company BP (British Petroleum). In another, the Spanish art activists Yomango sought to develop a social shoplifting movement as an anti-consumerist lifestyle choice based on direct reappropriation and the redistribution of wealth. Famously, the Yomango Group put on flash fashion shows in clothes shops of clothes that had been shoplifted from that store.

It was also during this period that newly developing forms of activist art began to intersect with emerging forms of Useful Art. Instead of using and repurposing existing art-world strategies and tactics to foreground and draw attention to key social, political and economic issues, those artists and activists who began to engage with Useful Art also intended to disrupt the smooth flows and logics of neoliberal occupation on its own terms. As we have seen in the example of Assemble's work with the residents and members of Granby 4 Streets CLT, the key aim of Useful Art is to provide working alternatives and real-world solutions to local issues and urgencies. Useful Art, therefore, provides a form of ground-up activism, one which enables artists and communities to disrupt and repurpose the mechanisms of neoliberal occupation on its own terms, thereby making available effective toolkits of micro-self-reliance and dissent which can be shared, recycled and used again. These new forms of Useful Art are, by their nature, critical of a system whose tools they redeploy in order to effect change. They are also defined within the asymmetric conditions of a neoliberal occupation which is equally dependent upon instituting its own false forms of deregulated social and economic freedom.

At the same time as this, the emergence of tactical and ground-up forms of Useful Art activism are happening at a time when the recent success story of global contemporary art is being tarnished by its realignment with neoliberal logic and by a radical and ongoing reduction of state funding. On the one hand, the withdrawal of government funding threatens a delicate ecosystem of local and grassroots arts initiatives which have been developing across Europe and the US over the last two decades. On the other, major arts institutions are again being looked upon to generate their own income, threatening the reaffirmation of blockbuster shows and the propagation of yet more conservative and populist art. Either way, those who make a living in the art world are effectively being asked to redefine themselves politically – and not necessarily along the traditional party lines of left or right.

To make artworks which simply seem to be ethical and communitarian in their crudest sense, engaging people in artist-run forms of social work, can only help to promote the cause of neoliberal political agendas by the back door.[39] Alternatively, any retreat into traditional forms or frameworks of aesthetic autonomy, or useless art, will only help to propagate the existing material and ideological forms of international economy and, more specifically, the continued development and growth of a commodity-driven art industry – an art industry which increasingly relies on the illusions of specialness and separateness from real life for the continued circulation of its luxury good.[40]

Useful Art and social change

Because of this, the kind of work that is now the work of Useful Art resides in the struggle to open up spaces of critical, social and political autonomy; spaces within which it becomes possible to reimagine the ways we live our lives. In the age of the global image, the difficulties of this task are immediately apparent – how to make Useful Art, and change the world, from within the condition of neoliberal occupation? However, as I have also argued, one of the most pervasive and persuasive aspects of our current condition of neoliberal occupation is that it has successfully reprogrammed, and monetised, the horizons of our imagination as well as our discontent. Those who identify as artists can stake no claim to live a life that is somehow integrally and ethically otherwise to those of the masses. Those who believe that art is something that is somehow automatically and innately beyond the grasp and capture of neoliberal occupation are at best deluded by, and at worst complicit with, the kinds of mechanisms that now structure and make sense of our every interaction.

Put this way, art has become just one tool among many in the negotiation of our futures and our dreams. That is why I argue that to use art as a tool for social change is not in itself an inherently anti-neoliberal act. Nor, would I argue, is Useful Art inherently a form of neoliberal complicity. Instead, I'm going to argue that it is no longer the tools we pick up to use (whether they be traditional or otherwise), or why we choose to pick up those tools (as good intentions are not the sole preview of the radical artist), but the way we use those tools that counts. It is in this sense that Useful Art enables us to rethink, reimagine, reposition and reuse art as a tool for collective, collaborative and constituent social, political and economic change.

2

Remapping the network: 1:1 Scale Practice and artistic activism

On 6 April 2023 I was invited to attend a midday meal at Tŷ Pawb, a hybrid art space, market place, food court and multi-storey car park in Wrexham, Wales. The meal itself was an iteration, or rather activation, of the project 'Tablecloth as a Toolkit', a collaboration between Owen Griffiths and Alessandra Saviotti, which was commissioned as part of the 'Horizon Garden' exhibition that ran at Tŷ Pawb from 28 January to 8 April 2023. I joined a varied group of stakeholders, which included Ian Bancroft, Chief Executive of Wrexham Council, Councillor Hugh Jones and artist and environmentalist Morag Colquhoun. We were also joined by our host and convenor, Owen Griffiths, and by fellow project initiator Alessandra Saviotti (who was able to join virtually via a laptop which was placed in the centre of the table on a rotating stand).

The meal itself, which was provided by food traders from Tŷ Pawb, was intended to act as a convivial space in which the invited group could meet and share ideas and perspectives as makers, doers, policymakers and activists alike. The aim of the meal was to harness these conversations as a means to think about and plan broader strategies for linking some of Tŷ Pawb's social growing initiatives to similar projects in the region and beyond.[1] To help spur these discussions, each guest was provided with a term or phrase on a napkin – such as 'solidarity' and 'resistance' – that each used, in turn, as a provocation for discussion within a broader 'map' of issues that included 'justice', 'activism', 'housing', 'culture', 'urban redesign' and 'slum clearance'. The napkins, in conjunction with a diagram of linked phrases which had been printed onto the tablecloth itself, formed the core components of the 'Tablecloth as a Toolkit'. A key idea was to record the discussions of this meal and to invite the same guests to return for a similar meal in five years' time, to review, rethink and replan these strategies.

As a broader context for these discussions, the 'Tablecloth as a Toolkit' was supported by a range of information. These included relevant case studies from the Archive of the Association of Arte Útil and a range of key examples.[2] Among them were 'GRAFT – A soil-based syllabus', a public garden and workshop project by Owen Griffiths based at the National Waterfront Museum in Swansea (which we will look at in more detail later in this chapter); 'Granby 4 Streets Regeneration Project', which we looked at in Chapter 1 via the work of the architecture group 'Assemble'; 'Company Drinks', a community enterprise based in the London Borough of Barking and Dagenham, which links the history of east London families 'going picking' for fruit and hops to the development of a new soft-drinks business; 'Incredible Edible', a social project initiated in the northern UK town of Todmorden in 2008 that began to use available and unloved spaces to grow food and teach communities how to cultivate vegetables; and Erlas Victorian Walled Garden, another growing initiative in Wrexham, North Wales, which uses growing and education as a way to provide meaningful daytime activity and work experience for disabled people.

During the course of the exhibition 'Horizon Garden', the 'Tablecloth as a Toolkit' was used to generate a range of discussions, projects and workshops that invited different communities, interest groups and visitors to Tŷ Pawb to use the exhibition as if it were an activist manual for change. Rather than simply presenting a curated collection of artworks, whose general theme was gardening, the ambition of 'Horizon Garden', for Tŷ Pawb Creative Director Jo Marsh, was to demonstrate how an exhibition does not need to be curated, or experienced, as an 'end point' – as a resolved presentation where viewers are asked to share in the conclusions of an artist, curator or institution. Instead, for Marsh:

> the exhibition can be one moment for dialogue, sharing, dreaming, planning and reflecting, within a long trajectory, in this instance around community growing as a response to shared urgencies of climate emergency, social isolation, loneliness and food poverty. At Tŷ Pawb the exhibition isn't King. 'Horizon Garden' is just one part of a constellation including the market, the roof garden and the wider network of community growers etc.[3]

What the 'Tablecloth as a Toolkit' project provides, when seen in its broader context of the exhibition 'Horizon Garden' – and, crucially, also within the broader plans for developing Tŷ Pawb as an art-led cultural hub – is an example of how hybrid solutions are emerging to address the once separate 'registers' of art and life. More importantly, it can be seen as an example of how activist artists, working together with directors, curators, politicians, council members, social entrepreneurs, community leaders, community members and ground-up makers, doers and thinkers, are setting themselves against the grain of centralised economically determined logic. 'Tablecloth as a Toolkit', 'Horizon Garden' and Tŷ Pawb can all be seen as forms of collaborative micro-resistance – as nodes in a growing international network of local solutions which is struggling against the impacts that the current condition of global neoliberal occupation has wrought upon local communities everywhere. And such projects and initiatives, I believe, offer us possible templates for change.

In this way, I would argue that Useful Art can disrupt the smooth flows of neoliberal logic and offer an alternative way forward, activating art practice as a tool for social, political and economic change. As I have also argued, such forms of Useful Art may not always employ the same materials, strategies or mechanisms of art as we know it or knew it to be. Nor, to many, might they be recognised as art at all. Instead, they tend to emerge when activist artists share their skills and creativity with other collaborators to address real-world issues on a real-world, rather than symbolic, scale. What I mean by this is that Useful Art can often be recognised or – as we saw with the example of 'Homebaked' with which I introduced this book – misrecognised by its use and adaptation of everyday life as the very material with which it works.

To make this point clearer I'd like to focus in this chapter of the book on the relationship of Useful Art to what the philosopher Steven Wright has termed '1:1 Scale Practice' (pronounced 'One to One Scale Practice'). This is a term derived from cartography (map-making) which Wright uses to distinguish a fundamental shift away from the symbolic and the representational in contemporary art practice. Beginning to think of our current condition of neoliberal occupation as a virtual and economic form of map offers us a way to understand how Useful Art, and forms of 1:1 Scale Practice, might also offer us the tools to reconnect with, and to reuse, what we might feel has been irrevocably lost.

1:1 Scale Practice and other stories

In his 2013 book *The Lexicon of Useful Art*, Stephen Wright begins his entry on 1:1 Scale Practice with the helpful observation that 'Art and art-related practices that are oriented towards user-ship rather than spectatorship are characterised more than anything else by their scale of operations: they operate on the 1:1 scale.'[4] What Wright means by this is that most art projects that seek to use art as a tool for social change in the real world, such as 'Homebaked' and Assemble's Granby 4 Streets project, tend to begin life as 'real-world' projects – so to speak – as opposed to art-based representations or re-presentations of what a world that exists outside museums or galleries should ideally look like.

To put this another way, rather than being paintings, sculptures, photographs, videos or art installations that only fully make sense within a gallery setting, '1:1 practices are both what they are, and propositions of what they are.'[5] As a result of this, instances of 1:1 Scale Practice appear in the real world as what they are intended to be – possible solutions that use art to directly address and affect social, political, economic and environmental problems and issues which exist outside any museum and gallery setting. So their existence as identifiable artworks within a museum and gallery setting is at best a secondary function of their 1:1 scale operations.

For Wright, this 'scaling up' of art as an operational tool for change runs counter to the tradition of modern art which, as he sees it, relies on the idea that the job of art is to present symbolic alternatives to the real world – a real world which, by extension, always exists somewhere 'out there', beyond the mechanisms and confines of an art world (the 'in here', if you like) that sought to re-present it. Again, as Wright puts it, 'by and large, the art of the twentieth century, like so many post-conceptual practices today, operated at a reduced scale; art was practiced as both other than, and small-er than, whatever reality it set out to map'.[6]

What is interesting here, for our discussion of Useful Art, is Wright's introduction of scale (or the different scales of art and the real world) and the function of art as a tool for negotiating that difference. But as we know, the assumption of art's traditional 'useless' role is no longer secure within the asymmetric condition of current neoliberal occupation, or what the Zapatistas would call the territory of the 'Fourth World War'.[7] On one hand, if the role of art is to tell us something about the world out there, then it follows that art must be something that is different to that world in the first place. On the other, if the once separate worlds of art and life have now become so inextricably entangled that there appears to be no discernible difference between the two, then what would (or could) art become in a world where its traditional roles and functions no longer apply? And it is precisely because of this that 1:1 Scale Practice can offer an effective way of working within that territory while enabling us to rethink some of those traditional terms and conditions governing our understanding of art.

As an illustration of his mapping concept for the scale of art against real life, Wright quotes from Lewis Carroll's 1893 story 'Sylvie and Bruno Concluded'. In this parable, a conversation takes place between a narrator and a character called Mein Herr, concerning the relative merits of a 'really useful' map – a map that grew so large that it eventually reached the scale of a mile to a mile. This 1:1 scale map, Mein Herr declares, has never been spread out because framers objected that it would shut out the light. So, as an alternative, Mein Herr explains that the country itself is now being used as its own map which, he assures the narrator, 'does nearly as well'.[8]

For Wright, this parable of mapping helps us to rethink some of the assumptions we have about art's fundamental role as a 'scaled-back' representation, or re-presentation, of something else – of art as a convention in which the artwork will always remain subordinate to the real it is intended to reference. Or, looked at another way, of an art that somehow occupies a special kind of aesthetic space which is both separate from, and superior to, the humdrum experience of everyday life. Wright goes on to argue that many of today's politically motivated art initiatives, just like Mein Herr's permanently folded full-scale map, are rendered useless precisely because they are still seen as representations and, therefore, remain firmly within the traditional understandings of the art world and the museum or gallery experience.

As I have already suggested, this observation about scale also helps us to think through some of the problems raised by Useful Art – especially when Useful Art, operating at a 1:1 scale, begins to blur or 'evacuate' the boundaries and distinctions that, for many, still exist between what is and isn't art. In the case of 1:1 representation, as Wright argues, the real is neither adequately mapped nor is it transformed. Instead, Wright argues that when 1:1 Scale Practices use the real world 'as its own map "all is transformed"'.[9] In such cases the representation is no longer subordinate to that which it represents, but becomes interchangeable with (and in some cases may even be superior to) that which it re-presents.

1:1 Scale Practice and artistic activism

To clarify this point Wright draws on an example first used by the artist and writer Allan Kaprow in his article 'The Real Experiment', published in the journal *Art Forum* in 1983. The article explores an intervention made by the conceptual artist Raivo Puusemp, where he successfully ran for Mayor of Rosendale Village, New York in 1975. Significantly for Kaprow, Puusemp's election followed from a campaign that proposed positive community involvement in the political process and, over the following two years, Puusemp applied what he had learned about working with people and communities as a conceptual artist to his new role. By working collectively with the local residents, Puusemp managed to solve the town's water and sewage problems.[10]

In addition to this, Kaprow claimed that, through Puusemp's actions as Mayor, the villagers of Rosendale began to spend more time together and, as a result, began to assume more responsibility as a community. Finally, Puusemp also helped his constituents to realise that their incorporation into the larger adjoining Township of Rosendale would effectively save their village without any loss of identity or local community. For Wright, however, the success of Puusemp's actions in Rosendale did not simply reside in their scope or social impact, but in the inseparability of his artistic gesture from his everyday act on a 1:1 scale:

> The exemplarity of what Puusemp did stems neither from the scope nor the impact of the action but rather from the inseparability of the artistic gesture from the everyday act in terms of scale. He was operating on the 1:1 scale. Puusemp approached politics as a social medium. One which has to be worked with and learned. *'Deliberate changes in political structure don't just happen,'* he argued, *'they are planned and occur because they seem inevitable. To make changes seem inevitable requires a clear structure and a systematic process.'*[11]

Useful Art

Here is a way for us to begin unpicking some of the problematic relationships that 1:1 Scale Practice may have in relation to (or rather between) the real world of non-art and the world of art as we know it or knew it to be. The separation of art and life has been a linchpin of both our understanding and experience of art since museums and galleries began to house and display artworks to their attending publics from the late eighteenth century onwards. But 1:1 Scale Practice offers a useful means to rethink our relationship to art beyond the consensual convention that artworks (or art objects) are special things made by special people – artists – who imbue those objects with the quality of art. Seen in this light, 1:1 Scale Practice also undermines the basic idea that an experience of art should be one in which we (as spectators) are asked to unpack and experience the aesthetic qualities that have been expertly created in artworks, or art objects, by artists. This leads us to a radical realisation: that 1:1 Scale Practices undo the expectation of us experiencing the special, aesthetic qualities of art. They do not need to be experienced aesthetically at all.

As if it wasn't exciting enough to start to rethink the Enlightenment protocols of artistic and aesthetic understanding that have governed our relationships to art over the last two hundred years, I would argue that Wright's analysis of 1:1 Scale Practice takes us even further. It also offers us a means to begin making new forms of Useful Art that seek to directly affect, rather than simply represent or re-present, the real social, political, economic and environmental world within which they operate. So 1:1 Scale Practice, as a key tool for Useful Art, can be an active process by which the real world is remapped, recoded, or even recopied. Instead of being a series of symbolic gestures, Useful Art on a local and everyday scale can be seen as a potential means of taking back forms of power and control.

Heidegger and the age of the world picture

In order to develop this idea further, let's look briefly at two other uses of the metaphor of mapping and picturing that have influenced my own experience of, and thinking about, art and its relationship to use over the last three decades. The first of these is an article, 'The Establishing by Metaphysics of the Modern World Picture', which was first delivered in 1938 to the Society for Aesthetics, Natural Philosophy and Medicine by the Philosopher Martin Heidegger.[12] In this article, Heidegger outlines the means by which the modern world had emerged from the Middle Ages by establishing a new concept – the sovereign individual or Enlightenment subject. This new form of self-determining individual (the idea that still drives most of our systems of law and individual human rights today) is, Heidegger argues, at odds with the previous conception of mankind as a social species – one that was subject to the divine rule of kings and queens and, ultimately, to God. However, Heidegger also argues that the very tools that enabled this historical shift – an objective belief in the accuracy and truth of scientific mapping and representation – also prevented 'modern man' from realising the true conditions of the modern age itself: that to understand the modern world, we must understand it as a map.

To put this another way, Heidegger argues that the newly found historical belief in scientific accuracy, which had enabled mankind to begin undertaking the project of accurately represent-ing or mapping the world, quickly became the only guarantee of scientific truth. What rapidly followed from this (for the first time in human history) was the belief that something can only exist as the 'truth' if it can be accurately and scientifically measured and mapped. Accompanying this was the parallel belief that anything else – any activity or feeling that cannot be accurately and scientifically mapped – would fall into the realm of subjectivity, inaccuracy and, at worst, from a scientific point of view, superstition. As Heidegger also argued, it is at this historical juncture – with the emergence of the 'Cartesian' subject often identified by the phrase 'I think, therefore I am' – that science, engineering and accurate forms of measurement and information exchange began to be conceptually separated from, and often privileged above, the subjective and poetic arts.

As Heidegger was already saying in 1938, this distinction – between the objective truth of science and the subjective vagaries of art – has become so culturally embedded in the way we think that it seems always to have been that way. We only need to glance at the example of how our education systems are separated into the sciences and the arts, with a privileging of the 'practical' subjects as a more guaranteed educational route to employability, to see the legacy of this historical shift at play. But as Heidegger also argued, this way of looking at the world – as separate realms of objectivity and subjectivity, as science and art – is relatively new and has not always been the case. We only have to look back at the 'mapping' projects of the Enlightenment, which re-emerge so clearly in Lewis Carroll's 1893 fable of a map which could cover the world at a 1:1 scale, to see how our modern world, and the ideologies that have grown with it, were produced.

Think of the race to accurately 'time' longitude at sea to give us precise locations of latitude. Or look at any 'map' of Africa or the Middle East made from the Western perspective of colonial conquest to see the long, straight lines of colonial territorial intervention. Or think of the abhorrent and pseudo-scientific photographic and archival projects that emerged during the period of nineteenth-century colonialism and empire, which sought to physically measure (and map) the facial features of a 'criminal caste' or to 'objectively' identify, from a Western point of view, the differences between the physiognomies of various ethnicities and races.

So, for Heidegger, the 'modern age' was distinguished both by a growing ability to accurately measure and map itself and by a growing ability to conceive and imagine itself in terms of its own picture. In the process of the Enlightenment's shifts, art began to lose its useful role and function within society as the means by which the power of kings, queens and religious iconography could be accurately represented. Painting, sculpture and drawing were joined by the new media of photography and film, while religion, power and ideology were made visible in more immediate ways that no longer required the special work of the traditional artist.

With the collapse of this old-fashioned 'use' for art, the West began to imagine that art occupied a special realm 'beyond' science. And this, for Heidegger, was the crucial historical moment when art became aesthetics. Perhaps more importantly, Heidegger also saw this new realm of aesthetics as a necessary and humanising balance to the 'Enlightenment subject' which was itself being formed within this move towards objective and scientific mapping. After all, if individual sovereign subjectivities could also be reduced to measurable, comparable and, ultimately, interchangeable components, then we would have allowed ourselves to become little more than machine parts. And, if we are little

more than measurable commodities, Heidegger's fear was that
we might allow ourselves to become devoid of those ineffable
qualities that make us human in the first place.

The importance of Heidegger's theory is that it also enables
us to rethink our current relationships to Useful Art and 1:1
Scale Practice. If art, as Steven Wright argues, has become a
scaled-down and supplementary activity in itself – something
that is now only capable of making imperfect representations
of a world 'out there' – then it too has become little more than
a form of mapping. And, if this is the case, then the aesthetic
realm – traditionally kept safe from the outside world within
the special experiential space of the museum and gallery – has
lost it its humanising ability, that of balancing out the objectifying
ambitions of all-pervasive science. Art, as we know it or knew
it to be, offers no alternative to our current condition of neoliberal
occupation. At best it offers us little more than imaginary alternatives to this occupation that can, in turn, be packaged and sold
to us as the commodified 'leisure experience' of art.

If this outlook seems a little bleak, it might also be helpful
to note that when I first used this Heidegger article in the 1990s
as a means to think through what art might be or need to
become, I simply assumed that it was still the Western ideology
of a predatory and objective science that most threatened our
unmeasurable subjectivity (if you like, our humanity). However,
I now recognise that the clearest threat to our humanity and
subjectivity are the instrumentalising forces of neoliberal economics. The success of neoliberalism relies on the acceptance that
everything – every thought, feeling, experience and hope – can
be measured and assigned economic worth. If it makes sense
in financial terms, the mantra now goes, then it is real, true or
worthwhile. And it is because of this that I would argue a

post-aesthetic shift to Useful Art and 1:1 Scale Practice – as shared and useful tools for remapping and remaking real-world social, political and economic change – is crucial if we are to resist the occupation of our humanity by the brutal and financialising logics of neoliberal economics.

Baudrillard: simulacra and hyperreality

This leads me, in turn, to our third parable of mapping. This time I'd like to turn our attention towards Jean Baudrillard's use of a tale from Jorge Luis Borges, in his 1982 analysis of what he called 'third order simulation' or 'simulacra'.[13] The Borges tale that Baudrillard cites is one of loss in which, again, cartographers draw up a 1:1 scale map – one so accurate in every detail that it covers every inch of the empire's territory. However, in this story, with the decline of the empire, the map itself begins to disintegrate until only a few shards and remnants remain as reminders of an imperial pride that was. For Baudrillard, this fable has come full circle within an age of digital representation. The territory of the real, he argues, is that which is now dissolving into memory – whereas the map remains as a testimony to the generation of a real without origin. This shift, for Baudrillard, has ushered in a new age of 'hyperreality', one in which territory no longer precedes the map or survives it. As a current example, in an age of constant photographic mapping of people's lives onto social media, there are certainly those who are real to us only in the digital world, and indeed whole communities of people whom we only ever encounter digitally.

In this scenario the true object (the human person behind the social media account, say) is no longer the fixed basis of representational activity, no longer the Enlightenment bedrock of measurable certainty upon which the truth of representation depends. Instead, Baudrillard argues that representations are now simply measured against each other in terms of equivalence, difference and interchangeability. (Does this person we have never met in real life look better in this photo, or that one?) Baudrillard argued (in the early 1980s!) that we have entered the realm of 'simulacra', a continuously shifting and endlessly manufactured realm of commodified image and information exchange. Our sense of the 'real' has now become fundamentally compromised.

If these ideas seem fanciful (and Baudrillard's ideas were not, and are still not, without their critics), then let's look back to the pivotal economic event we discussed in Chapter 1: the removal of the gold standard by President Nixon in 1971. This was a move which uncoupled our sense of monetary worth and value from a real and physical substance, gold, and which led, in turn, to our current age of neoliberal occupation: an age of conflicting false truths, internet extremism and precarious labour; a landscape dominated by algorithmically produced echo chambers and social-media info spheres; a global economy in which every point, click and swipe is monetised and resold as endlessly recombinable bytes of 'info-data'.

However, within this new order of 'hyperreality' and 'simulation', a world in which truth no longer needs an origin, Baudrillard still identified a lingering nostalgia for the one-to-one correspondence of meaning and reality. In the absence of this symbolic order, Baudrillard also argued that contemporary society had begun to remanufacture imaginary differences between reality and fantasy in phenomena like Disneyland. For Baudrillard, the childish fantasy world of Disneyland acted as a 'deterrence machine' – an imaginary realm of pirates, frontiers and impossible futures which provided the illusion that a real world still existed somewhere else beyond its borders. Instead, Baudrillard argued that no such real world now existed beyond the walls and car parks of Disneyland – all contemporary culture, he claimed, was now like Disneyland, an unreal network of images and signs governed by an endless circulation of commodities. In this sense Disneyland, for Baudrillard, acts as a placebo, as a misrepresentation that allowed us to indulge in the fantasy of a real world, still out there somewhere that, like the base metal gold, could act as a benchmark, a reality which guarantees and underscores our need for truth and material stability.

During this period, I would argue that major galleries around the world also began to function as Disney-like 'deterrence machines' – providing the comforting fantasy that the real world still existed somewhere beyond the borders of their blockbuster exhibitions and gift shops. During the 1980s and 1990s (as we have seen in Chapter 1) emerging brands such as Tate and Guggenheim began to capitalise on a newly emergent tourism and leisure market. At the same time, the harsh neoliberal economic climate of the 1980s and 1990s bit – which, as we have seen, forced museums and galleries to increasingly generate their own income streams. To create a market for the consumption of art, it became necessary for them to re-establish the separation between high art and the realities of everyday life. The traditional myth of the artist as 'shaman' – and of the artwork as a screen on which messages from a higher realm were made accessible to an everyday audience – would become the final fantasy of an art world that saw itself as being somehow separated from the conditions of its own neoliberal occupation.

In this scenario, the new neoliberal product of art – both as a commercially viable tourism and leisure experience and as an acceptable tool of urban economic regeneration – began to rely, somewhat ironically, on the selling point that art was a special kind of experience, separate from the world out there, and capable of commenting critically upon it. In doing so, these institutions, as well as the expanding critical and educational support networks that underpinned them, began to monetise the experience of art as an imaginary inoculation against the emerging condition of global neoliberal occupation. Armed with the new management speak of the cultural industries, in which the former languages of the avant-garde had been weaponised by the market place, visitors could now buy the reassurance that they were still, like artists, autonomous and self-regulating individuals acting within a thriving and expanding global democracy. At the same time, visitors to museums and galleries effectively began to be consumers of culture – quite literally buying moments they could misinterpret as escape to a place beyond neoliberal capture.

However, if Baudrillard is right, and our current condition is largely defined by our continuing process of virtual mapping, then let's say that forms of resistance can now be found in the shards and remnants of the once real that now lie rotting and discarded. Obviously, Baudrillard's analogy of a global map is only that, and the material and measurable realities have not vanished, but it does help us to face the fact that there is simply no inside out or outside in any more. Because our physical and virtual experiences have become so fundamentally and asymmetrically intertwined with each other, it is now impossible to expect that we can simply scrape away at the smooth surface of neoliberal occupation to find a neglected reality conveniently lying in wait somewhere below. Instead, I would argue that the shards and remnants of the once real have to be struggled over, renegotiated and repurposed by those artists and activists who seek to disrupt and corrupt global neoliberal occupation. I would also like to argue that newly emerging forms of Useful Art, which began to align strategies of 1:1 Scale Practice with existing forms of activism and social engagement during the 1970s and 1980s, also began to provide us with new ways of working that are capable of relocating and reconnecting us with these shards and remnants of the once real.

Reactivating the shards and remnants of use

As the emerging condition of neoliberal occupation became a global norm, a new generation of activist artists began to struggle over and reclaim forms of use and use value from the shards and remnants of a newly emerging economic order. More often than not these artists began to use 1:1 Scale Practice, together with more recognisable and familiar forms of art production, to activate networks of local micro-resistance, community re-empowerment and ground-up alternatives to the status quo. These new ways of working were neither intended to produce or lead to works of art in the traditional sense of the term (as objects or installations to be viewed and understood solely in terms of their aesthetic or monetary value). Nor were they the direct result of artists or institutions simply extending their logics and protocols of aesthetic understanding back into a 'real' world that somehow existed beyond the confines and purview of art-world autonomy and isolation. Instead, they offered new ways by which artists and communities alike could begin to use art as a tool to effect real social, political and economic change on their own terms.[14]

For example, from the mid-1970s onwards the American artist Suzanne Lacey, who coined the phrase 'new genre public art', began to blend performance, film, installation work and available forms of public media (such as print, radio and broadcast TV) with forms and strategies of direct social and political action. In doing so, she developed a hybrid art/activist practice that was not only able to highlight pressing social and urban issues, but was also able to collaborate with those communities in ways that encouraged the co-production of ground-up solutions to those same issues.[15]

In her 1977 work 'Three Weeks in May', Lacey shone a public light on the issue of rape in Los Angeles by encouraging victims to speak out publicly. As well as a visual representation of these issues – Lacey collaborated on the production of a large-scale public map which indicated where rapes had taken place and which was updated daily as new incidents occurred – Lacey also developed workshops, public forums, self-defence classes and art performances around the subject. A body of information, dialogue and opinion was then collated that could then be redistributed and broadcast through interviews that appeared in local newspapers and on local radio and TV.[16] In doing this, Lacey helped to develop a template for both her own practice and that of others that could be used, readjusted and reworked whenever and wherever required. For example, the internationally renowned Oakland Projects, which were instigated in 1991. As Lacey's own website puts it:

> Suzanne Lacy worked with scores of youth and adult collaborators to produce lengthy and large-scale public projects that included workshops and classes for youth, media intervention, and institutional program and policy development. The Oakland Projects are one of the most developed explorations of community, youth leadership, and public policy in current visual and public art

practice. The work was distributed on television, through lectures, in galleries, on documentary videos, and in articles and books.[17]

The Oakland Projects consisted of eight major 'works', all of which are listed and documented, with contextual and archival materials (such as video interviews, plans, photos, graphics and news articles) on an Oakland Projects website.[18] It should also be noted that each of the eight 'works' were, themselves, the result of long collaborations between Lacey, community members, collaborating artists, schools, government officials and policy makers. These collaborations also produced learning tools, school programmes and curricula (such as media literacy lessons for youth) which, in turn, enabled more participants to collaborate in the co-production of these works.[19] Lacey uses all the available tools and media at her disposal to grow long-term conversations and relationships around key issues that affect communities in contested urban environments.[20]

As a consequence, I would argue that Lacey's 'works' (and I have put Lacey's use of the term works in my own parentheses to emphasise this point) are not object-based 'works of art' as we know them or knew them to be. Instead, they act more as collaborative reworkings of these materials, resources and traditions (of both community and art alike) as a means of re-empowerment, re-engagement and solution-seeking activism. Lacey's work (or collaborative labour) also begins to help us to challenge, undermine and reimagine the normal operations of art as we know it or knew it to be – as a scaled-down representation of the real world – and, at the same time, of the terms, conditions and protocols of an art world that still fundamentally predicates itself as being distinct, in some way, from the world out there.

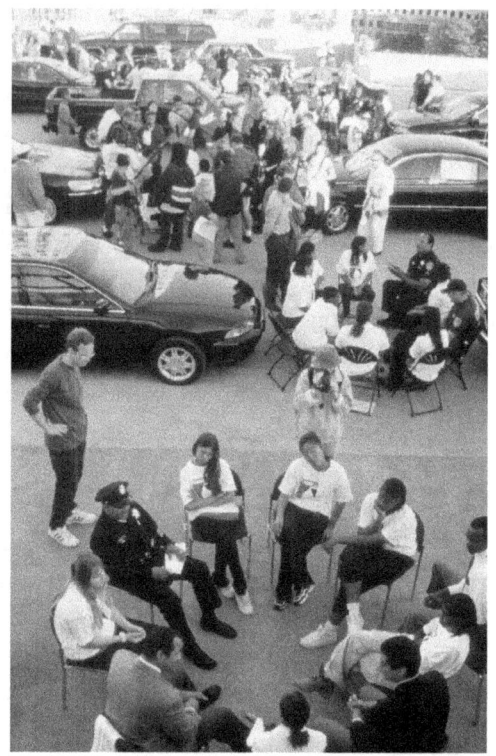

2.1 'Code 33—Emergency, Clear the Air!' from Suzanne Lacy, The Oakland Projects, 1997–99. Image courtesy of Suzanne Lacy

Like Lacey, Jeanne van Heeswijk develops forms of 1:1 Scale Practice that often result from her own long-term work with and within communities over a number of years. As an example, for the project 'Blue House' (2005–9), van Heeswijk acquired permission to use one of 18,000 new-build houses, constructed on the man-made islands of Ijburg in Amsterdam, as an experimental open site of community exchange and dialogue.[21] She invited architects, thinkers, writers, artists and academics from a variety of national and international backgrounds to work with neighbours and residents in building new forms of community network and infrastructure, introducing human connection into an otherwise highly planned and regulated environment. This allowed the new residents of the islands to grow forms of community that are otherwise impossible to implement during the design process of new-build housing estates.[22]

As well as a means of addressing social issues, and of allowing new communities to learn how to live together in more effective and altogether more human ways, 1:1 Scale tactics and practices have also been used by artists working with communities who wish to physically rebuild their existing urban and social infrastructures. So in the work of Theaster Gates, forms of 1:1 Scale Practice and social activism are combined with the reskilling and retooling of local citizens in the reclamation of their communities.[23] In the ongoing 'Dorchester Projects', Gates both inspired and helped residents in his home neighbourhood of Chicago's South Side to revitalise and regenerate the area.[24] Using his knowledge as a potter, and the idea of using what is in front of you, and ready to hand, to reshape the world around you, Gates began to buy cheap and abandoned housing stock in the Dorchester area of South Chicago with the ambition of collaboratively repurposing it.

Over the years, Gates and his community have rebuilt several buildings, including an old bank (now called the Art Bank), to develop a network of connected facilities and hubs for film, performance, dance, music, reading and publishing.[25] As Gates himself says, by thinking together with architects, developers, educators and community activists, and by using the skills of alternative entrepreneurship, economic and cultural redevelopment and placemaking, it has been possible to reimagine and reshape an abandoned and run-down community into a cultural destination.[26] In doing so, Gates has also actively contributed to what he sees as more complicated ways of thinking about the reshaping of cities.

These examples of emerging 1:1 Scale Practice begin to reveal a complex and significant shift towards new roles and uses of art within the landscape of our current condition of neoliberal occupation. On one hand, none of these practices rely, in any traditional way, on making scaled-down equivalences of the real world as a means to re-draw our attention to difficult and problematic social problems. Nor do these practices and projects simply use the terms and conditions of our experience of art to propose possible solutions that are hypothetical – as messages in a bottle, sent from the island confines of the world of art, and aimed at the shorelines and continents of the future. Neither do they yield objects or artworks that can be best (or only) understood within the confines of a museum or gallery space. In this sense they do not function from the 'outside in' or the 'inside out' – the frameworks of the art world are not required to understand them as art.

Equally, none of these artists or projects set themselves against the world of art. There is no sense that the world of art is to be shunned as an unnecessary and hierarchical hindrance. These artists use the existing tools of art, as well as the newly emerging protocols and possibilities of 1:1 Scale Practice, to make things happen in the world in ways that might not be possible if they were to adopt other more definable approaches (as community activists, social workers, architects or alternative entrepreneurs). But these forms of practice all still display a necessity, or perhaps more a need, to work across the once distinct gap between art and everyday life. This is because they rely upon the existing protocols of the art world to somehow remain identifiable as art works at all.

In this sense the projects of artist such as Lacey, van Heeswijk and Gates are neither imports from everyday life into the world of art, nor are they exports of art-world protocols into the sphere of the real. They seem to hover as hybrid practices that enable their collaborators and users to re-engage with taking back control of their lives, circumstances and environments through the existing protocols of that art world. In Lacey's work, collaborators co-produce forms of artwork and documentation that are consciously intended to be situated within museum and gallery spaces. This has the effect of using the art world to draw attention to issues while empowering those communities and collaborators to work within institutional environments that would usually preclude their participation as producers of art.

In the work of van Heeswijk the mechanisms of the contemporary art world which seek to step outside the museum and gallery space, such as the commissioning of art works in the public realm by biennials, provide a means by which communities can use art as a tool for building long-term and sustainable solutions to immediate social problems and urgencies. Gates, as an artist who is already internationally renowned for working across a range of interdisciplinary media, such as sculpture, pottery, performance and installation, uses his position to recirculate art-world value into urban regeneration. All allow their users to remap the territories of global neoliberal occupation in terms of their own specific, complex and located conditions – enabling them to use art to represent themselves to themselves, and each other, in ways that also allow them to remake and repurpose their ideological and material surroundings. However, none seems entirely able to shake off the guarantee of the art world to underwrite their real-world social, political and economic effect.

New activist tools for Useful Art

It is at this point that I'd like to re-examine some of the key issues that I raised by revisiting the work of Owen Griffiths and Jo Marsh, whose practices we met in the introduction to this chapter. Both, I would argue, provide recent examples of how Useful Art and 1:1 Scale Practice are being directly and self-consciously deployed as a means of direct community activism. In the first example, the work of artist Owen Griffiths will help us to gain more perspective on how artists are using Useful Art and 1:1 Scale Practice to re-empower communities and individuals who have been socially, politically and economically disadvantaged by the occupation of global neoliberalism.

More specifically I would like to look at two of the specific Useful Art methodologies – 'gleaning' and 'digging where you stand' – which Griffiths uses. In the second example, the work of Tŷ Pawb Creative Director Jo Marsh will, I hope, also begin to illustrate how forms of Useful Art are now directly impacting institutions who might wish to rethink and remake their own relationships to their local, national and international communities. I would like to look at how Marsh is developing and deploying the Useful Art methodology of 'taking it to market' to do this. Both examples offer ways of making work, and of working together, that run counter to the financially driven models of neoliberal museum and gallery management.

1:1 Scale Practice and artistic activism

Owen Griffiths: 'Glean' and 'Dig Where You Stand'

For the artist Owen Griffiths, Useful Art offers a means to work with communities to co-produce hyper-local activisms. These, along with all the other instances of Useful Art locally and globally, contribute to an ever-extending network of social re-empowerment and micro-resistance. Working closely with communities that occupy post-industrial landscapes and cities, such as his home city of Swansea in South Wales, Griffiths often refers to his work as the process of 'gleaning' and the act of 'digging where you stand'. For Griffiths, gleaning is derived from the historical need for rural labourers to sustain themselves and their families by looking for whatever was left behind in the cracks and furrows of a previous harvest and, in turn, by gathering and sharing whatever was found – that which was hidden but remained useful.

In 2017 Griffiths was commissioned to work on the project Tŷ Unnos, to celebrate the 800th anniversary of the Charter of the Forest, with the National Botanic Garden of Wales and the English grassroots environmental and education organisation Common Ground. Tŷ unnos, which translates as 'one-night house', is a centuries-old Welsh tradition which states that, if you build a house on common land in one night, and there is still a fire burning in the hearth by morning, then the land is rightfully yours.

Using Tŷ unnos as a both a starting point and inspiration, Griffiths collaborated with communities who live and work around the National Botanic Garden of Wales, as well as volunteers and visitors, in the construction of a building that explores what the histories of this tradition can tell us about current social and cultural disconnection from land. The Tŷ Unnos structure also remains as a both a permanent artwork in the collection of the National Botanic Garden of Wales and as a public forest school. What this illustrates is that, in the hands of Griffiths, the act of gleaning is a collective recuperation of skills and shared knowledge that have begun to slip from sight as a consequence of long-term social and economic decline. It is a 1:1 Scale Useful Art process in which communities rebuild from within while, at the same time, setting themselves against the grain of a global and networked neoliberalism that would reduce them to the economic wasteland of leftover rubble.

'Digging where you stand', meanwhile, involves communities reimagining and remaking the post-industrial landscapes and environments that they have inherited and now occupy. Borrowed (or gleaned) from a 1960s Swedish strategy for working with local history, Griffiths has developed this into a 1:1 scale operation of Useful Art. It's a strategy for excavating and analysing the complex relationships that exist between the people within communities, their physical places in the world, and the contexts of history and geography that make them unique. In the 2018 project 'Treherbert Skyline' Griffiths brought together over a hundred community members of Treherbert village, at the top of the Rhondda Fawr valley in Wales, to explore themes and issues of industrial heritage, climate change and existing structures of power.

Once a significant coalmining area, the Rhondda Valley fell into social and economic decline after major pits were closed after the loss of the 1984/85 miners' strike. 'Treherbert Skyline' invited community members to imagine long-term and generational change, sustainable business solutions and biodiversity that would draw upon radical Welsh history, lived experience of political resistance and a social reconsideration and remapping of existing resources. For Griffiths, 'digging where you stand' offers a way in which we can radically and collectively rethink how we might make our own historical legacy. Following the ideas of philosopher and co-collaborator Roman Krznaric,[27] who argues that we have already colonised the future as a depopulated dumping ground of ecological and technological waste and debt, Griffiths supports the idea of using 1:1 Scale Useful Art to provide and foster a better inheritance for our next generations.

As a practitioner of Useful Art, Griffiths deliberately sets these shared forms of collaborative working in opposition to the usual ways in which art, architecture and urban design projects are used as neoliberal tools in the redevelopment of economically challenged post-industrial environments. As we saw in Chapter 1, new strategies for developing urban regeneration projects, based upon the commercial viability of contemporary art as a tourism and leisure commodity, began to emerge during the 1990s and 2000s. These economically driven regeneration projects were, more often than not, formed by the development of short-term allegiances – between governments, councils, corporate interest groups and private investors – who all wished to benefit from repurposing post-industrial sites into global hubs for shopping, leisure and hospitality. Often, these developments were framed as cultural urban regeneration projects – in which 'genius' artists, architects and urbanists were seen as being capable of remoulding broken communities for the better. These artistic heroes were employed to impose their ideas and solutions on those same communities with little or no consultation. So both governments and private-sector interests were able to act as if they were providing future-proof solutions to long-term economic and social decline.

In contrast, the collective process of gleaning, and the micro-local act of 'digging where you stand', deliver the regenerative power back into the hands of the community. In Griffiths's work, the usual power structures and flows of economic regeneration can be reversed. However, as some of these projects become long-term and, in a sense, take on a life of their own, the traditional lines between artist, artwork and audience, as well as those between the strategies and methodologies of gleaning and 'digging where you stand', often become blurred and entangled.

In 2011 Griffiths began work on the longstanding 'Vetch Veg' project on the site of the old 'Vetch Field' football ground, which had housed Swansea FC from 1912 to 2005. Guided by the community, 2,500 square metres of waste ground, surrounded by tight streets of Victorian terraced housing, was transformed into a productive green space for growing, meeting, learning and exchange. The site now contains over a hundred planting beds where families, community organisations, charities, retirement centres and churches can grow their own food. The site also contains a kitchen, a pizza oven, polytunnels and a library. As well as preparing meals for one another, keeping chickens and growing their own food, the gardeners involved in the 'Vetch Veg' project learn skills such as cob-oven building and beekeeping.

Initially the project was considered to be short-term, due to a nine-month access lease that was granted by the local council. But due to the successful development of the project, and the fact that it was clearly playing a key role within the community that surrounded and used it, 'Vetch Veg' was granted a long-term lease. While 'Vetch Veg' continues as a community green space, and is now run by its members, the connected impact of such locally focused projects also extends far beyond the gardens

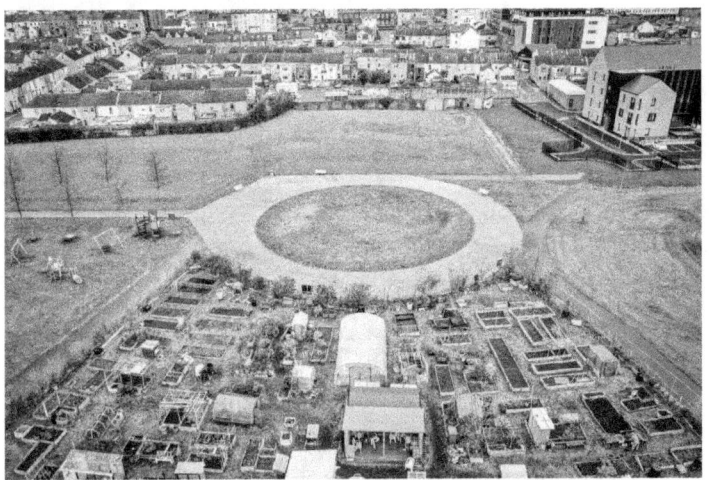

2.2 Owen Griffiths, 'Vetch Veg', Swansea, 2019. Image courtesy of
Owen Griffiths

themselves – the project has informed new Arts Council Wales
policy, encouraged the creation of the first Cabinet Minister for
Sustainability in Swansea, and encouraged public funding into
other community green projects in the city.

More recently, the principles embedded in the methodologies
of 'gleaning' and 'digging where you stand' were activated again
when, in 2018, Griffiths began working with Swansea's National
Waterfront Museum on the project 'GRAFT: A Soil Based Syllabus'. Co-collaborating with local communities, schools and
adult learners, the project has sought to enable communities
to grow food and explore making through the development of
an alternative curriculum. For Griffiths, this project provides
the basis for exploring and examining the production of a new
kind of 'practical pedagogy' – one which connects (or seeks to
reconnect) food, sustainable development and the creation of

green infrastructures within the environment of the city. As a result of this, the garden provides a place for people to grow food, cook, collaborate and learn, while providing templates for reimagining a post-industrial and post-COVID cityscape. Volunteers themselves are invited to join an integrated curriculum of outdoor learning and making which, again, is connected to food. All of the structures in the garden were built from scratch. As participants became users, they gleaned new skills and shared existing knowledge together.

In return, Swansea's National Waterfront Museum provides participants with accreditation, training and support to explore new skills thorough the project, which has been designed to be wholly participatory. In this way, Griffiths's practice begins to merge the tradition of ground-up education with that of permaculture.[28] Taking a reading of a specific locality and its resources (or digging where one stands) becomes a way for communities to reconnect, recycle and reuse what they have at hand, enabling them to rebuild and redesign the ways they live, with the tools they already have, in a way that allows them to rethink their relationships to identity, location and place. Key to this, for Griffiths, is also the long-term investment and relationships that can be built between himself, in his role as artist/activist, and the communities he works with. The aim of this long-term practice is to collaboratively create examples and models that will help to serve other communities in their pursuit of change and re-empowerment. This relies on the artist nurturing, participating in and developing not just dialogues with members of the community, but long-term friendships.

Griffiths's practice proposes a way of working with communities, in the co-production of long-term and functional 1:1 Scale Useful Art projects, that are capable of decolonising and dissolving

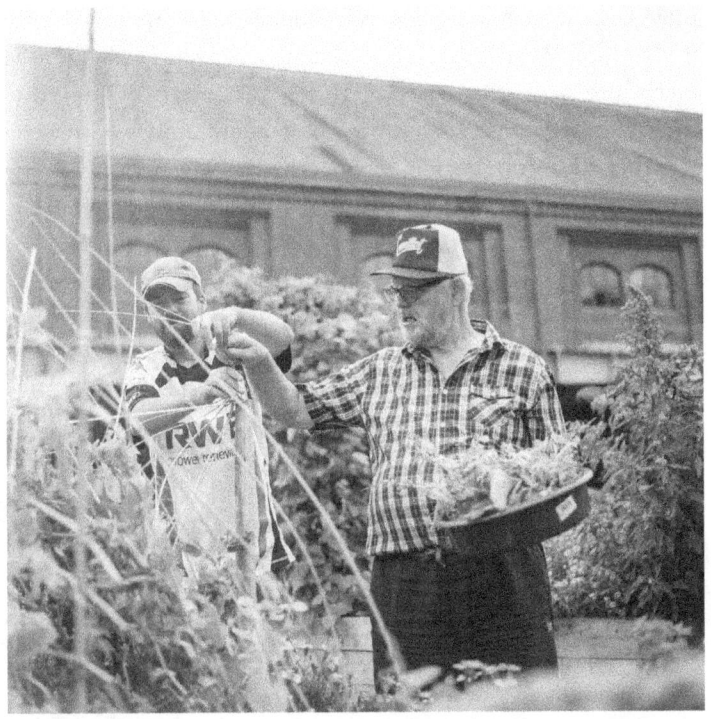

2.3 Owen Griffiths, 'GRAFT: A Soil Based Syllabus (a permanent edible landscape and education space, National Waterford Museum of Wales), established in 2017. Image courtesy of Owen Griffiths

our assumptions and prejudices about the planet and the future. Instead of seeing the world through a lens of endless growth on a finite planet – a short-term view that is wreaking havoc on our social, political, economic and environmental ecologies – Griffiths proposes that we make a stand, glean and dig together for ways that might allow us to co-design our communities from within. In turn, Griffiths also sees the practice of Useful Art as providing ways for overlooked communities to begin to participate in developing new forms of co-skilling that will enable them to tackle pressing urban issues on their own terms. Often, and through no fault of their own, these communities have been identified by local, regional and national governments as posing 'Wicked Problems' – a term which is used by design thinkers to denote a condition of such complexity and interconnectivity that it seems impossible to solve.[29]

However, far from admitting to some kind of powerless surrender in the face of overbearing complexity, what Griffiths offers here is a concerted way of working together which recognises that the problems we face are also the fault lines of struggle inscribed within the condition of global neoliberal occupation. In the face of over-simplistic local and national policy solutions to urban problems – which, over recent decades, have often played out in the breaking-up of communities, the demolition of their housing, and the resale of cheap land to large building companies – Griffiths points to ways in which we can work together locally and specifically, in the production of alternative ways of living, that recognise the connectivity and interdependence of these problems while rejecting the idealist need to find 'one-size-fits-all' solutions.

In this way, 'gleaning' and 'digging where you stand' – as processes of continual dialogue, ongoing process and the constant nurturing of productive friendships – are key tools to foster in times of multiple crisis, disconnection and the radical marginalisation of once connected communities. In turn, Griffith's long-term and 1:1 Scale Useful Art projects envision and imagine a world of usership and collaboration where practices of reconnection might help us to move from linear to circular economies – and, in doing so, addressing inequalities that more traditional forms of art, design and architecture propagate and uphold. So Griffiths often refers to the many projects he has undertaken with communities, in both Swansea and further afield, as forming small islands in a growing archipelago of Useful Art.

These islands of Useful Art, I would argue, can also be seen as instances of micro-activism in which the shards and remnants of use and use value can be struggled over and reclaimed from within our current condition of neoliberal occupation. To begin examining this idea of small local micro-activisms, formally or informally connecting into a growing network of alternative resistance and change, I'd now like to turn to the work of Jo Marsh.

Jo Marsh: Tŷ Pawb and 'taking it to market'

As we have already seen, Jo Marsh is the Creative Director of Tŷ Pawb, a Cultural Community resource in the city of Wrexham, North Wales. As a hybrid/intersectional space, Tŷ Pawb's key aim is to bring together both Wrexham's historical heritage as a market town with an ongoing socially engaged art agenda that plays out across shops, market stalls, a food court, a tiered theatre-performance space, two gallery spaces and a rooftop garden (which forms part of the attached multi-storey car park). Essentially, Tŷ Pawb – which opened in 2018 following support and funding from Wrexham County Borough Council, Arts Council Wales and the Welsh Government – began life as the potentially fractious bringing-together of two former entities that didn't really have anything to do with each other.

The first was the 'People's Market' which, having been built in the 1990s as the third market in a town that could only financially support two, had been identified for demolition. The second was Oriel Wrecsam (formerly Wrexham Art Centre), which had opened in the 1970s and had been denied funding for expansion in the 1990s due to public scepticism and a subsequent lack of local political support. In the late 2000s there was an appraisal of the options for potential sites for an expanded 'municipal cultural offer'. As a result of this the possibility of moving the Oriel, Wrexham's existing public space for contemporary and applied art, to the site of the flagging People's Market, began to materialise. The innovative solution to this was both ideological and architectural. Rather than keep the market place and the art space as separate, a new possibility emerged.

In consultation with the architect Sarah Featherstone, it was decided that a single dedicated art space would share a large indoor 'town square' with the footprint of the previous market and car-park spaces. This 'baggy-space' approach (as Featherstone called it) has allowed for a large degree of flexibility within the physical space of Tŷ Pawb between market stalls, food outlets, performance spaces and educational and exhibition programmes. Perhaps more importantly, as well as offering an architecturally interchangeable space, Tŷ Pawb has also begun to show how the traditional borders and boundaries between art, education, commerce and community can be broken down in productive ways. As artists, market-stall holders, educators and community members mix together, Tŷ Pawb has become a site in which new ways of working, thinking, making and doing together can be imagined. Interestingly, this comes to represent an ongoing 1:1 Scale Useful Art collaboration, active in the community, rather than a series of theoretical propositions for change. Delightfully, they have a stated commitment to foregrounding 'play' as a means of creatively working together across differences

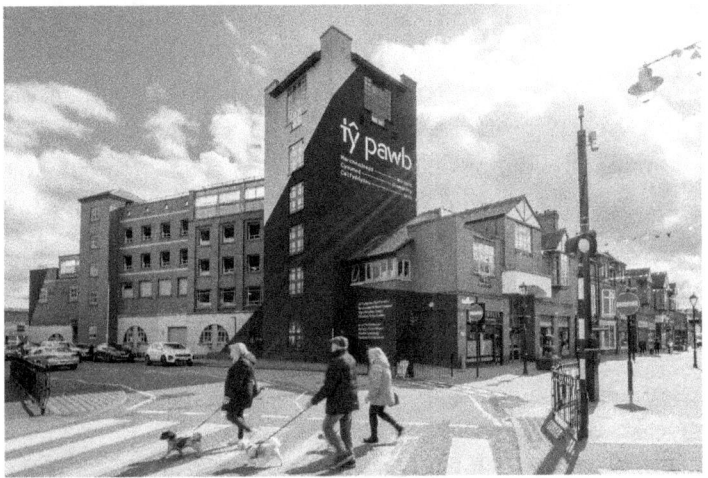

2.4 Tŷ Pawb, Wrexham. Image courtesy of Tŷ Pawb and Harry Meadley

of age, gender, ethnicity, sexuality and class. Tŷ Pawb is providing a shared and co-owned sense of what can be gained when formerly distinct spheres of social activity become leaky, unruly and creatively disobedient.

The significance of this approach becomes clearer when the broader context of Tŷ Pawb is considered. In early consultation with Wrexham Council, not only would the new Arts Centre occupy the site of the People's Market (and due to public demand find a way to include the market in its offer), the new hybrid space would also need to act as a way to link an emerging out-of-town shopping centre (Eagles Meadow) back into the historical town centre, thus helping to reactivate the centre itself. Tŷ Pawb not only sits at the junction of market, car park and gallery/theatre space, it also sits on the political and economic fault line of a deindustrialised town, suffering from the further impact of a post-2007 economic crash, and the expectation of linking a market-town heritage to future dreams of sustainable social growth through the funding of an 'art hub'.

In this context, the offer that Tŷ Pawb sought to provide was far more ambitious and far-reaching than the bringing together of art and everyday life (gallery space and market space), or a physical crossroads between old and new forms of commercial consumerism (the traditional pedestrian town centre and the peripheral and car-based retail offer). Instead, Tŷ Pawb also sought to provide a community hub through which sustainable, creative and long-term solutions to local issues and problems could be worked upon and addressed.

One of the first challenges that confronted Marsh was the complex knot of ideas, expectations and fears that potential users and stakeholders had in the new venture. To do this, she employed the services of Cardiff-based graphic design agency Elfen to run a series of public workshops – open to market traders, artists, politicians and locals alike – that would enable an open, inclusive and flexible rethinking of the new site's multi-function potential. The result of these workshops was both name for the site – Tŷ Pawb, which means 'everyone's house' – and the development of plans for a space that would allow for communities to discuss and action collaborative approaches to civic and social urgencies around, health, sustainability, environment, education and local identity.

Key to this approach was the opening of a dedicated 'Useful Art Space', or 'Lle Celf Ddefnyddiol' in Welsh, which is intended to be a space of play, dialogue and learning as much as a traditional gallery space. Its aim is to provide the context within which ideas are generated, artful solutions are sought, and ways of living together are imagined as shared futures. As 'Tŷ Pawb's website puts it:

> We have created Lle Celf Ddefnyddiol/the Useful Art Space because we believe art can be much more than something to look at or watch, we believe art can be a tool for social change. The transformation of this space builds on the Useful Art approach that has underpinned Tŷ Pawb since opening in 2018 and is at the very heart of our work. Central to Lle Celf Ddefnyddiol is the interaction between arts and markets: we want to harness the innate creativity of market trading, exploring commonalities between what is happening in the market hall and the work of artists at Tŷ Pawb.[30]

As well as being furnished with specially made structures that emphasise mixed use, re-use and play, the space hosts a range of developing community activities – Community Photography sessions, Family Art and Playwork sessions and Bom Dia Cymru, an initiative which sought to welcome the Portuguese Community into Tŷ Pawb – have seen local artists developing creative skills classes that led to the production of items that could be sold in the market place. Similarly, 'Make Yourself at Home' offered refugee and asylum seekers the opportunity to work with artist Ibukun Baldwin to learn textile, ceramic, printing, embroidery, accessory and product design skills, while also having the opportunity to make products that could be sold. In this project Baldwin shared her skills and convictions, gained through setting up her own business, that marginalised communities can address issues of neglect and need through working with the creative industries. One participant in the project has gone on to set up and sustain a successful business in Tŷ Pawb's market hall.

In many ways, all of these initiatives, as well as the hybrid concept of Tŷ Pawb itself, owe much to the vision of Jo Marsh,

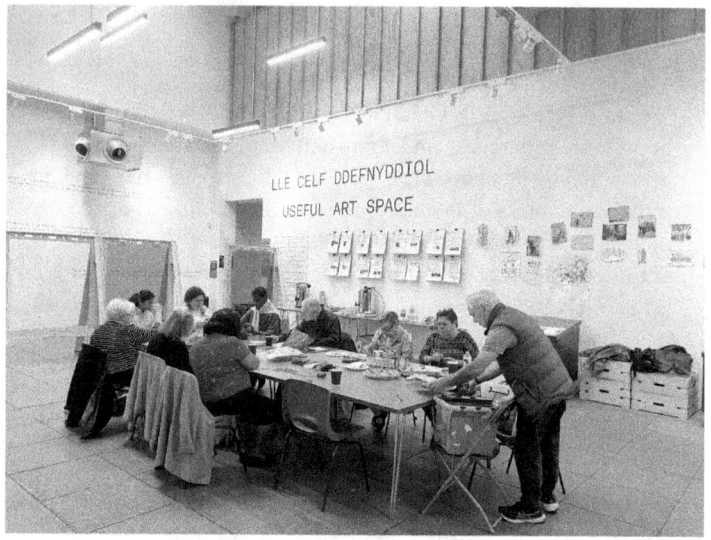

2.5 Lle Celf Ddefnyddiol/Useful Art Space at Tŷ Pawb. Image courtesy of Tŷ Pawb

who, as a means to help us think through and make through some of these complexities, has developed the idea of 'taking it to market'. For Marsh, the concept of 'taking it to market' is twofold. On one level it encapsulates simply what it says – 'taking it to market' as the idea of working creatively in a way that enables those skills to be traded and exchanged. On another, it allows us to begin rethinking some of the complexities that arise when art is used as an operational tool for developing 1:1 Scale Useful Art projects and solutions to pressing social issues. Marsh is aware that, in our current ways of thinking, art and exchange – or 'art' and 'everything else' as she deftly, but also bluntly, puts it – are more often than not seen to be mutually exclusive. However, Marsh also realises that forms of re-empowerment, using art as a tool for social change, won't always lead to each participant defining themselves as an 'artist' as we currently recognise the term. Rather than hatching an endless battery of individuals who might want to show, display or share symbolic alternatives to our current ways of living in museum and gallery spaces, Marsh proposes that Useful Art can be used by both communities and community members alike to open up conversations, exchange ideas, and to develop real-world, realistic strategies for change.

In this way, using art as a tool for change does not tally with the concern that Useful Art simply does the work of neoliberalism on its behalf, or is a misuse of art, as we know it or knew it to be, in order to solve social problems and issues whose responsibility should lie with the state. Instead, the idea of 'taking it to market' indicates a willingness to open up, examine and rethink some of the parameters that shape our experience of the world. By disrupting the usual flows of our common experience – in which the art world and the commercial world seem intractable consequences of our condition of neoliberal occupation – 'taking it to market' allows users of Tŷ Pawb to actively rethink and remake their relations to current circumstances.

Just one example of this is Tŷ Pawb trader Steve Tapp who, since being made redundant during the COVID pandemic in 2020, has made a business in refurbishing training shoes. Tapp's decision to step away from the security and stability of a corporate career and to effectively turn his hobby into his main source of income has also provided him with new levels of autonomy, possibility and fulfilment that were absent in his formerly stressful and highly regulated working life. Steve's choice to live a life creatively and artfully is characteristic of some of the key qualities that Marsh observes in Tŷ Pawb's community of market traders more generally – resilience, innovation, agility, immediacy, strong local connection, nimbleness, endless creativity, entrepreneurial spirit and an ad hoc approach – which, Marsh believes, can be learned, used and repurposed as key skills by both artists and community members alike. It is because of this that much of Tŷ Pawb's programming now emphasises a need to cross-pollinate between the formerly separate spheres of art and life to produce an effective and usable civically focused public space.

The idea of 'taking it to market' shows us some of the logics and ambitions that lie behind Tŷ Pawb's ongoing 'Maes Parcio Creadigol' or 'Creative Car Park' project. Initiated as a collaboration between KIM Inspire, Addo and artists Marja Bonada and Owen Griffiths, 'Creative Car Park' is a collaborative project in which the car-park floor above the gallery space of Tŷ Pawb has been repurposed as an experimental green space – one in which communities, organisations and artists can work together to imagine new forms of creative possibility. For example, the co-design and construction of an outdoor workshop, shelter and storage space was undertaken as a project which enabled community collaborators to develop new skills and confidence through building, willow weaving, mosaic making and ceramics. The site will be used to host events, gatherings, workshops, training and education initiatives that work closely with Tŷ Pawb's Useful Art Space. And, as we saw in the introduction to this chapter, 'Creative Car Park' will also offer an opportunity for creative-practice and action-learning initiatives to be used as a means of linking Tŷ Pawb and its communities with other garden spaces, community groups and Useful Art initiatives on local, regional, national and international scales.

Both Tŷ Pawb and the work of artists such as Owen Griffiths offer key examples of working with what you have to hand to re-equip and re-empower disenfranchised communities with the means to address and change their current conditions of existence. In doing so, and by activating methodologies such as 'digging where you stand', 'gleaning' and 'taking it to market', these 1:1 Scale Useful Art projects are enabling those communities to reconnect with those forms of the 'real' that have become all but lost under global neoliberal occupation. These reworkings of the shards and remnants of a past reality – where our possible presents and probable futures can be actively redefined and rethought – necessitate the repurposing and reuse of our civic and public institutions, such as museums, galleries and universities.

As I have already argued, these institutions can no longer simply offer autonomy or asylum: they are already shot through with the neoliberal logic of endless exchange. Yet, at the same time, they are not yet completely subsumed: they have not quite disappeared or morphed into the network of simulacra which defined our condition of neoliberal occupation. They present themselves as sites where the asymmetrical struggle of resistance can be effectively played out, where the use value of art can be reactivated in the struggle to repurpose and extend their role and function as hubs of resistance. In this sense our civic institutions of the Enlightenment, shot through as they are with historical baggage, can act as unlikely points of intersection, where different constituencies can collaboratively use art as a tool of negotiation and continual redefinition. And it is because of this that I would now like to examine how activist artists are deploying strategies of Useful Art and 1:1 Scale Practice as a means to imagine the institutions of the future.

3

Useful Art and the Useful Museum

On Friday 7 October 2011 I was sitting in the auditorium of the Van Abbemuseum in Eindhoven for the first day of the Autonomy Symposium. Set against the backdrop of the Arab Spring and the burgeoning Occupy/Indignados Movements, the debate included contributions from Jacques Rancière, Peter Osborne, Tania Bruguera, Gerald Raunig, Isabell Lorey, Thomas Hirschhorn, Ruth Sondregger, Kim Mereiene, Franco Berardi and Hito Steyerl. This three-day symposium was itself part of a three-year Autonomy Project, which I'd helped to organise with my colleagues at the Van Abbemuseum and other institutions.

The initial idea of the Autonomy Project was to test and reconsider the term 'autonomy', as it related to modern and contemporary art, in the light of recent neoliberal social, political and economic changes that were directly affecting the running and organisation of major museums and galleries. Key to this was a recognition of the increasing demands that local, regional and national governments were exerting upon museums and galleries to continually measure and evidence their economic and cultural viability. As museums and galleries were expected to bring in ever more visitors, and to demonstrate how this directly and indirectly affected their revenue streams (from ticket sales to tourism impact on local and adjacent service industries), the more they were expected to stage 'blockbuster' shows of the work of well-known artists – Manet, Monet, Degas, Matisse, Picasso, and so on – whose success, in turn, would be measured and calibrated in financial terms. This self-perpetuating loop, it seemed, was taking away the ability of museums and galleries to look beyond the crowd-pleasers and make space for experimental artworks, exhibitions and projects.

Therefore, the Autonomy Project set out to re-examine the problematic and contested meaning of autonomy itself. On one hand, the development of European Modern Art had depended on the idea of autonomy as a guarantee that art would be a special kind of experience that was separate from the hubbub of everyday life and its concerns. 'Art for art's sake' became, from the late nineteenth century onwards, the mantra of an avant-garde that saw art as something that operated according to its own specialist rules and systems. On the other hand, the term 'autonomy' suggested something independent: the possibility of a kind of shared civic space, encapsulated by museums and galleries, within which criticisms of the political and economic status quo could be developed and mounted. Within this context, the Autonomy Project marked an intention to look deeply and critically at this long-standing debate about the role and function of art in society at a time when the 'value' of art was running a genuine risk of being subsumed, as a series of measurable and economic functions, into the expanding portfolios of the global tourism and leisure industry.

What followed was a three-year project which saw established artists, thinkers, theorists, critics and philosophers work alongside undergraduate, postgraduate and early-career artists in an attempt to rethink some of the abiding terms and conditions of their practices. The Autonomy Project was organised around a series of summer schools, which took place at the Van Abbemuseum, the Dutch Art Institute and Liverpool John Moores School of Art and Design in 2010, 2011 and 2012, respectively. The aim of these schools was to bring together artists who were interested in developing and contesting ideas around autonomy from their perspective.[1] The outcomes of the project were published in a series of 'Autonomy Newspapers', followed by the first 'Manual of Useful Art' in 2012 and later 'Art and Autonomy' in 2022.[2]

For those involved in the Autonomy Project itself, the 'Autonomy Symposium' of 2011 marked a turning point in our thinking, scope and ambition in relation to emerging questions of Useful Art. Rather than just attempting to revivify the term 'autonomy' as a means to change things, the project looked towards the ideas of use, use value and usership as ways of radically rethinking the terms and conditions of what art, art institutions and our experiences of art could be or become.[3]

For my part, as one of the organisers of the Autonomy Project and as an editor of the *Autonomy Newspaper*, the early 2010s was a time when I began to wonder about the role of artistic autonomy and the idea that art should remain useless, as a kind of art-world short cut that somehow guaranteed, or at least underscored, art's claim to have either political or social relevance by default. As a result of this I also began to wonder about a series of questions which are still fundamental to my thinking about Useful Art and its relationship to use value and usership. As we saw in Chapters 1 and 2, this also led me to consider what would happen if we began to imagine that there was, in fact, no inside-out or outside-in to the condition of neoliberal occupation – no escape to a separate world-that-is-art. And, given this assumption that art is as stuck within the neoliberal rules of the real world as we are, I began to wonder what an art of resistance might look like if it were capable of escaping the gravitational pull of its assumed roles and functions within this new historical phase of neoliberal occupation. Some of my own questions began to be answered when, during the first day of the Autonomy Symposium, the Cuban artist and activist Tania Bruguera talked about her own work and practice in relation to Useful Art.

Useful Art and Arte Útil

Beginning with two examples of her own practice, 'Tatlin's Whisper #5' (2008) – in which two members of the UK mounted police were asked to demonstrate crowd control protocols on an unsuspecting audience in the Turbine Hall of Tate Modern – and 'Tatlin's Whisper #6 (Havana Version)' of 2009 – in which audience members were offered the opportunity to speak freely on a microphone for one minute each during the Havana Biennial – Bruguera talked about the need for artists to make forms of political art that were committed to instigating real world change, as opposed to propositions that could only be understood within the context of the museum or gallery. As an example, in the case of 'Tatlin's Whisper #5', Bruguera pointed to the possibility of offering museum audiences 1:1 scale access to the kinds of experiences (in this case being physically controlled by officials on horseback) that most would only have seen on TV. In the case of 'Tatlin's Whisper #6', Bruguera pointed to the possibility of using art to provide a political moment of free speech that would normally be denied to citizens in Cuba.

Following on from this, Bruguera began to ask a series of questions around what Useful Art might be, and the challenges that Useful Art might present to artists, audiences and museums alike: how does an artist straddle the dichotomy between doing political art and acting politically? How does an audience 'see' or experience Useful Art when it might not be object-based or even be played out in a museum or gallery space? What happens when an artist makes Useful Art that is beyond their own capacity to control or complete? Do artists become initiators of such work rather than authors – and what is the role of collaborators who also make the work? How is our experience, as well as our understanding of art, affected when there is no longer an audience in the traditional sense of the word – when a work of Useful Art plays out at 1:1 scale, in real time and in the real world? In the light of this, Bruguera also began to open up further lines of enquiry into how Useful Art might no longer need to be aesthetic, object-based or even legal but, instead, would be intended to provide workable solutions to real-world problems and social issues.

Bruguera's work helps us to examine the future of the conventional relationships between art, artwork and audience within the art/museum space. If there is no audience in the traditional sense for Useful Art, as Bruguera suggested, then what, exactly, would be their new role? How do we rethink our traditional relationships to art when audiences no longer simply experience or even use that art but, instead, begin to make (or in some circumstances even become) Useful Art themselves? And what might happen when dialogues are no longer about artworks but begin to happen via artworks – when political moments and interventions are made or activated through the collaborative production of Useful Art? In such cases, when do artworks begin or end, and who decides? And if Useful Art works are only activated when they are being used, what happens to them when they are deactivated? Can Useful Art projects have different lives, in different places and at different times – carrying different meanings, and different uses, to multiple and sometimes overlapping collaborators and instigators?

In full awareness of these contradictions and gravitational pulls – because as we know, there is no longer an outside-in or an inside-out to the art system within our current condition of neoliberal occupation – the director of the Van Abbemuseum, Charles Escher, agreed to address some of these questions. In collaboration with Bruguera, the museum itself staged a temporary and experimental alternative to conventional museum and gallery spaces. 'The Museum of Arte Útil' opened at the Van Abbemuseum in 2013. Rather than offering a symbolic representation of what a future museum of use might look or be like, 'The Museum of Arte Útil' was intended to act as 1:1 scale reboot of the operational systems which have underpinned the workings of museums and galleries since the Palace of the Louvre was first made freely open to the public in 1793. The opening of 'The Museum of Arte Útil' also led to the development of the Association of Arte Útil as an alternative online and offline network of global Useful Art activism. In turn, the growing idea that museums and galleries could become active hubs where Useful Art projects are generated subsequently developed into the idea of 'The Constituent Museum', where museums and galleries would become active sites for negotiating and propagating real-world change.

The Museum of Arte Útil

From 7 December 2013 to 30 March 2014 the Van Abbemuseum undertook a large 1:1 scale experiment in which it began to both imagine and make visible what a future museum based on usership might look and be like. The Museum of Arte Útil set out to develop some of Tania Bruguera's thinking from the Autonomy Symposium some two years earlier, and which had subsequently been developed into the eight criteria of Arte Útil (which we looked at in the Introduction to this book). Key to this was the opportunity to examine the current operational systems of museums or galleries, in their relationship to Useful Art and 1:1 Scale Useful Art practice, as a kind of framing paradox. On one hand, Useful Art and 1:1 Scale Useful Art practices depend on their representation within art museums and the art-world system if they are to be understood as art as we know it or knew it to be. On the other, it is difficult to understand and evaluate many of the roles and functions of Useful Art if we limit that understanding to our current protocols for identifying, experiencing and using art.

For example, and as we saw in Chapter 1, a facsimile reconstruction of the Granby 4 Streets Workshop/Showroom in the Tramway Gallery in Glasgow, as part of the 2015 Turner Prize-winning project between Assemble and Granby 4 Streets CLT, appears and functions in a completely different way to its real-world counterpart. Whereas the Tramway Gallery version only appeared for the duration of the 2015 Turner Prize display and allowed visitors to see and pre-order handcrafted objects made in the real-world workshop, the physical Granby 4 Streets Workshop functioned as an ongoing 1:1 Scale Useful Art project – an operational and community led business which employed

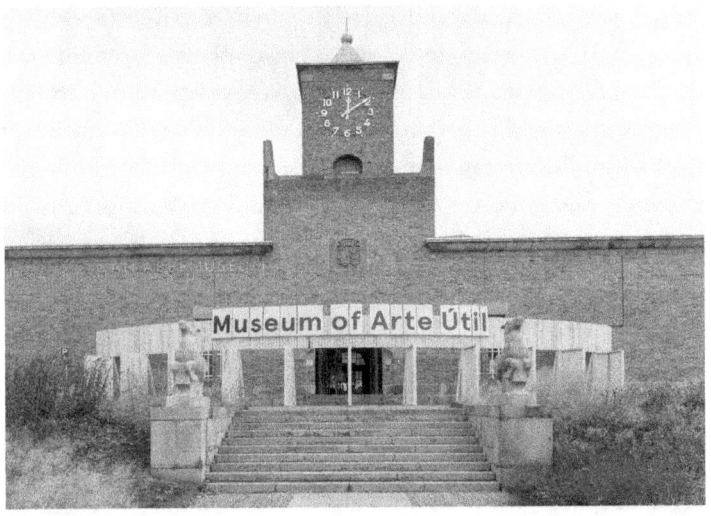

3.1 Museum of Arte Útil, Van Abbemuseum, 2013. Image courtesy of Peter Cox

and re-empowered local residents in the physical reclamation of their community.

Because of this, 'The Museum of Arte Útil' at the Van Abbemuseum was, in part, an attempt to shift some of the received ideas around the roles and functions of art and art museums within the condition of neoliberal occupation. The Van Abbemuseum itself was proposed as a site of interchange and co-production, where history and art could be collaboratively reused to imagine and make new forms of civic citizenship. Visitors to 'The Museum of Arte Útil' were given the choice of either paying a standard entrance fee or gaining free entry by agreeing to be active users of the show. As users, participants were asked to question their usual role as passive spectators and consumers of culture within a museum setting. Instead, they were asked how they could actively begin to help in transforming the Van Abbemuseum into a social power plant – a shared civic institution for input as well as output, where collective transformative energy could be generated for use in the world outside.

To aid this rethinking and revisioning of the traditional museum and gallery space, Bruguera and the curatorial team of the museum collaborated with the transdisciplinary design and building network Construct Lab to produce an alternative physical architecture for 'The Museum of Arte Útil'. They made a wooden circle which cut through the square rooms of the Van Abbemuseum's original gallery buildings, thereby challenging the white-walled cube experience of modern art. The same wood was also used to build tables, chairs, benches, discussion spaces and seminar spaces which would enable users to interact and activate the museum as social power plant. As well as presenting a new temporary entrance façade for the Van Abbemuseum, this physical rearrangement of the space enabled artists, designers, architects and local collaborators to think, discuss and build together. This resulted in the production of ten new temporary spaces out of materials that could be reused and reclaimed after 'The Museum of Arte Útil' had finished. The rooms of 'The Museum of Arte Útil' were themselves organised into seven 'Strategy' rooms – Use it Yourself, Institutional Repurpose, A-Legal, Space Hijack, Open Access, Legislative Change and Reforming Capital – two 'Analysis Rooms' – 'The Room of Propaganda, Legitimation and Belief' and the 'Room of Controversies' – and a central 'Archive Room' which housed a physical manifestation of the Association of Arte Útil as it then stood in 2013.

In view of this, both the physical and conceptual layout of 'The Museum of Arte Útil' was intended to challenge and subvert both the physical and conceptual means by which museums have traditionally organised their exhibitions and displays over the last two hundred years. Spaces were not necessarily intended to display finished artworks or objects of Useful Art. Instead, they mostly presented ideas, videos, drawings, diagrams and archival materials which signposted projects that were intended to have some real-world social, political or economic impact. In this way, the ten rooms of 'The Museum of Arte Útil', as the home of these signposts and plans, provide a blueprint that enables us to begin seeing and thinking about how Useful Art can operate in the world in multiple and complex ways. They also help us to imagine ways in which museums and galleries might operate differently without relying on the simplistic divide of useful versus useless art. Key to this was the open invitation for visitors to 'The Museum of Arte Útil' to become users – to discuss and contribute to the implementation of Useful Art projects beyond the scope and duration of 'The Museum of Arte Útil' exhibition itself.

The organisational structure of 'The Museum of Arte Útil'

At the centre of 'The Museum of Arte Útil' was a physical presentation of the Arte Útil online archive which, at the time, housed two hundred or so case studies. The case studies were displayed as printouts on a frame that users could take down and handle. Tables, chairs and writing materials were supplied so that individual or groups of users could consider the projects, discuss them with researchers and think through the case studies on display. Users were also asked to actively consider these case studies as an open-source toolkit, one that could be taken away and repurposed by users who wished to develop tactics and

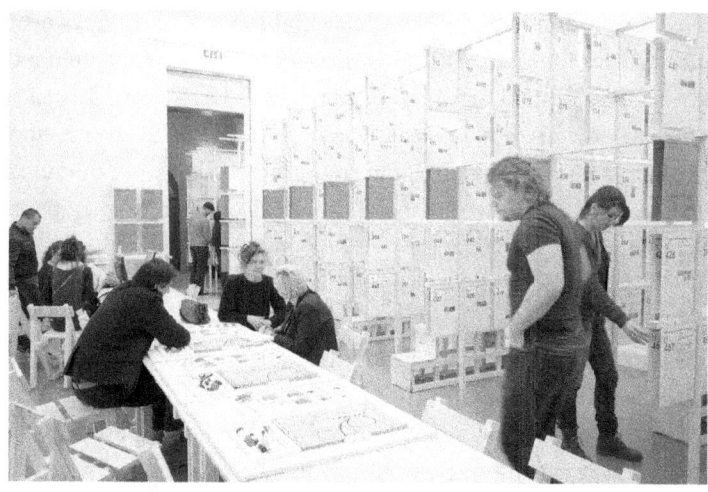

3.2 Arte Útil Archive, Museum of Arte Útil, Van Abbemuseum, 2013. Image courtesy of Peter Cox

methodologies for themselves and their communities. Users were also encouraged to propose their own projects for inclusion in the Association of Arte Útil archive. They were also encouraged to move away from the default mode of spectatorship – viewing the case studies as documentary evidence of completed artworks. Instead, they were asked to imagine them as a kind of fuel which would feed the museum as a social power plant. In order to activate these ambitions further, and to avoid the trap of simply using 'The Museum of Arte Útil' as a utopian representation of what art could or might be, a number of artists were invited to work with both the Van Abbemuseum and the city of Eindhoven, to propose and develop long-term projects that would foster ongoing relationships with local communities and organisations.

'Use it Yourself'

In 'Use it Yourself', which was the first of the seven strategy rooms of 'The Museum of Arte Útil', the idea of using both art and museums as tools for social change was raised. Going beyond the idea of Useful Art as a utilitarian alternative to useless and autonomous art, visitors were encouraged to think about how they might begin to re-empower themselves, and one another, by acting differently and using art as a tool to take matters back into their own hands. Examples of projects in this room included a re-presentation, for public use, of the artist duo Bik van der Pol's collection of 140 books from the now defunct publishers Loompanics Unlimited. The Loompanics books are a series of manuals and guidebooks on a wide range of topics and subjects that include how to start your own country, how to develop low-cost family food-storage systems and how to clear adult and juvenile criminal records.

'Use it Yourself' also foregrounded the work of Spanish social architect Santiago Cirugeda, initiator of the design and advocacy collective Recetas Urbanas, a group of architects, lawyers and social workers who seek to develop socially and ethically inclusive building projects by questioning the limits of legality within the city of Seville. More specifically, the room focused on the provision of a free, online and open-access toolkit developed by Cirugeda, which provides citizens with guidelines and instructions for building and creating spaces within the existing limits of legal infrastructures.

Children were encouraged to play in the 'Use it Yourself' room (which is something that was not usually tolerated or allowed in major museums at the time) and photocopiers were provided. This allowed visitors to make free copies of any of the Loompanics publication material on display, subverting the usual protocols of ownership and spectatorship, whereby museum objects are the property of the institution, to be looked at and not touched. Users were also encouraged to think about Useful Art in terms of an open-source repository of ideas, or toolkit of activisms, that can be exchanged, built upon and adapted freely without the usual constraints of artistic copyright or author permission.

'Institutional Repurpose'

The second thematic room, 'Institutional Repurpose', asked how institutions could change themselves if they were to become useful. More specifically, it sought to open up debates around what would have to happen to and within institutions to allow them to begin to use their own power, position and resources to directly tackle, rather than represent, urgent social issues. In addition to this, 'Institutional Repurpose' also asked what these uses might be – what could museums actually be used for?

To help unpack these issues it drew attention to the work of several artists who had collaborated with existing institutions in order to foster real-world social change. For example, the artist Paulina Cornejo had worked with Mexico's National Center for Crime Prevention and Citizen Participation. The funding this provided had enabled the production of the publication '100 Tácticas Creativas para la seguridad ciudadana' ('100 creative tactics for citizen security'), which presents a range of international projects that use art and creativity to propose solutions to social urgencies. As well as providing information on how such projects might be located and evaluated, '100 Tácticas Creativas' was also intended to provide an inspiration to other communities who might wish to activate their own solutions to local problems, as well as a toolkit for developing creative tactics and strategies.

Similarly, in his project 'Silent University', the artist Ahmet Öğüt worked with a range of international institutions to develop a university syllabus and open-access delivery mechanisms to provide educational opportunities for refugees, migrants and asylum seekers. Key to the success of this project is the involvement of refugees, migrants and asylum seekers, who have already gained professional and academic qualifications in their countries of origin as teachers. Provided with staff cards, student cards, attendance evidence and qualifications, teachers and attendees of the Silent University are able to gain help with the process of legal and cultural naturalisation in their new homes.

'A-Legal Strategy'

The third room, 'A-Legal Strategy', provided an opportunity to look at those forms of action and behaviour in which artists use their creativity to bend, evade or subvert the letter of the law to effect desired outcomes for social change. Rather than calling for Useful Artists to simply break the law, 'A-Legal Strategy' called, instead, for artists and communities to identify those specific areas where rules, structures and laws have failed the citizens they were intended to nurture and protect. Consequently, case studies included projects which identified and used the opportunities offered by legal loopholes and oversights in order to offer alternative support networks and services to the most vulnerable and under-represented.

For example, in their project 'Degenerate Political Art. Ethical Protocol', artists Núria Güell and Levi Orta created an anonymous corporation, 'Orta & Güell Contemporary Art S.A.', based in an offshore tax haven, as a means to benefit a group of activists. By passing on the management of the company, and its bank account, Güell and Orta enabled the activists to benefit from its a-legal status. Using the same regulatory loopholes by which big companies and multinationals avoid tax, Orta & Güell Contemporary Art S.A. allows those who use the company to avoid IMF (International Monetary Fund) and ECB (European Central Bank) regulations – effectively allowing artistic activists to use the tools of neoliberal occupation against itself in order to develop new forms of alternative economy.

In a similar vein, the project 'Immigrant Labor Issues' saw the Austrian collective WochenKlausur[4] use strict national visa laws, which allow artists to reside indefinitely in Austria as long as they can show that they are making a living from their art, to enable seven immigrants to stay and make social sculpture in the country. By identifying willing patrons who would subsidise the artists, and who would provide proof of their income, WochenKlausur enabled the refugee artists to remain as residents while preparing relief effort aid materials as artworks.

'Space Hijack'

The fourth strategy room, 'Space Hijack', built on the idea of A-Legality by examining artistic actions that seek to reclaim, take over and use public spaces which are becoming increasingly controlled, regulated and privatised under the conditions of neoliberal occupation. 'Space Hijack' also drew attention to the activism of a group of Australian women, the Victoria Street Residents Action Group (VRAG), who collaborated with the New South Wales Builders Labourers Federation (BLF) in the 1970s to place preservation orders on Kelly's Bush (the last remaining undeveloped bushland in the Sydney suburb of Hunters Hill). Further Green Bans, as they came to be known, involved hundreds of residents, trade-union members and other activists who lobbied to protect local land and buildings from private development. As a direct result, the activism of the VRAG and BLF helped to spawn a planning system and legal revolution in Australia which subsequently acted as a global benchmark for community-led rights.

Similarly, in the US during the 1970s, a group of activists who called themselves the Green Guerrillas began to throw seeds over the fences of vacant plots, growing sunflowers in the central reservations of New York streets and placing flower boxes in the windows of disused buildings. This developed into the creation of the Bowery Houston Farm and Garden in a vacant plot on New York's Lower East Side. In 1974, this was approved by the City Office as the Bowery Houston Community Farm and Garden at a rental rate of just $1 a month. Through workshops, classes and practical research into how plants can be grown in hostile urban conditions, the Green Guerrillas began to influence communities around the world who wished to work together to reclaim, rejuvenate and stabilise their local environments.

'Open Access'

The fifth strategy room, 'Open Access', examined alternative, deliberately inclusive modes of working. In these modes, access to knowledge, opportunities to learn and use of learning materials as tools of social change are considered to be an equal and shared right. Spanning different educational platforms and tactical uses of media, 'Open Access' looked at a range of current and historical case studies. These included Joseph Beuys's 'Free International

University (FIU) for Creative and Interdisciplinary Research', which was founded in 1973 and intended to be a completely open school, working outside the remit of academic and state systems, where people could work, research, communicate and organise. They also covered the work of the nineteenth-century English art critic and social commentator John Ruskin, who took issue with the worst excesses of industrialisation and its effects on both our physical environment and the dignity of labour, and who actively lobbied for free art education and museum access for all. Both of these examples were intended to highlight the use of art, education and science as openly available tools for social change that can, in turn, help to release the potential of individual citizens as active contributors to their communities.

To give another example, the project 'Free-Range Grain' saw the Critical Art Ensemble group examine and publicise issues around the exportation of unlabelled GM modified grain from the US, which enabled strict EU laws around importation to be circumvented due to pressures surrounding international free trade. In doing so, Critical Art Ensemble activated public awareness of debates around biotechnology, information technology, trade and mislabelling. Similarly, in 'Mirage: Disused Public Property in Taiwan', Yao, Jui-Chung + Lost Society Document (LSD) worked with university students to produce a study of disused public spaces know colloquially as 'mosquito halls'. Built at great expense in the 1990s, in the name of social welfare and recreation, these buildings had fallen into disrepair and disuse. Through a series of collective publications, students were able to use their academic work as an activist tool to force political re-engagement with this issue, develop citizen-led public debate and foster actions that would return such buildings to public use.[5]

Useful Art and the Useful Museum

'Legislative Change'

In 'Legislative Change', the sixth and penultimate strategy room, the ways in which artists had begun to force and mobilise real-world policy and legal change were considered. In a sense, 'Legislative Change' demonstrated how many of the strategies previously examined in 'The Museum of Arte Útil' could be combined to develop 1:1 Scale Useful Art practice at the level of local, regional and national policy-making and legal decision-making.

One example here was the project 'Theatre of the Oppressed: Legislative Theatre', where Augusto Boal used his position as city councillor (Vereador) in Rio de Janeiro to enable theatre to be used as a form of social and political change. Boal used 'Theatre of the Oppressed' techniques to give voters an opportunity to air their opinions through a 'transverse democracy'.[6] After 'spec-actors', who, for Boal, represent both the roles of spectators and actors in the Legislative Assembly, have discussed proposals on stage, the members of the Assembly can cast votes. The results of the votes from the Forum Theatre are then presented to lawmakers for approval. Boal used his governmental position with his knowledge of theatre and art to develop new ways of making participatory legislations which led, during his council tenure from 1993 to 1996, to the implementation of thirteen new laws.

In a similar use of dual roles, the artist and indigenous clan leader Djambawa Marawili collaborated with other artists from the Yirrkala region of Australia's Northern territories to produce the 'Yirrkala bark petitions' in 1993. These documents, now kept and maintained by the Queensland Art Gallery/Gallery of Modern Art, mark the first time that traditional documents, prepared by Indigenous Australians, were formally recognised by the Australian Parliament. This acknowledgement also marked the first documentary recognition of Indigenous peoples in Australian law. In this sense the Yirrkala bark petitions represent a direct use of art, for legal means, by an artist who is also a community leader. At the same time, their institutional and legal acknowledgement provides a template for how museums can hold and preserve documents as both artworks and an ongoing forms of legal community recognition.

The 'Legislative Change' room also presented the work of the 'Tams Year Ten' coalition (TY10), led by the activist Laurie Jo Reynolds, which saw a grassroots collaboration of artists, prisoners, ex-prisoners and family members lobby for the closure of the Tamms Supermax prison in Illinois in the US. In 2008, on the tenth anniversary of the prison's opening, the coalition launched a legislative campaign to call for it to be shut down. Originally the prison had been built to hold prisoners for a maximum of one year in complete solitary confinement, offering only one hour of exercise and a shower a day – no visitors were allowed, and all meals were eaten in the cells. But by 2008 over one-third of the inmates had been held in these conditions for a decade. Through a series of hearings, collaborations with legislators and negotiations with the Department of Corrections, the TY10 coalition finally brought about the successful closure of Tamms supermax prison in 2013.

'Reforming Capital'

The seventh and final of the strategy rooms, 'Reforming Capital', set out to examine artistic strategies that propose different ways individuals and communities might engage with production, economic exchange and debt. In the 'Proyecto Metero' project, initiated by Claudia Fernández, a team of artists, architects, designers, sociologists, psychologists and artists developed an art and design school structured around workshops for young homeless people living in extreme poverty. Homeless youths can produce and create design products which are then sold to raise funds for further youth-support activities focused on housing, health, well-being care and social empowerment. As a further outcome of these activities, children are given an opportunity to join a production market, using second-hand and recycled materials, which help to develop the skills needed to address local circumstances.

In the project 'The Rolling Jubilee', the activist group Strike Debt (OWS) used the tradition of Jubilee (shared by many Christian, Jewish and Islamic traditions) to reinvoke the idea of setting aside a time when sins are forgiven, debts are waived and prisoners are set free. As an organisation that grew out of the Occupy movements (which we looked at in Chapter 1), the 'Rolling Jubilee' set out to activate support to abolish other people's debts in the face of the growing US debt system (by which the 1 per cent continue to profit from the long-term debt of the many).

'Rolling Jubilee' use the legal constructs of the global financial industry – which allows companies to legally purchase debt as a long-term investment – to randomly buy and abolish people's debt at the rate of pennies to the dollar. Instead of purchasing debt to pursue debtors for profit, as certain companies do, 'Rolling Jubilee' immediately cancels purchased debt as a means to directly help members of the 99 per cent while highlighting the business of debt as an issue for open political discussion. As well as having raised $557,451 at the time of the opening of 'The Museum of

Arte Útil' in December 2013, and having abolished $11,153,855 of debt as a result, Strike Debt also published 'A Debt Resistors' Operations Manual', which helps citizens with advice on resisting debt as well as offering an opportunity to join the movement. At the time of writing this figure has risen to $31,982,455.76 as part of the Debt Collective Abolition movement.[7]

As well as providing case studies, 'Reforming Capital' also hosted a major 1:1 scale activation of the Grizedale Arts project 'Honest Shop'. Originally initiated as a village shop, in the town of Coniston in the UK's Lake District, the 'Honest Shop' is stocked with goods made by local producers – from farmed meat and vegetables to greeting cards and knitted items. Anybody who purchases goods in the 'Honest Shop' is asked to pay what they think is a reasonable price and to record their purchase in an 'Honest Shop' ledger. Some 80 per cent of the takings go to the producer of the goods purchased, while 20 per cent goes to the upkeep and maintenance of the 'Honest Shop' itself. The 'Honest Shop' brings local ways of making and using together more directly, while supplying an outlet for locals who might not be in a position to start up a business of their own. During the Museum of Art Útil, the 'Honest Shop' provided the opportunity for both locals and those travelling to the Van Abbemuseum to sell their wares for a fair price. 'The Honest Shop' also allowed the museum to begin rethinking its own strategies towards commercialisation and the role and function of museum gift shops, which now provide a major stream of income for museums around the world by monetising the brands of contemporary art and artists.

To offer a further opportunity to think through issues that were raised by the seven strategy rooms of 'The Museum of Arte Útil' and the material collated in the Museum's central

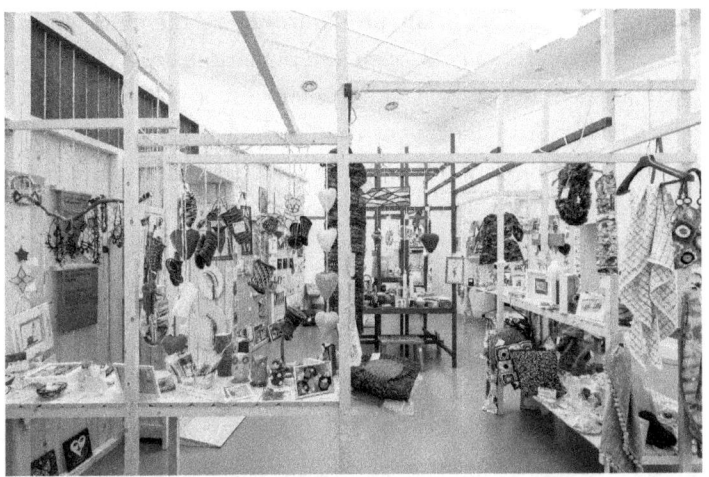

3.3 Grizedale Arts' 'Honest Shop', Museum of Arte Útil, Van Abbemuseum, Archives Van Abbemuseum, Eindhoven, 2013. Image courtesy of Peter Cox

archive room, two further analysis rooms were provided. In the first of these, 'The Room of Propaganda, Legitimation and Belief', some of the core questions about how to define and implement the eight criteria of Arte Útil could be discussed. Users were offered a single pulpit and a collection of source material and video interviews, which all addressed the questions around how Useful Art might operate within a major museum context. By providing access to these materials, the 'Room of Propaganda' also gave users the opportunity to formulate and make statements about their thoughts on Useful Art – thus providing users with the kind of platform in a public space that is more usually reserved for selected speakers.

The 'Room of Controversies', by contrast, was organised to resemble a people's parliament, with users facing one another during debates. The 'Room of Controversies' therefore focused more on the possibility of open and public debate. As a starting point, users were provided with four threads of public discussion, which were: Arte Útil, gentrification and misuse; Arte Útil, Activism and Sincerity; Arte Útil, social design and instrumentalisation; and Arte Útil, 2.0 culture and disobedience. As well as these threads, users could also suggest their own topics, and case studies from the Central Archive of Arte Útil could also be brought in for consideration and to provoke further analysis and dialogue.

Finally, during the closing stages of 'The Museum of Arte Útil', the materials provided for discussion shifted in focus towards the next stages of both this museum-based Arte Útil project and the wider Association of Arte Útil. Users were asked to debate what might be done to propagate projects such as 'The Honest Shop' and how to best recycle and reuse the materials left behind for the benefit of local communities.

Legacies of 'The Museum of Arte Útil'

Perhaps inevitably, 'The Museum of Arte Útil' also highlighted its own physical and ideological limitations. The current templates we have for experiencing and understanding artworks in galleries and museum spaces – as visitors are expected to become spectators of aesthetic value and worth – leave most visitors or users bewildered or unable to understand. As a result of this, simply looking at information about Useful Art projects, as if they were supposed to be art objects like any others, had the possibility to confuse and confound visitors even further. However, when the spaces in 'The Museum of Arte Útil' were activated

– through discussions, meetings, presentations, workshops or performances – the potentialities of Arte Útil became accessible and usable.

There were also problems with time. Because Useful Art tends to be slow art, activated and recognisable only in real time, the current rhythms and structures of running public museums and galleries began to get in the way. Most museums and galleries now rely heavily on an ongoing three-year plan of short exhibitions which maintain public interest. This partitioning of the exhibition experience into shorter commodities of public spectacle discourages longer-term thinking and collaboration with users and publics in the remaking of useful museums as social power plants. These problems made it apparent that those museums and galleries who chose to offer themselves as useful nodal points for the disruption of the current condition of neoliberal occupation would have to find ways to develop new strategies and tactics. This would be essential if any move from propositional (suggesting change) to operational (effecting change) models of art's use were to be implemented, and the obvious tools to use in that process are those of 1:1 Scale Useful Art practice.

One of the key concrete outcomes of 'The Museum of Arte Útil' was to instigate an international commitment between activist artists, curators, museum directors, thinkers and doers as to how such a power shift (between propositional art and operational art) might be achieved. And, as a direct result of these discussions, two 1:1 scale operational alternatives began to evolve, in the form of the online and ongoing Association of Arte Útil and the blueprint for a 'Constituent Museum' – Museum 3.0.

The Association of Arte Útil and Museum 3.0

The intention of the Association of Arte Útil (AAÚ) is to produce a continually evolving international online and offline toolkit.[8] The aim of this toolkit is to bring together and propagate forms of art practice which seek to have direct and lasting social, political and economic impact. The AAÚ originally developed out of a series of projects initiated by Bruguera at the Queens Museum of art in New York in 2010 which, in turn, led to the 'The Museum of Arte Útil' project at the Van Abbemuseum from December 2013 to March 2014. In 2013 the Queens Museum also launched an Arte Útil Lab and, since then, the AAÚ has grown into an ongoing international network of public programmes, workshops, symposia and events held at like-minded art museums and institutions across the world. More often than not, these take the form of 'Offices of Useful Art', where a range of institutions – from Salt in Istanbul, the Van Abbemuseum in Eindhoven, the Whitworth Art Gallery in Manchester, UK, Tate Liverpool and Liverpool John Moores University UK and Yamaguchi Centre for Art and Media Japan – agree to open part of their space as a temporary public resource for discussion, planning and exchanging ideas about Useful Art.

The online presence of the AAÚ also holds documentation of several exhibitions and workshops and multi/transdisciplinary events such as: 'Localist Worker' at Liverpool School of Art and Design in 2015; the AAU archive at Gallery Nova 2015; Granby Office of Useful Art at 148 Granby Steet, Liverpool, 2016; Re-articulating the Role of Aesthetics in Relation to Functionality at Catalyst Centre for Art, Science & Technology, London (2016); Escuela de Arte Útil (School of Arte Útil) at Yerba Buena Centre San Francisco (as part of the exhibition 'Tania Bruguera: Talking to Power') in 2017; the Useful School of art (Escuela de Arte Útil) at UMAC University Gallery in Mexico City in 2018 and the Coefficient of Art, Architecture and Mathematics and the Jane Addams Hull House Museum Chicago (as part of the Chicago Architecture Biennial) in 2019.

The online archive section of the Association of Arte Útil, which was first manifested physically at 'The Museum of Arte Útil' in 2012, has now also grown into an open-source platform with a selected archive-cum-database of Useful Art projects and other Arte Útil-related materials. The website also allows anyone to propose a project that might be added to the archive. Projects are usually selected for the online archive by a team of 'International Correspondents' (of whom I am one), who voluntarily meet to evaluate all submissions against the eight criteria of Arte Útil. The AAÚ archive is itself divided into sections such as 'urban development', 'scientific', 'economy' and 'environment', and the entries for specific projects (which can be downloaded as printable PDFs) are categorised in terms of their 'initiators', 'goals', 'users' and 'beneficial outcomes'.

Because of this, the AAÚ – the projects that constitute it and its call for an international movement of oppositional artistic strategies – also holds all the ethical and aesthetic dilemmas around Useful Art. In an art world where artworks are being replaced by experiences, passive audiences are giving way to active 'users' and museums are repurposing themselves as producers of new civic identities, AAÚ might simply seem to offer yet one more stark alternative to the established mechanisms of global contemporary art as a tourism and leisure experience. Moreover, at first glance it might also seem that the AAÚ is barely distinguishable from many other existing modes of socially engaged art practice. But I would argue that the AAÚ represents

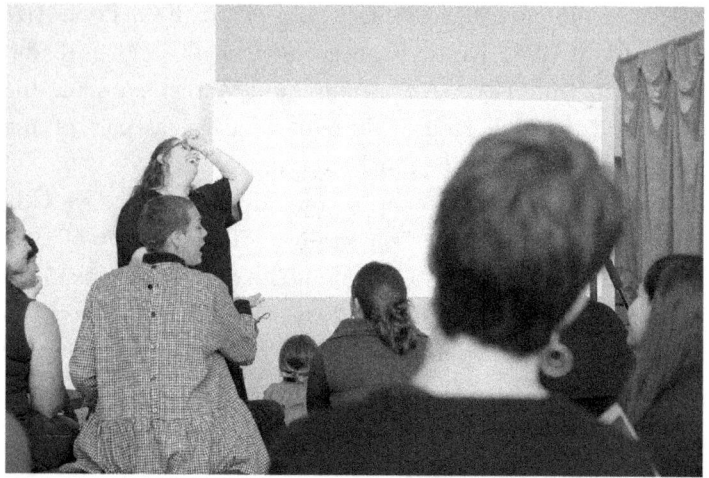

3.4 Installation view, Escuela de Arte Útil, a commissioned art project for the exhibition 'Tania Bruguera: Talking to Power/Hablándole al Poder', Yerba Buena Center for the Arts, San Francisco, 2017. Image courtesy of Yerba Buena Center for the Arts; photograph by Nando Alvarez-Perez

something more ambitious and far-reaching than the individual projects and practices that fall within its remit. The AAÚ is nothing less than a radical reorganisation of our relationship to art, artists, museums, galleries and their attendant 'art worlds' as we commonly know them – or knew them – to be. And, to this end, I would also argue that the AAÚ provides a helpful counterpoint to the ways in which we experience and think about our uses of art within the current conditions of neoliberal occupation.

The AAÚ and the practice of Arte Útil offer new ways to re-examine the changing nature and status of aesthetic autonomy.

Useful Art allows us to rethink and repurpose the work or labour of art as value of a new and different kind: use value, rather than aesthetic value. (We will look at this radical alternative in more detail in the next chapter.) The AAÚ also offers us access to a growing global community working and thinking like this, enabling us to share and repurpose pragmatic and realisable strategies of Useful Art that are capable of disrupting and reversing the instrumentalising flows of the commodity-driven art world. This activist–pragmatist approach, as Tania Bruguera herself said at the 2016 AAÚ Summit, should operate at multiple political levels.[9] For Bruguera, to be able to talk to institutions of power, let alone to harbour the ambition of changing their systems of operation, the AAÚ must itself be capable of operating at an institutional level. It is not enough to simply point towards a set of seemingly useful purposes that social art projects can engage with – which, for Bruguera, would be to infantilise the concept of Arte Útil. Instead, she argues that the focus must be on changing existing power structures rather than merely illustrating their current shortcomings through the tried and tested vehicles of art practice.

Bruguera's alignment of the AAÚ with the mechanisms of various international institutions, such as the Van Abbemuseum and the Queens Museum, can be seen as a deliberate and pragmatic attempt to change the way such institutions operate – a kind of activist approach at an institutional level. According to Alessandra Saviotti and Gemma Medina Estupiñán, who work closely with both Bruguera and the AAÚ via their ongoing role as educators and archival activists, working publicly with the archive has enabled them to begin rethinking the act of archiving itself as an activist tool for change:

As a result, we understood the possibility of the archive to become a porous mechanism thanks to the fact that it is both the result and the tool for research. Using the archive freely and adapting the selection of case studies according to the urgency of the moment, potentially enabled anyone to activate a curatorial process intended as a collective action. In this way, users (those being students, artists, social workers, or visitors) co-curated the sessions with us, adding discussion points and reflections on the distinction and overlaps between socially engaged art practices and other fields at a local and global scale.[10]

Seen like this, the kinds of projects that the AAÚ undertake with collaborating institutions, such as 'The Museum of Arte Útil', are not simply about finding new ways to stage more adequate representations of Useful Art and 1:1 Scale Art Practice within existing museum and gallery frameworks. Nor are they aimed at bringing social and political activity back into the museum and gallery space to make sense of them as art. Instead, they provide open-source templates for repurposing existing museum and gallery protocols that are no longer seen as fit for purpose.

At this point it is worth reminding ourselves that such activist ambitions are not intended to disrupt the current art world systems simply for the sake of change, but to recapture and re-occupy those systems as a means to resist the financialised and instrumentalised occupation of neoliberal capture. If art museums and galleries are to remain effective sites in which meaning can be contested and rethought, then they must be struggled over and fought for in ways which also contest the reduction of all cultural experiences to the common denominator of financial exchange. And, if this is so, then one of the challenges that we now face is how best to reimagine and remake a useful museum of the future, one that is capable of addressing this urgent task, with the tools that are most ready to hand. It is also worth remembering, given that many museum directors and curators work directly with the AAU evidence, that many institutions are themselves complicit in and willing to find new ways of rethinking and rebooting their traditional top-down operating systems. And one way of rethinking how and why this operational reboot might happen is offered is the concept of 'Museum 3.0', from philosopher and cultural activist Steven Wright.[11]

In the mid-2000s there was a move away from traditional spectatorship as the central experience for museums. This followed a change in how the internet was experienced. In the early phase of the World Wide Web (known as Web 1.0), websites only offered static information to an audience of visitors who could only look. In the shift to Web 2.0, audiences switched from passive visitors to active users who could generate and share content. More recently, in his book *Toward a Lexicon of Usership*, Steven Wright argues for a new phase of museum usership, which he calls Museum 3.0. This is because museums are currently undergoing a fundamental crisis in self-understanding.[12] He argues that this crisis is manifested in the oscillation between traditional spectator-based museum display and new forms of active and participatory usership. On one hand, art museums still represent physical and conceptual organisational architectures which are largely top-down. Directors, curators and exhibition teams work with collectors and artists to make shows which, in turn, deliver or broadcast a message to be received by an audience. Usually, a team is employed to communicate the more complex cultural messages embodied within museological art exhibitions to a largely uninitiated public audience in accessible language. Through this act of mediation and social engagement, Wright points out, museums are now embracing aspects of 2.0 culture in which their own legitimacy is becoming contingent upon visitor experience, feedback and input. The crisis occurs because while embracing 2.0 culture, museums are also showing a reluctance to develop new models of physical and conceptual organisational structures which are themselves based upon use – the infrastructure, or operating system if you will, that is really needed to support a shift towards usership over spectatorship.

One of the key reasons for this reluctance to shift towards new museological models of usership lies in an understandable antagonism towards the economic demands of neoliberalism itself. On the one hand, the condition of neoliberal occupation would reduce every kind of experience to one of measurable financial transaction. This has been often played out over the last forty or so years across the territory of culture. As institutions such as museums and galleries are increasingly put under pressure to generate their own income, the public experience of art and culture becomes one that can be bought in bite-sized pieces. Subsequently, ticket sales for popular blockbuster shows and exhibitions are increasingly relied upon to keep larger institutions afloat.

Set against this is the tempting idea that museums and galleries, despite their clear co-dependence upon neoliberal forms of income generation, can still offer a kind of sanctuary from the gruelling incursion of economic necessity. Consequently, the idea that museums can still somehow represent a special kind of autonomous or useless space, in which artworks and aesthetic contemplation can act as a form of resistance to neoliberal instrumentalisation and commodification, continues to be played out.

However, this is a neoconservative bunker mentality, one that ignores the conversion of leisure time into surplus value by the culture industry – think of how every visitor to a museum is now a measurable 'footfall' statistic. The useless aesthetic space is not autonomous: it's a commercialised, instrumentalised one. In sharp contrast to this, Wright argues that it would be better for us to adopt a bolder strategy:

> What may be required is to rethink the conceptual architecture of our evolving institutions from a perspective outside the public / private binary – repurposing tools, categories and opportunities inadvertently made available to new ends. Here again the category of usership ... comes to mind. In contemporary 2.0 culture, usership generates both content and value; indeed, it is a locus of surplus-value extraction, for it is rarely if ever remunerated. In this respect, 2.0 culture is both a promise, and a swindle. For the time being, 3.0 names the prospect of fulfilling that promise.[13]

For Wright, users are neither owners nor spectators. A museum 3.0 would be a museum where usership and not spectatorship would be the key experience. Wright envisages the 3.0 museum as being 'like a kind of walk-in toolbox for usership', a place 'where user engagement – user wear and tear – was explicitly acknowledged as generating value, and as such was entitled to share that value'.[14] While creation and use are often separated within the current political economy, Wright argues that within a museum 3.0 they might be made to merge. He concludes that usership doesn't have to mean only consumption or destruction of art but has the capacity to become production itself. 'Usership', he argues 'is creation socialised, and as such engenders a surplus.'[15]

If Wright's ideas here seem somewhat counter-intuitive – after all, how can museums and galleries 'pay' their visitors for usership? – it may be that we are ourselves trapped in the neoliberal monoculture of thinking that remuneration can only be offered in, or measured by, financial means. And if we only allow ourselves to think in terms of exchange value, then we deny ourselves the opportunity to begin thinking about Useful Art in terms of use value. A better question might be: what can you gain by working together to make communities and societies a better place to live and be, and by doing so in ways that can't be measured by money?

We will look at the relationship of Useful Art to use value in more detail in the next chapter, but in the meantime, it is worth remembering that institutions of art don't simply need to offer us toolkits or examples of Useful Art. Museums and galleries can offer us places and methods to learn, and to teach each other, deft and sophisticated ways of working together within complex environments. Museums and galleries should offer places of sharing and communities of learning in which we can begin to build forms of real alternatives within an interconnected world. This, in turn, would mean that museum and galleries begin to shift towards modes of operational, rather than symbolic, use, becoming sites, or civic power stations, through which we can begin to take back some control over the building of our longer-term ecologies and economies through the act of 'living artfully'.

Beginning to think and imagine how such shifts and changes could actually happen formed part of L'Internationale Consortium of museum and galleries project 'The Uses of Art: The Legacy of 1848 and 1989'. More specifically, this project looked at how to draw upon the often overlooked resources of historical alternatives to autonomous and useless art during moments of political and social revolution, as a means to begin using art as an activist tool for social change.

The Constituent Museum

By 2013, L'Internationale Consortium of museums and galleries had begun to consider different kinds of models for how museums and galleries of the future might operate under the condition of neoliberal occupation.[16] Facing some of the challenges that 'The Museum of Arte Útil' sought to address, L'Internationale Consortium wished to consider ways in which museums and galleries could collaborate – sharing information, knowledge, resources and ideas – without simultaneously losing their national, regional or local identities. L'Internationale Consortium wanted to combine and coordinate their resources while avoiding the trap of collapsing into a global contemporary art brand like Guggenheim or Tate. Thematically, 'The Uses of Art' project (as it came to be known) looked back at the long history of European civil society – from the revolutions of 1848 through to the digital and economic revolutions of 1989.

As we saw in Chapter 1, the collapse of the Eastern Bloc in 1989 saw the beginnings of the social, political and economic climate of neoliberal occupation we are struggling with today. As a result of this, and in contrast to the usual adoption of a bunker-mentality belief in the power of aesthetic experience and useless art, 'The Uses of Art' project also looked ahead to new ways of working, such as those explored in 'The Museum of Arte Útil', which would enable museums and galleries to consciously activate Useful Art as a means to shape real world futures and conditions for the better.

In 2013 I was invited to lead the 'Constituencies' research strand of this project which, via a series of seminars, workshops and collaborations, took place over four years in Liverpool, Eindhoven, Ljubljana, Istanbul, Madrid, Barcelona and Middlesbrough. We recognised up front that any attempts to cascade information about the research and exhibitions programmes of L'Internationale Consortium museums and galleries would always be hampered by the fact of their existing institutional structures. Put another way, no matter how many internationally recognised projects, collaborations, publications, discussions or community-led projects these museums and galleries undertook, if the top-down structures of their organisational mechanisms remained, then all they were really capable of producing would be increasingly sophisticated versions of one-way broadcast. In a sense, both 'The Museum of Arte Útil' and the development of the Association of Arte Útil had underscored what many of those who worked in the museum and gallery sector already knew – that visiting museums and galleries to experience and learn from art, as we know it or knew it to be, and taking those lessons back into the real world of everyday life, was an anachronistic one-way street.

At the end of the day, the existing mechanisms of major exhibition planning – which often lock in economically viable short-term exhibition programmes some three years in advance – could do little more than replicate the Western Enlightenment ideology of museums and galleries as sites of passive experience rather than active participation. That such a conception of a museum or gallery was hopelessly out of step with the growing demands of diverse communities, increasingly able to produce forms of culture for themselves, appeared to be a given.

What was also pressing during this period were some bigger challenges to economic and political norms that had begun to break through the smooth surface of the global neoliberal dream. The Russian occupation and annexation of Crimea and its military support for pro-Russian separatists fighting in Ukraine (which, as a former Eastern Bloc country, had indicated a democratic willingness to join the European Union) signalled a physical shift in the remapping of Europe. During 2015, and as a consequence of ongoing conflicts in Syria, Iraq, Libya, Afghanistan and Eritrea, the flow of migrants to Europe increased exponentially, as refugees began to use perilous land and sea routes.[17] In the same year, the resulting debates around migration and ethnicity began to reach toxic proportions during the lead up to the UK's Brexit referendum of 2016.[18] The failure of global neoliberal economic policies to deliver their promises continued in the EU sovereign debt crisis, which had begun in Greece, Italy and Spain shortly after the global economic collapse of 2007. Meanwhile, the growth of the alt-right movement and the election of Donald Trump as US President in 2016 also triggered a growing awareness of direct political manipulation that was being carried out via social media platforms such as Facebook, Twitter and Instagram.

It was against this political backdrop that the Constituencies research strand of L'Internationale Consortium discussed the questions of future museums and the role and function of art. What became clear in those discussions was that museum directors and head curators who were either involved with L'Internationale or who shared similar convictions wanted their institutions and collections to play key roles in maintaining the possibility of democratic and peaceful change. Stacked against the possibility of such institutional change, however, were those very hierarchies of institutional management and cultural norms which made the tactical and day-to-day transition towards more participatory uses of art next to impossible. As a result of this, the group undertook to not only envision and encapsulate a broader set of aims and goals for such institutional transition, but to look at how changes could be brought about by a slow process of micro-activisms and tactical implementations within museums and galleries themselves.

This shift of focus to a ground-up approach for long-term museum and gallery change was the basis of what came to be known as 'The Constituent Museum'. Instead of subscribing to monolithic and entrenched notions of the role of art within society, which echoed the hierarchies of power and control that had underpinned the European Enlightenment, we began to imagine the Constituent Museum as a place in which change could be implemented through long- and short-term collaborations with shifting constituencies of users. And key to this reimagining was the idea that a Constituent Museum would, itself, always be one constituency among many – open to a continual and negotiated feedback loop of evolution through use and usership. This, in turn, would mean that Constituent Museums would have to open up and rethink their existing hierarchical managerial and operational systems, while simultaneously renegotiating their role, function and meaning in an open dialogue with users and constituencies that visited them.

Over the four years of the Constituency research strand, L'Internationale Consortium worked alongside invited thinkers and members of the public to address the key question: 'what would happen if museums put relationships, rather than objects, at the centre of their operations?' The results of this research were published in the book *The Constituent Museum: Constellations of Knowledge, Politics and Mediation – A Generator of Social Change*, which was edited by John Byrne, Elinor Morgan, November Paynter, Aida Sánchez de Serdio and Adela Železnik.[19] The Constituent Museum book was designed to look and feel, and also to be used, as a manual for social change. Instead of using the budget provided for the publishers, Valiz, to include colour images of projects, the research team, in collaboration with the designers George & Harrison, opted to insert a cluster of yellow pages to reproduce statements, quotes and photocopy-style illustrations. Our ideal was that somebody somewhere might pick up the book and use it to develop some similar small, manageable and tactical projects that might help their own local museum or gallery to open up to Constituent operations.

Constituent Museum collaborations

The research around The Constituent Museum also had some identifiable and real-world impacts amongst L'Internationale museums and galleries, as well as some of their collaborating and partner institutions. The Van Abbemuseum began restructuring both their collection policy and board of collectors to include constituency members from a full range of ethnic, gender, class and LGBTQ+ representation. It helped to shape the museum's 'De Werksalon' (Living Room) project, which ran from 2016 to 2020, in which one floor of the collection wing was dedicated to developing constituent practice and the principles of Arte Útil. The 'De Werksalon' project brought in local Eindhoven-based groups who are themselves connected to important contemporary social, political and economic issues. These groups were considered constituencies by the Van Abbemuseum, rather than communities or visitors, and worked with curators and staff to develop a series of one-year or multi-year programmes.

The aim of engendering these relationships with the museum was to give space to a range of constituent voices, using the museum's collection and facilities to work on topics they themselves define as relevant. Several constituent groups from Eindhoven were invited to choose themes and develop presentations

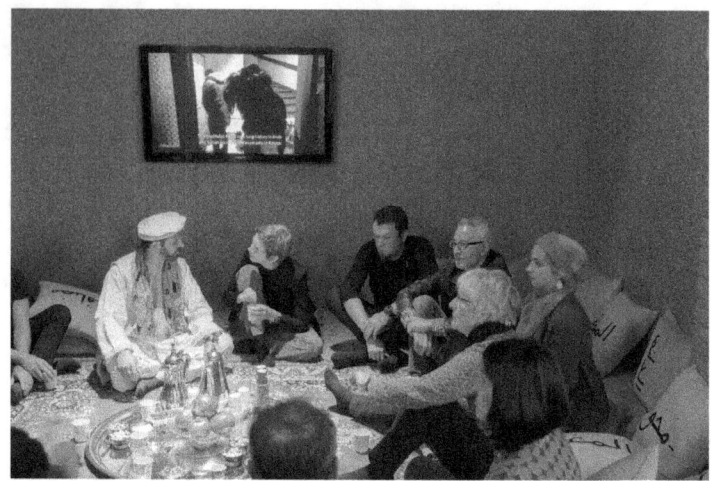

3.5 Sandi Hilal and Alessandro Petti Al-Madhafah, The Living Room, Positions #4, Van Abbemuseum, Archives Van Abbemuseum, Eindhoven, 2019. Image courtesy of Perry van Duijnhoven

which became part of the 'The Way Beyond Art' exhibition, which opened in 2017, organised around the three key themes of land, work and home. The constituent groups were considered to be both custodians and fellow curators who could help the Van Abbemuseum use its collection to tell new stories that directly connect with local communities and their specific identities. Currently the museum is reflecting on how a Constituent approach can become central to the running of museum operations as a whole.

In 2018 the Van Abbemuseum also collaborated directly with the Whitworth Art Gallery (UK) on a project called 'The Constituent Museum: Collecting Relations and the Transformational Potential of Arte Útil'. The intention was to radically rethink what Constituent art institutions of the future might become and how they might function. By using the principles of Arte Útil, the Van Abbemuseum and the Whitworth have sought to radically transform their core protocols (which, as with most museums, are rooted in the nineteenth century) by redrawing relationships with local constituency groups, creating agency for them to inform the museums' collecting, curating and presenting.[20] In order to do this, each institution employed a specialist Constituent curator, who collaborated on the development of a public programme for their own institutions as well as shared projects.

During this period, I was the Whitworth Art Gallery's researcher and writer in residence, looking deeply into the question of repurposing and reformatting the Whitworth as a Constituent Museum. Working with Alistair Hudson, the director at the time, my focus was to develop a series of theoretical and practical strategies and tactics that would enable the Whitworth to begin the process of moving from a symbolic to an operational mode of Constituent Usership. Beginning in March 2019, and coinciding with the launch of an open and constituent exhibition, 'Joy for Ever: How to use art to change the world and its price in the market' (which also celebrated the 200th anniversary of John Ruskin's birth), the Whitworth began publicly realigning itself as a Constituent Museum based on the principles of Useful Art. As a constituent collaborator I was able to participate in, and contribute to, a series of discussions and workshops with curatorial and management staff of the Whitworth Art Gallery, the Manchester Art Gallery and other collaborating institutions and artists. By drawing on the historical past of the Whitworth – which was initially opened in 1889 as a public resource for the education and cultural benefit of the working women and men of Manchester – this project aimed to continue an open and public rethink of current museum and gallery operating systems.

Our purpose was for the Whitworth Art Gallery and the Manchester Art Gallery to be open-source manuals and toolkits for how museums and galleries can become new kinds of public art institutions: useful museums that aim to share and use public collections and programming policies as tools for ground-up social, political and economic change. In 2021 the Whitworth opened a public Office of Arte Útil which would host workshops, discussions and constituent maker spaces that would connect with its exhibitions programme. The Office of Arte Útil also hosted rotating displays of case studies from the Association of Arte Útil Archive, which speak to other projects in the gallery and also act as an open-source toolkit for local constituencies to use in developing their own community-based projects in collaboration with the Whitworth.[21]

Post-exhibitionary practice

For Alistair Hudson, the term that best came to encapsulate both the necessity and ambition for this operational shift was 'post-exhibitionary practice'. Writing for the L'Internationale project 'The Glossary of Common Knowledge', he argued that this term offers a clear way to begin thinking through the end, or perhaps more precisely the cultural handover period, of the age of Western global dominance. For Hudson, we have a duty not only to question ourselves, but also to 'disrupt our habits and our comforts, even the deepest ones', as we seek to find new way of rebalancing the world and its economies and ecologies:

> Building a constituent-led museum is part of this troubling. Opening up power and control to voices and actors beyond the purview of the established cultural classes has begun the transformation of our institutions, from closed autonomous zones to active civic agencies. The working classes, the Global [South], disenfranchised populations. But the inherited museological architecture, both physical and conceptual, is a hard one to move on or redesign, especially when it has worked so well for so long, and still does.[22]

Hudson points out, quite simply, that before the relatively recent (200-or-so-year-) history of exhibition making, societies and cultures all over the world had used what we now call art in many different ways and across many different activities – from ritual to agriculture, craft, food and architecture. Seen like this, the era of the exhibition, initially marked by the Great Exhibitions of the nineteenth century, simply signalled one more cultural shift in our uses of art as museums and galleries became places within which new public and civic identities could be negotiated.

As large numbers of people began to migrate from rural areas to the newly forming cities of the Industrial Revolution, and as traditional urban centres such as London and Paris grew exponentially, collections of art that were open to the public and free to view began to change our ideas of what art is, what art does and who art is for. However, Hudson argues that the legacies of these very specific uses of art, and the concepts that have come from them, such as works of art, spectatorship and aesthetic experience, are inevitably shot through with the industrialising cultures of Western colonialism that fuelled them.

From early displays of pots, sculptures and religious icons uprooted from their original contexts to the development of a Western modern art based on leisure, consumption and market value, art has been systematically plucked from daily life and stripped of its use value. In opposition to this, Hudson sees the Constituent Museum as a philosophy 'which really seeks to take our institutions from a state of autonomy, controlled by a few, into the broader [ecology] and economics of society; an idea that strives to work with the widest number of people for the greatest benefit':

> the key to this pursuit is the work to make art and its institutions more relevant and useful to the communities and networks around them. In this it has been the work with people in real time, in processes that are part of their own localised economies and cultures, that has succeeded most: projects to change environments, thus enabling political agency, provision of food, technology, housing, healthcare, education. The exhibitions of these institutions have been a mechanism, a tool, in this process, to convene and model ideas – but not the endgame. This concept of the 'Useful Museum' reverses the usual polarities, so the exhibition works in service of the public programme, where once the public programme worked in service of the exhibition.[23]

While director of the Whitworth and Manchester Art Galleries, Hudson helped to instigate a range of reuses of the space. These include the sculpture gallery at the Whitworth becoming an experimental classroom, Hudson's own 'Director's Office' becoming a dedicated prayer room and quiet space for therapy sessions, and the conversion of a gallery space at the Manchester Art Gallery into a space for monitoring the development of local children from birth to the age of 5.

As well as this Hudson began to encourage curatorial forms of rethinking whereby planned exhibitions could be repurposed from moments of spectatorship into opportunities for use. Notably, a long-term plan to show the work of Suzanne Lacey, whom we encountered in Chapter 2, was reconceived as a manual for future social change. This meant that four key projects were reconfigured by Lacey in collaboration with new constituents and users of the Whitworth and Manchester Art Galleries. So a collaborative reimagination and retelling of Lacy's 'Oakland Projects' became a programme of youth work and education in Manchester using the Whitworth's Office of Useful Art. In 'Across and in Between', communities and residents from both sides of the internal Irish border, which was established in the early 1920s as a political solution between the North and South of Ireland, were encouraged to playfully explore issues of identity, partition, landscape and change against the fractious background of Brexit.

In 'The Circle and the Square', communities of people from South Asian and white heritage, who had become separated in the ex-textile town of Pendle in the north-west of England, worked together to reinhabit disused mill spaces through the formation of choirs and song. Finally, 'Uncertain Futures' saw Lacy work with a constituency of Manchester-based women aged over 50 to analyse and highlight the shared inequalities of gender, age, race, disability and migration status which they faced. This project developed into an over-fifties women's advisory group which was able to work directly with Manchester City Council's Work and Skills Team.

For Hudson, the period of the exhibitionary is fundamentally entwined and entangled with those hierarchical cultural logics which seek to impose Western narratives of knowledge and power – what art is, who can make art, how art can be experienced and who is allowed to share in that experience. Aligned to this is an educational system and a professional class of art-system employees – from artists, museum directors and curators to volunteers, educators and audiences – who participate in the upkeep and propagation of those narratives and logics. By asking the question of what a transition towards a post-exhibitionary epoch might be like, Hudson is also asking us to consider how we might better use what we already have to hand, as a means to develop new and necessary forms of activist collaboration, co-labour, curiosity and care.

Such a shift, from symbolic to operational forms and uses of art and art institutions, would also need an accompanying theory of Useful Art to allow us to begin tracing and implementing this process of curious change. A theory of Useful Art would also allow us to identify those practices, both individual and shared, which are capable of moving against and through the grain of neoliberal occupation. Whilst there is nothing about Useful Art, either as a concept or practice, which automatically immunises it from the logics of neoliberalism that it would set out to challenge and change, any risk of complicity should not prevent us from developing Useful Art as an activist form of counter-neoliberal occupation. Instead, we need to begin thinking of ways in which we can do more than simply identify what good (and bad) forms of Useful Art might be and start to work out how it can be evaluated, shared and activated in ways that avoid that complicity.

4

Useful Art and use value

It's Sunday morning, 14 January 2024 and I'm sitting in Grizedale Art's Lawson Park Farm watching and listening to activist and artist Fernando García-Dory over a live stream. Since 2004, García-Dory, a long-time collaborator of Grizedale Arts, has developed and sustained an internationally renowned Shepherd's School, in the Urrieles mountains of northern Spain. The school, which attracts participants from all over the world, is a yearly opportunity for city dwellers to learn shepherding and cheesemaking skills from long-term shepherds. As well as encouraging those who would like to relocate from the city to the country and addressing the real-term decline in shepherds in northern Spain, the Shepherd School offers an opportunity to challenge romanticised images of the rural and to excavate political and economic issues of landscape, space management, ownership and cultural value.

Dory's work echoes some of the key principles that underpin the methodologies that Grizedale Arts' Director, Adam Sutherland, has helped to instigate over the last twenty-five years. Evolving from the Grizedale Society's programme of land art and site-specific forest sculpture, which ran from 1969 to 1999, Grizedale Arts has, under Sutherland's stewardship, developed into a highly experimental organisation that initiates and facilitates cultural activities across local, national and international scales. As their website succinctly puts it:

> Over the last two decades Grizedale Arts has become an acclaimed and influential model for a new kind of art institution, one that works beyond the established structures of the contemporary art world … Central to our ethos is the pursuit of valuable function for art, which we explore through commissioning, curating, making and education. This means that many of our projects put craft skills, collaborative production and the expertise of non-artists at centre stage.[1]

To kick-start this rethinking of art's social role and function, Grizedale Arts simply began by asking artists what kinds of things they would do if they decided to make themselves useful. Grizedale also took the step of not providing traditional studio spaces to artists who decided to work with them on commissions. Far from opening the floodgates to a stream of predictable utilitarian and applied art projects, this Useful Art approach has led, over the last quarter of a century, to the development of both short- and long-term experimental ventures by artists who have themselves fostered new lines of inquiry.

As a long-term collaborator of Grizedale Arts I've been aware when writing this book of the profound impact these new lines of enquiry have had on me, and others, who have been involved with these projects. As an institution which has set out to evade the capture of the art world's 'established structures', Grizedale Arts have helped to remap what a territory for the deployment of Useful Art might look like beyond the historically entrenched binary of art versus everyday life. Through innovative commissioning programmes, by which artists and communities alike are encouraged to improve their own and each other's lives and environments through their uses of art, those working with Grizedale Arts have begun to rethink and renegotiate the terms and conditions of what art now is or could become.

Simply asking what artists might do if they were to do something useful has opened up a series of corresponding questions, which help us to use art as an activist tool for implementing real-world change: what can artists begin to do as citizens? What would art look like if it were not reduced to monetary imperatives or the need to 'inform' the masses from the dizzying heights of culture? What would happen if artists didn't necessarily commit to producing luxury consumer goods for a global art market? How do artists begin to meaningfully work with their contexts and communities?

Often, the results of these enquiries have seen a wide range of artists and artists' groups take the opportunity to work in very different ways and in very different environments to those that typically define their practices.[2] They also offer us, I would argue, an opportunity to speculate about what new ways of thinking about and evaluating Useful Art might be like if they were based on use value rather than aesthetic value. Such a shift, from thinking about Useful Art in terms of use value rather than aesthetic value, would also allow us to explore and reactivate the contributions of philosophers such as Fredric Jameson, Franco ('Bifo') Berardi, Jacques Rancière and George Yúdice as a means to examine how we might recognise and evaluate the kinds of Useful Art that escape our more conventional systems of artworld recognition and worth.

Grizedale Arts and Useful Art

Grizedale Arts is based in the Coniston area of England's Lake District. Once a network of farming and mining communities, the Lake District is now a designated area of natural beauty – the Lake District National Park is a UNESCO world heritage site and, as such, it represents a precariously contested site of conflicting ideologies, interests, stakeholders and mythologies. The Lake District has a legitimate claim as the birthplace of Romanticism: William Wordsworth, Samuel Taylor Coleridge, Thomas De Quincey, Thomas Arnold and John Ruskin all made their homes there for periods during the nineteenth century, and Percy Bysshe Shelley, Sir Walter Scott, Thomas Carlyle, John Keats, Alfred Lord Tennyson, Matthew Arnold, Felicia Hemans and Gerald Massey were frequent visitors. By way of postmodern homage, the University of Cumbria runs a master's programme in 'Literature, Romanticism and the Lake District'. Due to the rapid expansion of rail networks across the UK during the mid-nineteenth century, the Lake District can also lay claim to being one of the world's first destinations for mass tourism.

Today, the Lake District is managed and fought over by the National Trust, the Forestry Commission, a number of local councils, local and national business interests and environmental pressure groups. It is a place where a dwindling community of farmers and agricultural workers rely, often begrudgingly, on the income generated by a constant flood of hill walkers, mountain bikers, campers, potholers, rock climbers, hang-gliders, sailing enthusiasts, day trippers and weekend want-aways. As a result of this, artists working with Grizedale Arts frequently address issues of culture, the tourism and leisure industry, economic sustainability and employment. The work of Grizedale Arts is also consciously embedded within a complex and shifting network of local, national and international agendas concerning the relationships between art and social regeneration. Operating from Lawson Park Farm, a site overlooking Coniston Water, Grizedale exploits an amalgamation of freely available low- and high-tech methodologies to engage and interact with communities around the globe. Here, the emphasis is no longer on the production of tangible art objects but rather on the production of ideas, solutions and new knowledge.

From 2011 Grizedale Arts worked on a series of interrelated projects with the constituents of the nearby village of Coniston to restore and repurpose the Coniston Institute as a Community Hub. Originally established as a Mechanics Institute in the 1860s and rebuilt by the art critic and social provocateur John Ruskin in 1878 (after he had moved to Brantwood, his home in the Lake District in 1872), the Coniston Institute became both a village hall and a prototype arts centre. As well as a bathhouse, the Institute provided a kitchen, library, billiard room, theatre and artists' studios for the use of local residents. Following the model of other Mechanics Institutes, which sprang up across Britain, Canada and the US from the 1820s, the Coniston Institute was designed to provide both educational opportunities to the working class of the area (during the eighteenth century Coniston was a well populated mining village) and, in the eyes of Ruskin, to act as a new form of social hub where life could be enriched through art.

Housing educational collections of minerals, fossils, antiques, pictures and architectural ephemera, the Coniston Institute also offered a place in which useful craft and design skills could be learnt and exchanged. By reconnecting with this history and reimagining it as a way to improve the social and economic life of a rural village in the early twenty-first century, the new Coniston Institute evolved to include a restored theatre stage, a new kitchen, a self-service library (designed by artist Liam Gillick), an 'honest shop', in which villagers could sell goods and services for a fair price (a version of which appeared in the Van Abbemuseum's exhibition 'The Museum of Arte Útil' in 2013) and a restored reading room which hosted events, discussions, presentations and village meals.

Over the next decade, the repurposed Coniston Institute played host to numerous projects which sought to use art as a tool for social change. In 2011, Grizedale Arts commissioned 'Child's Play', a musical written by singer, songwriter and former Kinks front man Ray Davies, which aimed to provide a narrative of the hopes, and subsequent frustrations, which have been shared by many in the UK since the Festival of Britain in 1951. The Festival of Britain was a national exhibition that celebrated the country's arts and culture in the immediate post-war period. It led to the creation of the South Bank Centre arts complex in London. For Davies, 'Child's Play' offered an opportunity to assess shifting class relationships in Britain while celebrating the role that community can still play in small villages and urban settings alike.

Performed by a group of ex-students from the John Ruskin Secondary School in Coniston, 'Child's Play' also formed part of a larger project (initially proposed by one of Grizedale Arts's artists-in-residence, Alexandre Singh) for artists to write and perform plays in collaboration with children. In 2012 local users of the Coniston Institute were invited to take part in Grizedale Arts's project 'The Colosseum of the Consumed', which took place at that year's Frieze International Art Fair in London. The Colosseum in question was a purpose-built wooden amphitheatre, designed by the Yangjiang Group,[3] which allowed viewers to watch performances and presentations by artists, chefs, food historians and critics while, around the Colosseum, shops allowed artists, community groups and Coniston villagers to sell homemade produce and promote ideas for alternative eating.

By providing a space for locals to trade their wares within the established commercial art world, the intention of 'The Colosseum of the Consumed' was to offer possible alternatives to this seemingly fixed system of aesthetic value exchange – a possible world in which artworks and artists' projects could have multiple lives as artworks, experiences, events, legacies and useful activities. As a result of this, 'The Colosseum of the Consumed' offered a template for another kind of world in which people from different backgrounds could meet and interact with Useful Art in different ways – a world in which Useful Artists, artworks and art institutions would begin to dissolve into their communities.

A year later, some of these ideas and alternatives for rethinking and remaking art as a useful and essential component of everyday life were again played out when artist Laure Prouvost won the 2013 Turner Prize with the Grizedale Arts-commissioned video installation 'Wantee'. Originally intended for inclusion in the Tate's 'Schwitters in Britain' exhibition of the same year, 'Wantee' was made in Coniston by Prouvost in collaboration with local craftspeople, pupils of the John Ruskin School and members of the Coniston Youth Club. Drawing its title from Schwitters's partner Edith Thomas, who was nicknamed 'Wantee' because of her habit of asking, 'want tea?', Prouvost's project followed the fictional story of her own grandfather, who, like his close friend Schwitters, was an early twentieth-century conceptual artist who relocated to the Lake District during the Second World War.

Being less famous than Schwitters, Prouvost's narrative develops around the struggles that her fictional grandfather had with his own wife, who, unconvinced by the status of his sculptures as art, wanted to see them put to more functional use. Prouvost's 'Wantee' project was filmed at a set built in the gardens of Grizedale Arts's Lawson Park Farm, in collaboration with members of the Coniston Youth Club. The set represented the artist's desolate living room before he escaped, never to be seen again, via a secret tunnel to Africa.

After winning the Turner Prize, Prouvost's project returned to the Ruskin Museum in Coniston, this time staged as a retrospective of her grandfather's work. This reimagining of the Turner Prize-winning installation featured new work by Prouvost, made with Grizedale Arts and pupils from the John Ruskin School, which included original works by Schwitters, loaned from the Lakeland Arts Trust Abbot Hall Art Gallery collection, as well as artefacts from Schwitters Merz Barn site at Elterwarter. Similarly to Assemble's 2015 Turner Prize win (in collaboration with members of Liverpool's Granby 4 Streets Community Land Trust), Prouvost's Turner Prize success in 2013 was seen by locals, villagers and users of the Institute as Coniston winning the Turner Prize. Likewise, the reimagining of the 'Wantee' Project in the John Ruskin Museum in Coniston (which forms part of the footprint of the Coniston Institute building) was welcomed as a homecoming of the project, something that had been made together by artist and villagers alike.

Useful Art and use value

The Farmer's Arms, an inn for the twenty-first century

More recently, Grizedale Arts has collaborated with local communities and constituents to instigate The Farmer's Arms project. The Farmer's Arms is a public house, reputed to be one of the oldest in the Lake District. Its location at the top of the Crake Valley has made it a historical hub for travellers, traders, farmers and, in more recent years, tourists, to rest, meet and eat. However, by 2018 the building had fallen into dereliction, and in 2020 locals held an open meeting which resulted in the Farmer's Arms being registered as an 'asset of community value'.

In the UK, this is a legal designation, defined under the Localism Act of 2011, which means that land or property is deemed important to a community and, therefore, is granted additional protection from speculative development. In collaboration with the community, Grizedale Arts tendered a bid. By instigating a local, national and international on-line funding campaign, Grizedale Arts successfully raised the capital to buy and begin renovating the property as a hybrid public house, hotel, arts centre and community hub. Grizedale Arts also worked with local communities and constituents to reimagine and remake The Farmer's Arms as a viable and useful community asset. Based on the Ruskinian philosophy that a life lived creatively and artfully can lead to developing forms of creative and artful community, The Farmer's Arms sets out to be an inn for the future, the hub of a thriving community, enhancing the lives of locals and visitors alike.

The Farmer's Arms seeks to offer paid working opportunities to locals while also offering project and volunteer opportunities to anyone who might wish to contribute. As well as selling

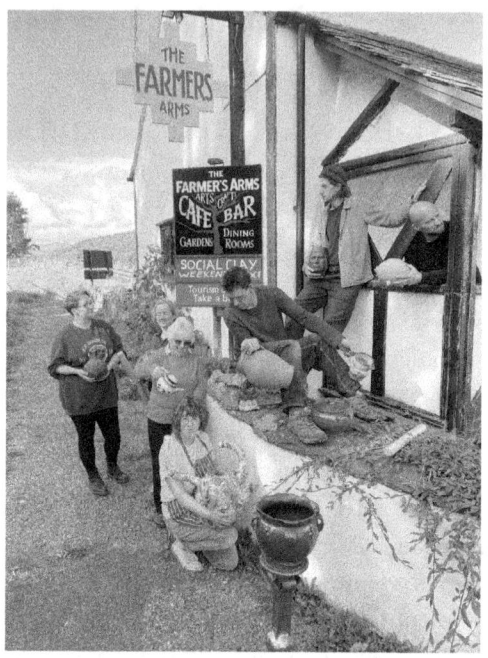

4.1 The Farmers Arms, Grizedale Arts, 2020. Image Courtesy of Grizedale Arts

reasonably priced, home-made and locally sourced food, it offers accommodation and a range of classes, workshops, talks and events that both locals and visitors can contribute to and enjoy. This is supplemented by an honesty shop and a range of long, short and medium projects that are evolving to ensure the future growth and development of The Farmer's Arms as a sustainable and shared local asset. These include plans to regenerate the six acres of surrounding farmland by removing sheep grazing and enhancing its biodiversity and running a monthly gardening school which will help to grow fresh produce for the kitchens.

Useful Art and use value

An outdoor oven, designed by Hayatsu Architects and built by students, currently provides an early example of the concrete outcomes that will emerge from running schools in architecture and self-build techniques. The aim of these architecture and self-help schools will be to co-produce and make new buildings and facilities that will enable the Farmer's Arms to develop further educational and social programmes which, in turn, will activate the gardens and workshops as accessible learning spaces for all ages and skill levels. Plans also include pop-up shops and creative start-up spaces, intended to support existing local business, and aimed at fostering new forms of local entrepreneurship and circular economy. As well as encouraging experimental uses of micro-agriculture and food projects, The Farmer's Arms intends to foster community skill-sharing and learning as a means to develop and coproduce circular ecologies of recycling and waste re-use, with the aim of becoming carbon neutral.

Useful Art, use value and artistic activism

It is difficult, when confronted with a project as nuanced, complex and open-ended as those of Grizedale Arts to know how, or where, to begin accounting for it as art at all – if, by art, we still mean the material or immaterial production of an object or event with a relatively identifiable beginning and end point. Projects such as 'The Colosseum of the Consumed', 'Wantee' and 'The Farmer's Arms' seem to be far in excess of the current models and protocols for identifying either their aesthetic or ethical worth. At the same time, such projects seem to be so embedded within the contexts of their production that it is almost impossible to disentangle them from the hubbub of everyday exchange which they occupy. Any attempt to disentangle such works of Useful Art is immediately faced with an archaeological task – identifying significant fragments of the work and hierarchically piecing them back together in ways that would make sense within our current frameworks of understanding.

How is it possible to account for the relationships between the manifestations of Prouvost's 'Wantee' project, in both the Turner Prize and the Coniston Institute, without automatically privileging the work of Prouvost herself? Or how is it possible to account for the discursivity and impact of 'The Colosseum of the Consumed' project without privileging the 2012 London Frieze Art Fair as the site of the project as an artwork? And how is it possible to account for the temporal dimension of 'The Farmers Arms': the research, the building, the ongoing workshops and classes, the community activation as well as the day-to-day attention to running a pub as a financially viable concern? Does its value lie in the building, the business, its web presence or in the constant interactions of its many community members, constituents and users?

Privileging any one of these aspects of the project seems likely to miss some of its more subtle nuances: the temporal/geographical shifts which make real sense of the work; the historical and social relationships between the Mechanics' Institute in Coniston; the work of Grizedale Arts as a commissioning agency based at Lawson Park Farm; the rereading and reactivation of Ruskin or the foregrounding of everyday political forms of resistance in The Farmer's Arms itself.

Looking at the work of Grizedale Arts, what becomes immediately apparent is that many our existing forms of analysis and evaluation are simply not up to the task of helping us to understand or evaluate Useful Art. The conventional tools that we currently deploy keep returning us to the familiar binary impasse of useful versus useless art. Nor are these problems simply due to artists and curators beginning to take on the role of social workers, or the side effect of contemporary art's modish fascination with involving audiences in the production of socially engaged artworks. The key problem, I would argue, in beginning to interpret and evaluate such complex works – or perhaps, more accurately, the temporal and social unfolding of such work – is no longer to be found in the persistent question of whether they might be art or not. Instead, it is to be found in the growing proximity between the working practices of artists and their audiences within an increasingly deregulated and deindustrialised society – and the concomitant inability, or refusal, of the art world to either accept or deal with this situation.

As I have already indicated, one way to do this is to begin examining Useful Art works through the lens of use value rather than aesthetic value. To do so would not be some kind of surrender to the utility of the market; instead it would be a step towards acknowledging that multiple theorists and artists have already begun to speculate about what an art of resistance within the condition of neoliberal occupation might be or become.

The use value of Useful Art

The working practices of artists, which were once dissimilar enough from the working practices of blue- and white-collar workers to appear special, are now shared and understood by the majority of people who go to look at artworks in galleries or assist artists in the production of their work. As we have already seen, the very procedures that neoliberal economies have deployed to produce the false freedoms of the creative economies have also implicated artists within the regimes of capitalisation that they try to resist. And, I would also argue, this proximity of contemporary artistic work to the labour patterns of audiences for art has quite explicit consequences for any possible theorisations of Useful Art. At its most blunt level, the action of deciding to become an artist doesn't make much of a difference now in terms of how one might live out a lifestyle or construct a livelihood. The idea of the free, self-determining bohemian – most succinctly characterised by the image of the artist with an easel strapped to his back in Courbet's 1854 painting *Bonjour Monsieur Courbet* – has given way to the image of the artist attached to their laptop, mobile phone in hand, enquiring about a recent residency or funding application, while waiting for the latest video edit to render and, simultaneously, worrying about the effects that emerging AI technologies might have on issues of copyright.

According to the Italian philosopher and theorist Franco 'Bifo' Berardi, the historical demand of workers for freedom from industrial constraints has been answered by the 'flexibilisation and the fractalisation of labour'.[4] Berardi's concern here is the destabilising effect this has had on individuals and communities alike who have been affected by precarious and unstable labour under the condition of neoliberal occupation. This has taken the form of cutbacks in social spending, the dismantling of social protections, de-taxation, industrial downsizing and the outsourcing of production. The result of this process, Berardi argues, has been a growth in recombinant labour (flexible forms of labour which are no longer closely connected to particular industrial processes, and which can be easily moved from one place to the other and 'recombined') and the 'fragmentation of time-activity'.[5]

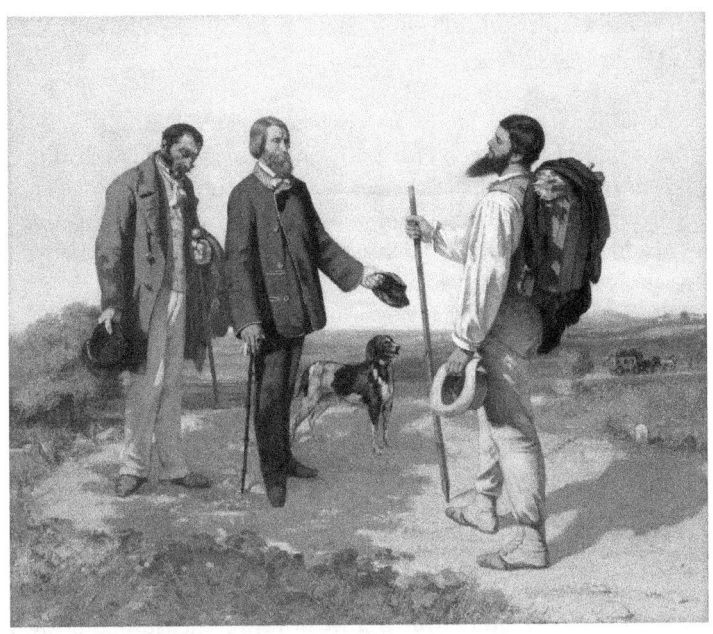

4.2 Gustave Courbet, *The Meeting* or, *'Bonjour Monsieur Courbet'*, 1854

In an increasingly digital and networked economy, capitalism no longer has to pay for full-time life-long labour, or to cover the cost of its needs (therefore freeing itself of the necessity to provide the conditions of subsistence and reproduction of its labour force). Consequently, the labourer has become an 'interchangeable producer of micro-fragments'.[6] For Berardi, it is now the mobile phone which 'is the tool that best defines the relationship between the fractal worker and recombinant capital'.[7] In this scenario the self-organisation of cognitive labour seems to offer the only plausible form of resistance to neoliberal oppression.[8]

As Berardi beautifully, but somewhat nihilistically, puts it in his book *After the Future*:

> Let us think of the crowd of people sitting in the subway every morning. They are precarious workers moving towards the industrial and financial districts of the city, towards the places where they are working in precarious conditions. Everyone wears headphones, everybody looks at their cellular device, everybody sits alone and silent, never looking at the people who sit close, never speaking or smiling or exchanging any kind of signal. They are traveling alone in their lonely relationship with the universal electronic flow. Their cognitive and affective formation has made of them the perfect object of a process of desingularization.[9]

What Berardi describes here is an experience that is, at times, familiar to us all. Over the last twenty years the condition of neoliberal occupation has had profound effects on everyone – how we live our lives, how we relate to ourselves and one another, how we perceive the world, and how we measure our own self-worth. And this experience isn't something that can be simply limited to the young, those who have experienced touch screens and social media platforms since birth. While I can remember the experience of high unemployment when I was a twenty-something in the 1980s, I'm now in the small percentage of those lucky enough to have what would have once been called a 'real and steady job'.

Even so, my life as an academic has witnessed a decisive shift to the continual 'measurement of deliverables' and the accompanying logic of the Excel spreadsheet. Again, measuring outcomes and having tools to aid organisation is no bad thing in itself, it is just the feeling we all now have of being controlled by those imperatives and tools – of not making choices that can't be accounted for in numbers or preventing ourselves from acts of creative spontaneity in case they might not stack up financially – that is marking the difference.

While it is probably true to say that we have all had the experience of only being able to do the things we can afford in our free time, the condition of neoliberal occupation has ushered a much more invasive phase of this experience. Now our free time, bought at the cost of our own labour, is also becoming financialised by the demands of producing evidential and measurable outcomes. From academics being asked to constantly audit their research and artists having to evidence required 'auditable indicators' when competing for funding, to the financialisation of domestic hobbies as online business opportunities, the time and space for creative spontaneity seems to increasingly diminish.

At the same time, the erosion of civil liberties, unionised protection, freedom of speech, political alternatives, racial and cultural tolerance and all forms of social safety net has been rapid during these decades. And their continual erosion, as governments seek to 'balance the books on our behalf', shows no sign of abating. Under these circumstances it is little surprise that the majority of those involved in the current art-world system continue to foster the illusion that aesthetic experience, and useless art, can still offer a meaningful sugar-rush fix of Disneyland-esque alternative radicalism – of believing that museums and art galleries are among the last places in which we can symbolically think against the grain. All we have to do is queue up and pay admission, and convince ourselves that, somehow, this is not the same as other experiences offered within the globalised service industry sectors of tourism and leisure.

And it is also understandable, for the same reasons, that concerns might emerge about Useful Art as a placebo for neoliberalism, little more than a thin ideological gloss over the job of willingly doing the dirty work of neoliberalism on its behalf and in its absence. However, Useful Art as a tool of activist social change – as a counter to the counter-insurgency of neoliberalism, as the Zapatistas would have it – takes a decisive turn when we begin to think it through in terms of use value rather than aesthetic value. Rather than surrendering to the condition of neoliberal occupation, thinking in terms of use value, as opposed to aesthetic value, also allows us to consider how Useful Art can oppose the instrumentalising neoliberal monoculture of exchange value. The use value of Useful Art, I would argue, resides in the tactical capacity for radical artists to develop real-world strategies, rather than symbolic alternatives.

Reimaging the work or labour of art

Admittedly, it is still quite difficult to think of use value and work as being part of the project of contemporary art – let alone its central tenet or a means by which to identify and evaluate its potential or worth. This would seem especially so, since to make the most useless possible kind of work would still appear, to many, to be the most obvious way to defeat the commodification of art. But to think about the use value of art in this way is to set up entrenched positions between utility and non-utility – that is, use value belongs to applied art whereas art's 'artness' depends upon the condition of its non-utility. The thought and writing of Karl Marx are helpful here. As Fredric Jameson has recently reminded us, the Karl Marx of *Das Kapital* was quite keen to bracket use value off from exchange value when thinking about the commodity.[10] Marx argued that use value did not matter one jot to the capitalist who wished to sell commodities – that the capitalist would only ever consider use value in so far as it could assist the profitable sale of units. It's interesting to note that Marx used the terms 'work' and 'labour' in very different ways. 'Work' is the physical activity over time which creates use value ('quality'), while 'labour' is a commodifiable capacity which can be exploited by the capitalist system and used to produce exchange value ('Quantity').

As Jameson points out, Marx equated the idea of useful quality with the body and physicality, work and time – while quantity and vagaries of the mind or soul are negative, serving only the purposes of capitalism. For Jameson:

> Use value is therefore quality; it is the life of the body, of existential or phenomenological experience, of the consumption of physical products, but also the very texture of physical work and physical time … Quality is human time itself, whether in labor or in the life outside of labor; and it is this deep existential constant that justifies that Utopian strain in Marxism which anticipates the transformation of work into aesthetic activity … from Ruskin to Morris.[11]

The ethics of Useful Art as a political tool for change

What Marx also presents us with here is the now familiar ethical and moral hierarchy that places the productive (bodily, useful) over the ideological (abstract, useless). His separation of use value and exchange value in the commodity form also marks a historical juncture. This is the point at which any calls for a future beyond capitalism begin to rely centrally on the concept of use value and, more often than not, on ethical forms of work and labour, serving the worker and not the forces of capitalism as an inalienable human right. It is at this historical moment

– roughly the mid-nineteenth century – that we begin to witness the opening-up of the familiar gap between art and life. And it is within this gap that the possible complexity (and the potential use value that the work or labour of art could embody or represent within this complexity) begins to get lost.

The rapid industrialisation that characterised the nineteenth century also brought with it the affordable availability of mechanically produced goods and services to an increasing middle- and working-class market. From prints of Pre-Raphaelite paintings, household ornaments, decorations, books, comics and, by the end of the nineteenth century, sound recordings, wireless broadcast and film, the distribution and consumption of cheaply produced mass culture rapidly became a social norm.

In response to this, many began to fear that mass-produced culture would have a detrimental effect on a rapidly changing society. And this concern itself began to elicit two distinct and contradictory responses. On one hand, critics such as John Ruskin and artists such as William Morris worried over the long-term effects that a loss of traditional craft skills would have on a growing population of factory and office workers. Seen in this light, Ruskin's support of Mechanics Institutes as art and craft-based educational resources open to all, as well as Morris's commitment to the handcrafted production and design of household goods and architecture, can be seen more as an anxiety that a growing industrialised population was losing its ability to produce its own conditions for living. On the other hand, a growing 'art for art's sake' movement, which saw the production of useless and aesthetic art as the only possible rebuff to the detrimental effects of industrialised mass production, also began to emerge. Epitomised by writers such as Oscar Wilde, the 'art for art's sake' movement claimed that artists were special kinds of people who could step outside of, or see beyond, the crushing conditions of industrialised life. Both sides of this growing divide were, perhaps somewhat ironically, based on the same goal: that of seeking a solution to what they perceived to be the long-term detriment of industrialisation on the human condition.

Somewhat paradoxically, it is also from this point onwards that it becomes possible for there to develop a European avant-garde which has as its goal the reuniting of art and life. Under this unificatory logic, both art's autonomy (as a resistance to the onslaught of mechanised industrialisation) and art's utility (as a means of harnessing the power of mechanised industrialisation as aestheticised revolutionary potential) begin to be offered up as possible avant-garde solutions to this division. By returning to the past in this way, it becomes easier to see the complex legacy that we have inherited from this period – a complexity which is obfuscated by the overly simplistic notion of an art/life, useless/useful divide.

The historical consequences of this bifurcation for the role of art in the West have been profound. At one extreme, art and culture came to be seen as little more than a functional reflection of the true economic driving forces of history (with the con-comitant assumption that an analysis of culture could provide a key to understanding these material driving forces). At the other extreme, an emerging mentality of art for art's sake saw political and ethical value in this separation, arguing that art and culture should be isolated from the material necessities of everyday life and held within an autonomous, aesthetic field. The political argument for this position was that art and culture had to be protected from the corrupting forces of industrialised capital if they were to remain a viable vehicle through which to imagine any kind of alternative utopian future.

This latter position, initially propagated by Alfred H. Barr, Jr's development of a white-cube museum space (as the most appropriate arena to experience autonomous works of art) and an accompanying historical narrative of -isms (underpinned by a commitment to the pursuit of technical radicalism as a viable artistic end in itself) is still largely with us today. It was Barr, for example, who did much to shape our expectations, understandings and experiences of modern art. After taking over the directorship of New York's recently formed Museum of Modern Art in 1929, he encouraged the move towards a white-walled gallery space, which privileged and foregrounded paintings and pedestal-based sculptures, and which provided minimal accompanying information by way of the artist's name, the name of the artwork and its year of production. The idea of this was to encourage an exclusively aesthetic experience of modern art, which was separate from the historical, social, economic and political conditions of everyday life. The legacy of this curatorial initiative can still be seen in most modern and contemporary museums and galleries, such as the Tate and the Guggenheim, and in the yearly tradition of art-school degree shows, which still largely adhere to this format.

However, there is a more discernibly left-wing, and often overlooked, lineage in opposition to both of these polarities (art as an expression of its socio-economic context or art as a separate, emancipatory and autonomous field). This tradition proposes the value of art and culture as the physical embodiment of work and labour, and for art and craft to be used as a means of protecting the moral and ethical ownership of work and labour against the instrumentalising and brutalising forces of mass production. Emphasising craft, design and making – and extending from John Ruskin and William Morris to Constructivism, Bauhaus and beyond to the work of Bruguera, the Association of Arte Útil and Grizedale Arts – this strand of art history also provides the conceptual framework within which the two seemingly irreconcilable positions of useless and Useful Art have traditionally met: the qualitative and ethical bodily work or labour of art.

Both traditions see the possibility of individual creative work or labour as something that is qualitatively distinct from the regulated and industrialised demands of quantitative wage labour. For the 'art for art's sake' movement, the kind of creativity or expression which is captured in the brushwork or paintwork of, say, a Van Gogh or a Jackson Pollock, is evidence of the possibility of human creativity despite the demands of financial and mechanical instrumentalisation. For the Arts and Crafts movement, the propagation of skill and labour, which is embodied in the shared production of a better environment, evidences a way of life which is no longer subject to the imposition of pre-produced and commercialised living. By insisting on the co-dependency of art and everyday life, and on the use value of art as its distinguishing trait, I would argue that this lineage encompasses both the scale and ambition of Useful Art today.

Bearing this in mind, asking what kind of work makes up the labour or work of art, is not necessarily to refuse the possibility of aesthetic autonomy. Nor is it an attempt to seek out another way of maintaining art's identity by singling it out as a special type of activity that is somehow distinct from all others in capitalist society. Instead, by asking the question we attempt to identify how artists, critics, curators, writers, radicals and others are attempting to open up spaces of radical community self-reliance, however short-lived these may be, within the current condition of neoliberal occupation. It is an attempt, therefore, to define a territory within which the relationship between Useful Art and everyday life can be understood as complex forms of interaction and, because of this, analysed more clearly.

Stealing gold from the gods

To give another view on this position, it's useful to look at how the philosopher Jacques Rancière has used Gabriel Gauny, an unlikely French political writer, to challenge existing languages of power and control. Gauny, Rancière informs us, was a nineteenth-century floor layer and prolific writer.[12] However, only one of his pieces of writing was published during his lifetime. It appeared in one of the many revolutionary journals which sprang up during the 1848 revolution in France.

In this piece, Gauny describes the complex attitude of a skilled worker who believes that he is less exploited than a day labourer. The skilled worker, who is allowed to get on with his job in his own time, as long as the outcomes are perfect, feels himself to have more ownership of his labour than an unskilled labourer who is constantly monitored by his bosses. This gives the floor layer an illusory sense of freedom and emancipation – in the sense that he knows that his so-called freedom is won at the expense of spending more time and effort over his labour than is necessarily required. On the other hand, the skilled labourer derives a real (not illusory) and secret pleasure from this delusory emancipation which, he knows, is won at the cost of his own exploitation. In the light of this, Rancière argues that Gauny's story represents 'both a tiny shift and a decisive upheaval in the understanding of the relationship between exploitation and delusion'.[13]

What is interesting here for our discussions of the relationship of Useful Art to use value (as forms of real-world micropolitical dissent) is that, for Rancière, texts such as Gauny's do not merely represent everyday experience through symbolic description; they also reinvent the everyday through the reframing of 1:1 scale individual experience. This 1:1 scale reframing of experience not only has an objective effect upon us as individuals – either positive or negative or both – but also helps to frame and make sense of those experiences. Or, to put this another way, as well as providing us with the raw data need to understand what is around us, these experiences also provide us with the toolkits, shared knowledges, ideological positions and forms of understanding that enable us to make sense of the world in the first place. They shape the effect that real world has upon our constantly evolving senses of being while, at the same time, framing the kinds of effects that we, as individuals and communities, can have upon those environments and experiences that we share.

This complex and ongoing set of intersectional relationships is a condition that Rancière often refers to as the 'distribution of the sensible'. For him, the distribution of the sensible is not simply about what we understand, it is about who is allowed or expected to do and think what:

> a relation between occupations and equipment, between being in a specific space and time, performing specific activities, and being endowed with capacities of seeing, saying, and doing that 'fit' those activities. A distribution of the sensible is a matrix that defines a set of relations between sense and sense: that is, between a form of sensory experience and interpretation which makes sense of it. It ties an occupation to a presumption.[14]

If we think back to Homebaked, the community bakery initiated by artist Jeanna van Heeswijk, we encounter something that was never intended to appear, or even be re-presented, in a gallery or museum space. Instead, we are looking at an ongoing process in which local residents use the opportunity to collaborate with an artist to redevelop a disused bakery as a community resource. This has allowed that community, and the individuals who form that community, to successfully renegotiate and recircuit local and government policy which, without consultation, had marked out the area for demolition. Such a shift, from symbolic and propositional art to operational Useful Art on a 1:1 scale, has enabled both a physical and conceptual reframing of real-world conditions on a ground-up and micropolitical level.

Whereas classical Marxist theories would say that uncovering the ideological misrepresentation of exploitation would ensure the revolutionary uprising of the proletariat – a job which the historical avant-garde, deploying shock tactics and strategies of symbolic disruption, saw itself as being especially well placed to do – Rancière argues that the 'schema of knowledge and ignorance, reality and illusion, actually covers up a mere tautology: people are where they are *because* they are where they are, because they are incapable of being elsewhere'.[15]

In other words, people do not occupy specific roles and functions in the world because they either ignore, or are simply incapable of perceiving, the reasons why they occupy those positions in the first place. Instead, people occupy specific roles and functions – and are frequently unable to make meaningful or sustainable social change – simply because they already occupy those allotted positions within an established social framework. 'The point', argues Rancière, 'is that those who have the occupation of workers are supposed to be equipped for that occupation and for the activities that are related to it. They are supposed to be equipped for working, not for peripheral activities such as looking around and investigating how society at large works.'[16]

The acceptance of inequality, or the schematic organisation of occupations which we are encouraged to believe is our norm, has, for Rancière, been historically resolved for through the 'egalitarian mode of the story'.[17] The mode of the story both frames and explains real relationships of inequality. The key example he uses to illustrate this is Plato's two reasons for why workers should remain in their place. First is a temporal and material argument: workers should remain in their place because they have no time to go elsewhere – their time is taken up by work. Second is a mythological reason: the gods mixed iron in the make-up of workers and gold in the make-up of the aristocracy, those others whose job it is to deal with the common good. By combining mythos with logos, fiction with fact, a particular distribution of the sensible is established and maintained. If we allow ourselves to think of our current condition as one of neoliberal occupation, then the role of the networked and precarious labourer, locked within capitalist structures of instrumentalising exchange, then it is only a small leap to imagine Plato's aristocracy as the golden 1 per cent who now control over 99 per cent of wealth.

For Rancière, the worker in Gauny's text begins to invert the logic of his allotted place, not through the revolutionary rupture caused by a sudden understanding or knowledge of his position, but by becoming '*less aware* of exploitation and pushing aside, thereby, its sensory grip':

> It is a subversion of a given distribution of the sensible. What is overturned is the relationship between what is done by one's arms, what is looked at by one's eyes, what is felt as a sensory pleasure, and what is thought of as an intellectual concern. It is the relationship between an occupation, the space-tie where it is fulfilled, and the sensory equipment for doing it. This subversion

> implies the reframing of a common sense. A common sense does
> not mean a consensus but, on the contrary, a polemical place,
> a confrontation between opposite common senses or opposite
> ways of framing what is common.[18]

This reframing of common sense allows Rancière to remind us that the generalised idea of the worker's voice is derived from multiple voices, continually reframed across the distribution of the sensible at a given historical period. As with the example of Gauny's letter, these activities are primarily accomplished through common forms of reading and writing.

For Rancière, reading is not simply the passive activity by which pleasure and knowledge can be gained from a fixed text; it is a form of the redistribution of the sensible which is activated through writing. Writing, in turn, is an activity in which words or signs are continually released from narratives of mastery, from fixed social structures which would seek to impose consensual forms of meanings upon them and become available to anybody. And what Gauny does, in a further letter to his friend Ponty, is to recommend reading as a means to secure freedom. 'Plunge into terrible readings. That will awaken passions in your wretched existence, and the labourer needs them to stand tall in the face of that which is ready to devour him.'[19]

Reading, in this sense, becomes for Rancière a means by which the labourer can steal some of the symbolic gold, formerly mixed only in the souls of his masters, and thus contribute to a redistribution of power. The activity of reading and writing does not simply make messages or representations available; it makes passions available. In turn, Rancière argues that it is the triggering or arousing of these passions, and not simply the messages imbued in literature by particular authors, that makes the activities of reading and writing political.

In doing so, Rancière also consciously avoids the trap of projecting a future revolutionary and proletarian class – a mythologised class somehow standing at the ready to free itself from the shackles of capitalist oppression (when, and only when, it is brought to the full consciousness of its own servitude by enlightened bourgeois revolutionaries). Instead, he weaves a more plausible picture of everyday micropolitical dissent – a reuse of the existing languages of mastery made by a class that is already fully conscious of its own fixed position within the hierarchies of power. For Rancière, this (already existing) class of fully conscious workers, who are willing to reuse a language that is always too mutable and porous to be owned completely by the hand of their masters, contains within it more revolutionary potential than an idealised and abstracted proletariat:

> A worker who had never learned how to write and yet tried to compose verses to suit the taste of his times was perhaps more of a danger to the prevailing ideological order than a worker who performed revolutionary songs ... Perhaps the truly dangerous classes are not so much the uncivilized ones thought to undermine society from below, but rather the migrants who move at the borders between classes, individuals and groups who develop capabilities within themselves which are useless for the improvement of their material lives and which in fact are liable to make them despise material concerns.[20]

What Rancière offers us here is a means by which it becomes possible to conceive of Useful Art as a micropolitics of resistance. The political content of Useful Art is no longer identical with, or reducible to, the symbolic content of art as we know it or knew it to be. Nor is its potential or impact dependent upon symbolically identifying and uncovering falsehoods which belie the real conditions of subsistence and exploitation – our current condition of neoliberal occupation is all too apparent. Instead, Useful Art, like Gauny's story, operates as a new common language by which the meaning of previously fixed signs and symbols can again be struggled over and redistributed to form new meanings and possibilities.

As we have already seen, in the examples of Homebaked and Grizedale Arts's The Farmers Arms, the shift from symbolic art practice to operational forms of 1:1 Scale Useful Art practice enables communities and individuals involved in those projects to develop and participate in forms of real-world micropolitical resistance. By digging where they stand, residents have begun to reclaim their agency from within the peripheral shards and remnants of neoliberal occupation. And by gleaning resources from what would otherwise be left behind in the waste of the post-industrial periphery – skills, abilities and shared knowledge bases, as well as the physical material of disused bakeries and public houses – those communities have also begun to reclaim and reactivate the use value that is embedded in their environments. This, in turn, has enabled those communities to begin sharing their own knowledge resources, and learning from other communities in similar circumstances, as acts of shared resistance. By acknowledging the systems and structures of power with which we are all complicit, and by recircuiting and reusing those systems against themselves, these communities of users begin the process of stealing gold from the gods: of repurposing the tools and languages that usually frame and delimit them as a means to live otherwise from within.

This process, this production of new possibilities and meanings, is where we can locate the use value of Useful Art – as the kind of work or labour that art now is or can become. In this sense we can begin to understand Useful Art and its methods and strategies as a common resource, rather than as an art-world category of a traditional kind. We don't aim to use it as a category to identify and recognise new forms of art because it is instead a tool for recapturing and reimagining use value, as socially produced work or labour, within the uneven and unequal distribution of neoliberal power and control. And this continual reuse and reconfiguration of the possibilities offered by language, technology and existing architectures and protocols is the kind of work, or labour, that Useful Art has now become.

Connection and conjunction – returning poetry to the body

Franco 'Bifo' Berardi offers a fascinating way to think about use value and the production of meaning in his book *The Uprising: On Poetry and Finance*.[21] Here, he links the radical deregulation of neoliberal capital to the increasing abstraction of language from the body. He does this by drawing a direct line of historical lineage between the 'art for art's sake' insistence of nineteenth-century Symbolist poetry – in which the word, decoupled from its equivalence to a real-world referent, was free to stand on its own – to President Nixon's 1971 decision to decouple the value of the dollar from its material equivalence in gold. Berardi sees the antidote to this lying with a growing proportion of society who will withdraw from the rules and regulations of neoliberal economic occupation:

> These people will abandon the script of individual consumption; create new, enhanced forms of cohabitation; establish village economies in metropolises; withdraw from the field of the market economy; and create community currencies.[22]

He argues that neoliberalism's deregulatory logic relies on the possibility of endlessly connecting and reconfiguring language into regulated, meaningless components. As the endless financialisation of our leisure time and private lives spills over from increasingly unpredictable and precarious working models – from zero-hour contracts to the financialisation of every point and click of our mobile screens into reusable and resellable data – we increasingly become interchangeable components in an endless web of financial exchange. In radical contrast to this, Berardi suggests that we adopt open, porous and poetic uses of language as an endlessly unfolding means of understanding ourselves and one another through evolving forms of communication and growth. As a consequence, Berardi proposes that the new job of the artist or poet is to return forms of mutable and productive language to the physical and social body.

More specifically, Berardi's insistence on the distinction between abstract and material uses of language consciously replays the distinction that Marx intended to make between a bodily and ethical use value and an abstract and instrumentalising exchange value. Clear parallels emerge here. On the one hand, between connective, abstract forms of neoliberal language and the quantitative abstraction of exchange value. On the other, between conjunctive and productive uses of language and the material, bodily necessity of use value. The use value of language provides a means to challenge the established status quo through the production of new social meanings. In this scenario, the job of the artist or poet becomes the work or labour of Useful Art, keeping language alive when there are no longer any simple distinctions between art and everyday life. If this is the case, then it also follows that the work or labour of Useful Art is no longer to unite, bridge or combine the seemingly irreconcilable gap between useless and Useful Art. Instead, Useful Art operates as a form of social possibility, identifiable in terms of use value rather than aesthetic value, within an already networked and saturated world of deregulatory and delusory logic.

At first glance, Berardi may seem to be offering us little more here than the possibility of romanticising the activity of labour itself through the act of returning language to the body as some kind of ethical rebuff to the dehumanising consequences of capitalism. However, I would argue that just such an insistence on the collaborative production of labour, as something which is activated through the very mechanisms of collaboration and constituency, is essential if we are to think and act beyond our current impasse. If this is the case, then collaborative and constituent uses of art would provide us with the means to challenge the status quo.

So here is one answer to the question of what kind of work, or labour, the work of Useful Art has now become within the condition of our current neoliberal occupation: the job of returning an instrumentalised and abstracted language, reconfigured as a porous and mutable form of poetry, to the physical and social body. But how, we might then ask, is it possible to imagine (let alone effect) such a strategy within a dispersed and networked society that already suffers from alienation, instrumentalisation and abstraction on every level? And how can we even begin to imagine forms of resistance and organisation, based upon the use value of Useful Art, when all forms of traditional organisation and resistance (class, race, gender, religion, sexuality, party affiliation) seem to be collapsing into each other under the weight of flexibilisation and the exploitation of precarious labour (think here of Berardi's earlier description of the precarious and alienated worker, subsumed in technology, travelling on the Underground towards the equally precarious industrial and financial districts of the city)? How does one radicalise, collectively or individually, when all faith in the mechanisms of inherited political affiliation would seem to be lost? And what would make such a shift towards new forms of activist art both necessary and possible?

Towards a praxis of Useful Art

The work of George Yúdice suggests a way of activating the possibilities of Useful Art.[23] Following the approach outlined in Néstor García Canclini's book *Art Beyond Itself*,[24] he maintains that art now functions within and across a range of disciplines that are no longer confined by the art-world systems of production, distribution, evaluation and worth. For Yúdice, 'art is no longer only in museums and galleries but has migrated to other areas (media, fashion, social action, investment funds, urban revitalization, new technologies, security, recovery programs for at-risk youth, etc.)'.[25] For this reason, he suggests that activist artists should begin looking for their collaborations beyond the established borders of recognisable and institutionalised silos of expertise towards other diverse communities, 'particularly those at a remove from hegemonic Western cosmology'.[26] What Yúdice is interested in opening up here – and this is essential for developing any theory of Useful Art that is capable of reading forms of 1:1 scale activism in terms of use vale rather than aesthetic value – is a shift away from existing forms of institutional critique:

> the frame is more ambiguous and there is no finger pointing; that is, the effectiveness of the project is not based on the smug disclosure of the dubious if not deplorable underpinnings of the art institution (museum, gallery, biennial, etc.) while nevertheless living off and gaining cultural capital in that institution.

> Rather, it [*the work or labour of art*] gets involved in the problems
> that arise due to its interpolations into the flows, constituting a
> learning experience.[27]

Arguing that Useful Art should adopt, repurpose and reuse the
flows of neoliberalism against themselves as forms of interrup-
tion, Yúdice points towards what he terms a possible 'politics
of intermediation' that

> reproduces neither the hegemonic control by governments, large
> business enterprises or large NGOs ... not to speak of the naiveté
> of Internet enthusiasts who believe that the distributed networks
> of the web have eliminated intermediaries simply because people
> get to upload their own contents.[28]

So, instead of art projects which provide symbolic alternatives to
current situations, or those which simply enlarge the frame of art
(a process by which any means of activity can become art simply
by a 'like or as' comparison to existing forms of art practice
that have already been validated through the mechanisms of the
institutional art world), Yúdice is interested in those activations of
Useful Art in which all parts of a project (be they art or otherwise)
can merge into a 'whole situation'. In doing so Yúdice is also
providing us a way to flip or invert our usual preconceptions
that art, if it is to be art at all, needs to be anchored in some
way to the existing protocols of the art world. Instead, like the
Museum of Arte Útil or the idea of Museum 3.0, Yúdice enables
us to begin thinking of Useful Art as something that does not
necessarily need to belong in a museum or gallery at all. Instead
Useful Art can be seen as more of a shared resource, or toolkit,
for activating real-world change. And this real-world change
can take place whether the project belongs to, or activates, the
normal protocols of the art world or not.

If we look again at Homebaked or The Farmers Arms we see two similar activations of existing resources (a bakery and a pub) as a means for a community of users to regain and share some agency over their lives from within the current condition of neoliberal occupation. As is often the case, and as I have experienced in group conversations with students and artists alike, it is often easier for people to initially accept Homebaked, rather than The Farmers Arms, as a work of Useful Art. This is simply because it is easier to link Homebaked to its initiation by an artist – in this case Jeanna van Heeswijk – and to place it within a known art-world context – in this case Liverpool Biennial 2012.

Situating Homebaked like this allows us to see a Useful Art project as an art project by surrogate extension. It plausibly exists, as all other familiar artworks that we encounter, as a derivative of a familiar aesthetic Eve moment – when an artist forges aesthetic value into an artwork which can subsequently be extracted by a spectator in a moment of aesthetic experience. However, as there is no individual artist, so to speak, in the development of a project like The Farmers Arms, it can be harder to see as an example of art as we know it or knew it to be. Instead, what Yúdice offers us is a way to experience both Homebaked and The Farmers Arms as instance of Useful Art in the first place, regardless of their relationship to art as we know it or knew it to be. Whether we encounter Homebaked or The Farmers Arms as observers, users or both, or whether we encounter them on site, on-line or as re-presentations in a museum or gallery, we have an opportunity to approach them in terms of their potential as use value rather than aesthetic value. To put it another way, as instances of operational possibility and impact on the real world as opposed to observational or propositional representations of that world.

Yúdice also opens a door through which we might be able to rethink and reconsider the two-centuries-old paradigms and confirmation biases of an art world that currently limits the potential of what Useful Art could be or become. Effectively, this would also mean that the currently identifiable frames of the art-world system are subsumed within those projects that are capable of fully merging into their surroundings (for example, a bakery that is also a work of art) but also capable of testing a whole range of social, political, economic, urban and environmental structures and assumptions against each other. On that basis, Useful Art projects no longer need to be identifiable as isolated art projects at all – at least not in the sense of our current understanding of what art was or used to be. Instead, they begin to be identifiable as activations of counter-neoliberal activism and social use value, signalling what Useful Art can become.

Viewed like this, it could also be argued that Useful Art practices already exist in the world, just in ways that may not be possible for the art world to account for in terms of their similarity to aesthetic or useless art. Not only does this mean that a history of Useful Art could be written, it also means that the examples which might populate such a history may not always be examples that we currently see as art at all. As Yúdice also argues, the production of Useful Art in this scenario no longer requires a will to flee, or reframe, the existing institutions of art as we currently know them or knew them to be (a strategy that in any case would suggest the existence of an uncorrupted institution of art from which such flight would itself be possible).

Instead, Yúdice suggests that we begin looking towards those kinds of practice that are not only capable of placing the 'institution on the same plane as a range of others', but that are also capable of operating critically within 'a necessarily relational world'.[29] Both Homebaked and The Farmers Arms, and other instances of Useful Art that may be similar or dissimilar to them, offer us an opportunity to rethink the limits of our current conceptions of art while allowing Useful Art to function in the real world as a shared resource of activist change.

The approach that Yúdice offers here shows how the work or labour of Useful Art can have both direct and indirect political, social, economic and historical effect as a complex form of operational, rather than symbolic, interaction. Yúdice refers to this kind of practice as 'interpolative dissemination', where something that is 'apparently 'non-art' is inserted into the flows of institutional process and causes productive trouble elsewhere (his examples are 'journalism, media, law, public policy, policing, urban zoning'), and spins off into other projects in other places.[30]

For example, if we reconsider Grizedale Arts beyond the idea that the social projects it helps to instigate somehow inherently do more 'good' than those negotiated around closed forms of art-led collaboration, and instead consider them in terms of use value, then we can also begin looking beyond the collation of information that simply legitimises their existence as art as we know it or knew it to be. Instead, we can begin to rethink Grizedale Arts in terms of a hub, or node, of micro- resistance – one in which different forms of usership (from observation to active engagement and reuse) are offered and enacted against the grain of our current neoliberal occupation. We can also begin to understand Grizedale Arts not as 'art' (in whatever extended format the art-world system has sanctioned), but in terms of an active community, or fluid constituency of users, who are continually co-creating and re-producing their own terms and conditions of living via dialogue, association, affiliation and use. In turn, what this offers is a possibility to evolve and co-produce a corresponding theory and practice of Useful Art, as well as the use value of the work or labour of art, which enables us to rethink these issues through and alongside the very problematics and challenges they begin to activate and unfold. Or, as Yúdice would have it, much can be learned if we are prepared to be nimble enough, and stay close to, new forms of practice as they flow through, between and across the existing flows of neoliberal capitalism.[31]

In order to discuss this, again with students, artist and curators alike, I have often thought about the gathering of connective possibilities of Useful Art in terms of a metaphor from nature: a murmuration, or concatenations of murmurs. Rather than thinking of a bold and centralised strategy for developing forms of thinking and action around Useful Art – as if the scope of its ambition was to be another form of 'ism' in the A to Z of contemporary art – we could instead think of Useful Art in terms of fleet, flexible and context-specific moments of micro-activism, identifiable in terms of their counter-neoliberal use value, which organically resonate with one another in the same way as a flock (or murmuration) of starlings does when they gather. The murmuration of Useful Art contains endlessly complex patterns of use, usership and use value tracing through and across the flows of neoliberal occupation by means of sharing, collaborating and learning together through acts of located doing and making otherwise.

Such a view allows for the possibility of evolving a non-hierarchal and decentralised theory of Useful Art based on moments, or murmurs, of activist use value, when individuals and communities alike share toolkits that might allow them to steal gold from the gods. By mapping and sharing toolkits, solutions and methodologies for activating real-world social, economic and political change, we can begin to provide an open-source commons of knowledge exchange, enabling constituents and collaborators in different circumstances and conditions to begin the task of taking back control and re-empowerment within our current condition of neoliberal occupation.

5

Useful Art and the power of the local

It's Saturday, 20 August 2022 and I'm sitting in the audience for the first of two Arte Útil round tables at the documenta fifteen Contemporary Art Exhibition.[1] What distinguished documenta fifteen from previous iterations of the exhibition was that it was not curated by an individual with an established reputation in the contemporary art world.[2] Instead, it was curated by ruangrupa, an Indonesian collective who were co-ordinating a major international art exhibition for the first time. As a curatorial principle, ruangrupa had chosen to activate the organisational and sharing model of the *lumbung*, or collective rice barn. In Indonesia, *lumbung* is both a physical structure and a method by which a surplus harvest is stored and shared by the community who grew it. In the light of this, ruangrupa offered *lumbung* membership to artists and collectives who agreed to share, organise and distribute the resources made available to them by the infrastructure of documenta as a way of sharing ideas, launching projects and developing new networks and templates for using art as a tool to live and think otherwise.

The presence of ruangrupa at documenta fifteen formed part of Tania Bruguera's INSTAR project, which began in 2015 as an activist protest/performance in Havana, Cuba with a collective reading of Hannah Arendt's 1951 book *The Origins of Totalitarianism*. Conceived as both a location for action and a verb meaning 'to instigate' or 'to institute', the intention of INSTAR is to operate across and between the fault lines of art and activism. It also aims to provide a model of an alternative institution that operates collectively and consensually, one which is guided by freedom of speech, human rights and respect for basic working conditions. For its participation in documenta fifteen, as part of the organic and self-regulating structure of *lumbung*, INSTAR activated projects in both Havana and Kassel, Germany which took as their inspiration the Russian Constructivist poet, journalist and playwright Sergei Tretyakov, one of the founders of the short-lived Russian Revolutionary journal *LEF*. During the period following the Russian Revolution of 1917, Tretyakov produced a tool for social information exchange, which he called 'operational factography'.

This took the form of a mural-sized newspaper whose intention was to help communities of farm labourers co-ordinate and visualise their activities.[3] Using 'operational factography' as a starting point, Bruguera and INSTAR produced ten exhibitions for documenta fifteen, each lasting ten days, which would act as a platform for Cuban artists whose works are usually censored by the Cuban government, and would also address issues surrounding the restitution of historical legacy.

On the Saturday in question, and as part of INSTAR's processes of operational factography, members and collaborators of the Association of Arte Útil Network were invited to discuss how 'Arte Útil could be understood as a movement, a praxis, a meta-artwork, a method to look at how art has been used as a tool in society to instigate change starting from the XX Century'.[4]

The panel was asked to focus on the idea of an ecology of usership in art practice. This ecology would encompass active processes that tend to oppose the idea of finished art objects and passive spectatorship – that is to say, the features of the kinds of projects we've seen in this book, such as artist-led community hubs for learning and sharing, rather than thought-provoking paintings or objects to look at. In opening this debate, Steven Wright made what I thought to be an astonishing and poetically potent observation about ruangrupa's curation, or rather use, of documenta fifteen as a whole – that this was the moment when 1:1 Scale Art Practices had 'slipped their mooring'.[5]

For Wright, documenta fifteen might be the last time when such practices would be encountered within a classical museological art framework, however radicalised that framework had become. In seeking collaborations with other things and other ways of working in and beyond the current art-world system, and by jettisoning their specificity as art as we know it or knew it to be, the projects represented in documenta fifteen had ramped up their 1:1 scale operations to such an extent that the whole mismatched encounter had become a 'joyous clusterfuck'.[6] What Wright meant by this is that documenta fifteen had willingly participated in the act of exceeding its own borders, boundaries and operational systems to such an extent that a decisive turning point had been reached. The art world had painted itself onto the end of a diving board, Wright argued – it would have to leap into a world beyond its own current limits, or wait for the paint to dry before climbing back down.

We are in a moment of 'no turning back' jeopardy, a moment which clarifies many of the arguments around Useful Art that we have examined so far in this book. Do activist artists use art to change the world or is it art's job to remain one of symbolic proposition? And, if it is to be the former, then how do we begin to rethink, remake and recognise what art could be or become as a toolkit of real-world social change? Wright argued that 1:1 Scale Useful Art practice had broken free of the existing museological frameworks of the global contemporary art system. These practices could now not only be encountered in other spaces and contexts, but could be made compatible with any number of other activities, times and places. They would no longer be encountered or identified simply as artworks, instead using art as a tool to make contributions to projects and activities in the real world that would not be possible without these artistic interventions and strategies.

The discussions that followed Wright's observations tended to expand upon and elaborate his 'edge of the diving board' metaphor – would the art world jump, or climb down? I like to imagine a patchwork fleet of pirate activists, setting sail to recapture and repatriate those territories that have been lost to the condition of neoliberal occupation.[7] These pirates are engaged in a long-term struggle in which Useful Art allows artists, activists and constituents alike to reimagine and remake themselves and their environments otherwise. However, as we know, for Useful Art to function as an activist tool of resistance would necessitate the development of a new praxis of Useful Art – based on the qualitative social production use value rather than on the quantitative exchange of aesthetic value – one which will have to be grown, nurtured and tested through collaborative effort. This means forsaking an ideal 'place beyond' which can only be accessed through art and, instead, envisaging an ongoing and participatory praxis: the work of art is now the 'work' of art. It is the struggle, the labour, the activity itself, and not a marble figurine or a painted mural held within a white cube with an entry fee and a gift shop. Its value is usefulness, not aesthetics or exchange.

It is curious to me, as I write this book some two years later, that Wright imagined 1:1 scale projects to be non-specific. He saw contemporary art practices operating on a 1:1 scale as by default acting as toolkits for others to use. They would have to combine an assemblage of components which could, in turn, be recombined and reassembled by others. On one hand I find this interesting because Wright uses ideas we've seen before about recombining component parts of things.[8] On the other hand, this observation of 1:1 scale (and Useful Art more generally) as a kaleidoscope of borrowings, relays, repurposings and assemblage more closely resembles Franco Berardi's idea of conjunction than connection; a space in which new forms and ways of being together can grow and be nurtured, a space in which poetry can again be returned to the body.

Looking at this another way, the resistance that the art world has to letting go of the centrality of things identifiable as art as we know it or knew it to be reminds us that, as an industry, it has still not encountered anything like a Napster moment.[9] The contemporary art-world system, I would argue, still runs on a linear, Darwinian model – anything can be art, or be claimed to be art, as long as it can be traced back or likened to a moment of aesthetic experience – it always assumes a spectator who, on confronting a fixed, separate and closed object, is somehow able to extract the aesthetic value previously imbued into that object by the labour of an artist.

However, by using art as one tool among many in order to produce instances of radical and anti-neoliberal community and re-empowerment, Useful Art becomes an open-ended and porous process. Instead of producing objects that might teach us how to symbolically imagine a world that might never be, Useful Art opens up a constantly shifting network of micro-re-empowerment and self-reliance. Useful Art can help us to carve out spaces of curiosity, friendship and collaboration from within our condition of neoliberal occupation. These spaces, in turn, can be seen as interlinked and co-produced laboratories, or classrooms, in which we can learn our way out of our condition. By operating collectively, sharing knowledge and co-producing the work that is now the work of art, we reclaim levels of control or participation that are increasingly denied to us, subverting the ways by which neoliberalism has weaponised and redeployed art against our common communities via management speak and measurable alienation.

Looking at the bigger picture, I see an opportunity to reopen a struggle for meaning over the terms and conditions of how we might live otherwise. By resisting the flows of neoliberalism and creating a new and collaborative form of art-in-the-world beyond the art world, we find the means and potential to resist the reduction of our imagination into singular, fixed and measurable memes and bytes of meaning. We can move beyond what we are told 'art' could possibly be to imagine something radically different. In this sense, Useful Art offers us ways of keeping meaning alive by opening up fractures and fissures of use value which cut across and through the smooth surface of symbolic exchange, opening wormholes that allow us to connect and create spaces of micro-resistance from within.

Like a growing relay of murmurs of resistance, concatenating slowly into a murmuration of global potential, resource and re-empowerment, Useful Art as a movement and collective gives us a means to wriggle free of the grip of an instrumentalising and financialised neoliberal logic that is now driven by new forms of nationalism, nation-state politics and the re-emergence of strongman leaders. Because of this, it is more important than ever to activate Useful Art against these real and ideological reimpositions of borders and blockades.

Useful Art offers us a way to reimagine a global infrastructure that is participatory and local. It offers us a means by which we can take back control of the political through forms of micro- rather than macro-dissent. Instead of offering another form of symbolic resistance and protest, it asks us to begin remaking and reimagining now, to find ways of loosening the grip of financialised power and reimagine a version of the local without nationalism, and a version of the global that is free of neoliberal- ism. Like those border crossers who, as Rancière imagines, steal gold from the gods and redistribute power, Useful Art provides a means for individuals and communities alike to dig where they stand and refashion alternative futures from the remnants and waste of extractivist commodification.

By way of example, we can examine four projects, or rather ongoing instances of Useful Art practice. These are not fixed, finished, determinable and comparable objects – instead, the aim here is to open up a kind of dialogue with these projects, as part of a curious and ongoing relationship that I already have with them, and to invite you along as fellow travellers. They are overlapping, interweaving and, at times, interchangeable solutions to local and immediate problems that I prefer to think of not as artworks, as we know or knew them to be, but as solutions that share recombinable approaches that could, in themselves, inspire further use, repurposing and reapplication in times, locations and spaces that have yet to be imagined.

Rather than trying to identify core aspects or values of these projects that mark them out as Useful Art as opposed to useless art, or which emphasise their use value as opposed to their aesthetic or exchange value, I will ignore these things as remnants of a system driven by the established art world and try to briefly escape its gravitational pull. In spite of this interesting moment of jeopardy and potential, I'm pessimistically convinced that the existing system will find a market-driven set of reasons for climbing back down from the diving board. Now, perhaps more than ever, the world needs artists, creatives, activists and constituents who are willing to jump, to make the dive and use art as a means to change the world.

ruangrupa, *lumbung* and documenta fifteen

If ruangrupa's curation of documenta fifteen provided the moment when art slipped its mooring, then underpinning this slippage was a sustained attempt by ruangrupa to alter the operational systems of documenta fifteen, its home town of Kassel and the exhibitionary logics which still dictate the current art-world system. However, on visiting documenta fifteen and looking at accompanying literature, both online and in print, it is easy to be filtered back into the position of a spectator observing, or trying to understand whether the projects exhibited or presented are art or not. As we have already seen from the Van Abbemuseum and Tania Bruguera's 2013 exhibition 'The Museum of Arte Útil', the current art-world system has an ambivalent relationship to the idea and practice of Useful Art. Unless an institution like the Van Abbemuseum wants to actively engage with Useful Art as a means to change its current role and function, shifting from a place of spectatorship to a site of active usership, then a documentary reconstruction of Useful Art projects, often out of place within a new location or context, does little more than exacerbate their existing incompatibility.

The experiences available within the current art-world system – spectatorship and aesthetic exchange – and Useful Art – usership and use value – seem to repel each other like oil and water. However, looking at ruangrupa's use of documenta fifteen as an opportunity to instigate new (useful) forms of thinking, making, doing and community – around the five-yearly cycle and inescapably institutional and instrumentalised nature of the Documenta exhibition/festival itself – I would argue that we begin to encounter another kind of experience altogether. What ruangrupa set out to do with their curation of documenta fifteen was to instigate a series of local, national and international structures and *ekosistems* (Indonesian for ecosystems), community networks and affiliations of knowledge and skill sharing. If successful, it was hoped that these *ekosistems* would begin to grow, self-generate and interconnect with other *ekosistems* both before and after the hundred days of the exhibition itself. They encourage a shift away from, and beyond, the moment of art-world spectacle in this way – when press, media, artists, curators and visitors from all over the world converge to celebrate the stellar spectacle of the global contemporary art system.

ruangrupa and domestic scale

Drawing their name from *ruang*, which means space, and *rupa*, which means visual form, the conceptual, ideological and physical framework of ruangrupa (it is never spelled with a capital R) resulted from an activist and practical imperative to create a sustainable environment for developing new forms of localised cultural engagement. In Indonesia's post-New Order period, which began to emerge after the overthrow of President Suharto's repressive and bloody dictatorship in 1988, ruangrupa developed organically as a loose affiliation of like-minded creatives who cut their teeth organising gigs, DJ-ing, making local radio broadcasts, developing socially engaged practices and undertaking infrastructural interventions within their own immediate environment. Unlike many arts collectives that emerged in the Global North, and which based themselves in the abandoned warehouse and factory districts that surrounded post-industrialised cities, ruangrupa began on a local and domestic scale:

> We wanted to meet, gather, do projects and research, show things and make them public. Everything gradually grew out of this need … we moved into a small house and that's where we also worked … The little house was a private domestic space where we initiated everything, between friends. Ruangrupa was completely different from those alternative spaces and artist initiatives in Europe that used post-industrial spaces or larger warehouses. Not just ruangrupa, but many other initiatives in Indonesia started in houses that were part of residential areas. That's why our vocabulary is also a domestic one from living spaces. We use words like living room, gathering, hospitality, because they fit well with our practice that was born out of the private, the public, the living, and the in-between. Everything is so entangled that you can't separate it. We're integrated into a neighbourhood, and our projects and ideas are inspired by our existence, survival, and struggle in a city like Jakarta.[10]

The group's founder members embraced an ethic of self-sufficiency and self-reliance, finding ways to marry their interest in living artfully with the practical necessity to co-produce a basic living wage for their membership. Their members did not belong to, or wish to belong to, a global art system modelled on star artists – who are contracted to private galleries and who make work for an international art market. ruangrupa wished instead to make work that was connected to community, inclusive of that community and of benefit to that community. It was at this point that they began to experiment with the *lumbung*, or rice bar, metaphor.

Initially *lumbung* was a way to think through the management of financial resources into a central and accessible account, but their efforts towards centralising financial resources soon became complicated, partly by the accompanying idea that anything they could use as a resource would be financial, or at least measurable in financial terms. Instead, ruangrupa began to move to the development of more decentralised models for resource-sharing that were not simply financial and which also included human resources, space and equipment. Decentralisation of shared resources also began to foster the emergence of more local autonomy, allowing smaller sub-groups and individuals to use some of the collective resources in ways that could respond more tactically to specific neighbourhood urgencies within an agreed overall context of need and activity. As the documenta fifteen handbook states:

> Since 2013, we – ruangrupa with other Jakarta-based collectives – have tried to build ekosistems based on an understanding that even a group of people, a collective, cannot stand alone, but must purposefully play a part in their larger context – just as in nature, where different species have their specific functions and roles to keep an ecosystem in balance.[11]

The Gudskul Ekosistem, for instance, emerged in 2018 as an 'informal educational platform … established with two other collectives: Serrum and Grafis Huru Hara'.[12] Gudskul pools a range of physical and economic communal resources – finance, space, equipment and knowledge sharing – which enable many

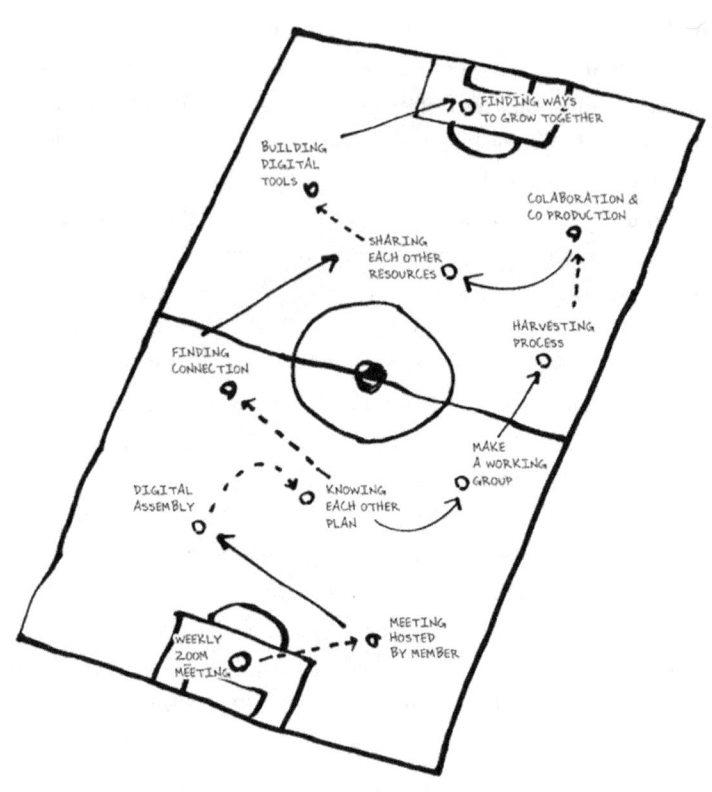

lumbung
building

5.1 ruangrupa *lumbung* diagram, The football field: drawing by Daniella F. Praptono; text by Indra Ameng. Image courtesy of ruangrupa

members and collaborative groups, from a wide range of disciplines and backgrounds, to develop projects together. The Gudskul Ekosistem website states:

> We believe that the idea of sharing and working together is one of the more important platforms for the proliferation of art-cultural work … This study is open for artists, managers, curators, researchers and cultural practitioners who are eager to develop collective and collaborative based artistic work model. Gudskul will become a common learning space for art-cultural agents who wish to contribute in local context while at the same time involved in international dialogue.[13]

Based on these values and priorities, ruangrupa made a collective decision not to approach documenta fifteen as simply a large-scale and visible exhibition space. Instead, they invited documenta fifteen to become part of their journey, refusing to adopt or mimic the mechanisms and agendas of Western European art-world protocols. Instead (or as well), ruangrupa wished to use the platform of documenta fifteen to offer possible alternatives to the existing art-world system: to move away from the emphasis on individual expression, spectacular moments of international exhibition and the value extraction of the international art market. They had in mind the Gudskul Ekosistem as a kind of template for what documenta fifteen could become. However, they also knew very well that any specific way of working in one local context could not simply be carried across as a working model to another location.

This was a big task, to make *lumbung* the core of an international artworld event and have it exceed the hundred days of the exhibition itself through the implementation of new and sustainable ekosistems. For this plan to work, they would need to instigate a long-term collaborative process, and invitations were initially sent to five individuals in Kassel, Amsterdam, Jerusalem and Møn (Denmark) who would form an artistic team. Next, fourteen groups were invited to take part in a *lumbung*-building process that would continue beyond documenta fifteen. These groups became known as *lumbung-inter-lokal* members. Subsequently, over fifty artistic collectives and individual practitioners, who became known as the *lumbung* artists, also joined in the building process. When the global COVID-19 crisis hit, most initial meetings had to be held on-line. In accordance with previous, though always flexible, *lumbung* building processes, larger meetings, called *majelis*, were convened regularly for all members, out of which smaller working groups emerged. ruangrupa consider the majelis to be shared learning spaces, in which decisions are reached about how to share and distribute resources according to need. So collective decisions were reached about how to organise and activate documenta fifteen as a *lumbung*, and how to grow new forms of collaborative resources that would be necessary for the long-term growth of an international post-documenta fifteen *lumbung*.

Through this flexible system of meetings as learning spaces, the collaborating groups and individuals were part of an open and accessible curatorial process, dissolving more dominant notions of artistic authorship and ownership. One of the key aims or hopes of the project was that ekosistems might be capable of escaping the gravity of more exploitative and extractivist art systems and biennial circuits. Because most of the collectives that formed the *lumbung*-inter-lokal came from contexts in which state institutions had failed, new ideas began to form and around sustainability, autonomy, circular economy and currency.

Consequently, discussions also began to emerge through the majelis meetings around where or what 'the art' is. The *lumbung* members' working methods are rooted in life, 1:1 Scale Useful Art practice and forms of necessary ground-up activism. They needed to resist the institutional pressure of the European art-world system, based on consumption and spectatorship, to use documenta fifteen as an opportunity to present objectifications, snapshots or clarifications of their collective and process-based practices. The majelis system of workshops fed understandings back into larger group meetings of all members (called majelis akbar). Via this structured system, new forms of confederation and solidarity emerged which allowed for members to share resources for the production and curation of document fifteen on a micro-level while, on a macro level, discussions could be had about issues that affected the development of the new ekosistem as a whole. The collective response to the accusations of antisemitism that were levelled at documenta fifteen: statements were issued, on behalf of all members and documenta fifteen, that rejected all forms of antisemitism and racism while emphasising freedom of expression across all disciplines including art.

Global ekosistem as local activism

Although the documenta fifteen ekosistem was impressively global, its evolution was also, of necessity, rooted within the specific context of the city of Kassel. As well as providing meeting spaces and curatorial access to artists and collectives involved in Documenta's *lumbung*, ruangrupa wished to extend the same opportunities of friendship, conviviality, co-production, co-learning and ownership to local constituents of the city and the region. In order to do this, as soon as COVID-19 pandemic restrictions allowed, two ruangrupa members and their families moved to Kassel. By integrating themselves into day-to-day life there, taking their children to school in the city, getting to know local communities and identifying existing ekosistems, ruangrupa were able to evolve and share further mechanisms for meeting, exchange and making that, they hoped, would lead to long-lasting infrastructural change and new forms of connective ekosistem that would continue to evolve independently in Kassel after the exhibition had concluded. For example, in one of Kassel's vacant former city-centre department stores, ruangrupa opened up a ruruHaus, a kind of living-room space in which locals from Kassel were invited to collaborate and experiment with artists and collectives. ruruHaus provided a space for exchange in which locals and their communities could freely and openly meet with participants of documenta fifteen and, through the methodology of *lumbung*, could themselves shape and take part in the hundred days of exhibition.

Knowing that documenta fifteen would still initially be viewed and experienced through the lens of a global contemporary art event, and that the ekosistems and *lumbung* would be judged, by many, in terms of spectatorship and spectacle, ruangrupa chose to invert public expectations through their use of allocated Documenta buildings. The Fridericianum, one of the oldest and most established museums in Europe, and the space where most visitors to Documenta over the last sixty-five years have expected to see star artists presenting the most prestigious and marketable work, was turned into Fridskul (or *Fridericianum as School*). Instead of a location for static display, the Fridericianum building as Fridskul became a site in which an ever-changing programme was co-produced by artists, thinkers, makers and communities from across the world and from Kassel itself. Those working on projects talked, collaborated, cooked, ate, drank and slept in Fridskul. This gave visitors to documenta fifteen a very different

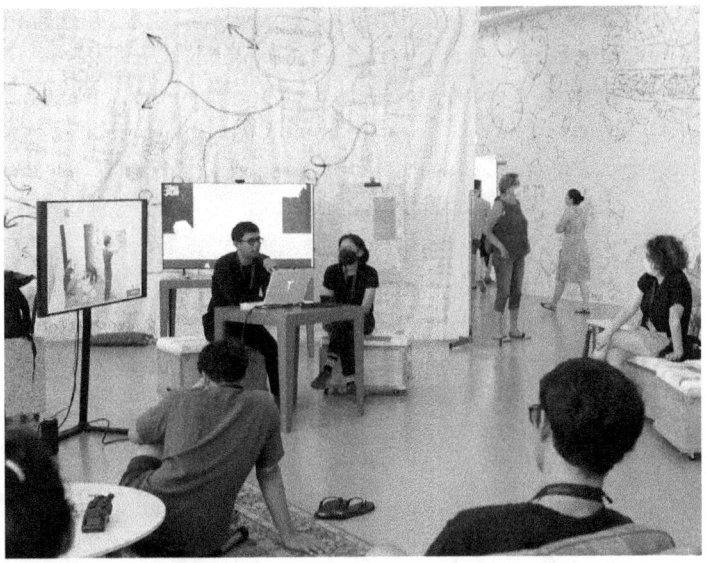

5.2 ruangrupa documenta fifteen, Gudskul/Fridericanium. Image courtesy of ruangrupa

experience. Instead of quiet reverence, visitors would be invited to participate in an atmosphere of conversation, exchange and knowledge production which was often punctuated by the smells of cooking and the sound of children playing.

They also paid careful attention to new mechanisms for mediation of knowledge between the exhibitors, its visitors and the host community. Instead of individuals being employed to translate and communicate previously fixed and established ideas about what is exhibited or put on display, ruangrupa initiated a team of one hundred locals and international volunteers who were known as *sobat-sobat* (which is Indonesian for friends). The sobat-sobat hosted artists and collaborators and, through their own interests and perspectives, were invited to contribute and participate in the creative process of building *lumbung*. Instead of developing a separate public outreach programme, sobat-sobat were invited to help develop moments where visitors and participants alike could plug into and develop the harvest of *lumbung* across all locations within the exhibition.

Harvesting the lumbung

Harvesting, for ruangrupa, is the collective process whereby any outputs – be they artworks, conversations, publications, new collaborations, solutions, plans, ideas or any other physical or immaterial resources – are pooled as a store of surplus for common use and reuse. As ruangrupa's intentions were to invite Documenta to join them in their ongoing process of *lumbung*, those involved in the development of documenta fifteen produced the online resource, lumbung.space.[14] The lumbung. space platform provides *lumbung* members, affiliates and associates with an opportunity to continue the international growth of the *lumbung* through connecting together all its various manifestations. Outcomes – from videos, images, on-line debates, podcasts, publications, seminars and workshops – can be uploaded by members and shared.

Another method for *lumbung* harvesting, which grew out of majelis discussions in the lead up to the hundred days of documenta fifteen exhibition, was *lumbung kios* (kiosks in Indonesian). Envisioned as a decentralised network of self-organised kiosks through which *lumbung* members and groups can sell their products, *lumbung kios* also provides a means through which alternative economies and sustainable support systems can be explored and co-developed. They have adopted the feral trade model, in which goods are shipped, hand-to-hand, by individual collaborators who happen to be travelling in the right direction.[15] *Lumbung kios* also provides an on-line and off-line opportunity for surplus profits – whether that be money, knowledge or shareable resources of any kind – to be stored in the *lumbung* barn and to be redistributed, according to need and requirement, decided though the mechanism of further majelis discussions and debates.

By inviting Documenta to join and extend an international network of activist ekosistems, I would argue that ruangrupa intentionally and politely inverted the usual logics and operating systems of the global contemporary art world. Instead of using documenta fifteen as a major platform to show and display their work and working methods, ruangrupa chose to offer an alternative model of organisation and collaboration via *lumbung*. They offered an open-source toolkit by which the art-world system might begin to think and make itself otherwise. In doing so, ruangrupa also presented a way of experiencing and being with Useful Art projects that fundamentally challenged how we expect to experience and understand art as we know it or knew it to be.

Far from a symbolic illustration of an activist alternative, documenta-fifteen-as-*lumbung* offered a template for producing ekosistems that could be repurposed and contributed to by other users in different contexts and circumstances. Thus ruangrupa effectively plugged a blueprint for accessible and participatory change into the global exhibitionary model of display and spectatorship – one that has dominated the Western art experience since the first Venice Biennale opened in 1895. Disrupting and reimagining the fixed logics of an entire monocultural global art system, they harnessed the collective potential that a myriad of local, thoughtful and compassionate perspectives can bring.

Renzo Martens: CATPC and the White Cube

Since 1989, when biennial culture began to spread and propagate a kind of homogenised leisure-culture version of art across the globe, contemporary art has played a major role in the regeneration of post-industrial cities around the world, including my own city of Liverpool. One of the phenomena of biennial culture has been its frequent commissioning of short-term, socially engaged art practices which have a tendency to spectacularise and aestheticise the complex living conditions of those who are invited to participate in the production of such works. That such projects also tend, almost by default, to encourage the short-term participation of communities who are situated on or within the fringes of the Global North has only exacerbated this form of colonialism through contemporary art.

For example, in his 1999 work *8 People Paid to Remain inside Carboard Boxes* the artist Santiago Sierra employed low-paid workers, offering them 100 quetzals, or US$9, to conceal themselves in boxes at the G&T Building in Guatemala City. When the work was repeated a year later as *Workers Who Cannot be Paid, Remunerated to Remain inside Cardboard Boxes* at Galerie Peter Kilchmann, Zurich, Chechen refugees were paid in secret so as to avoid German legislation (which stipulated that exiles could not earn more than 80 marks a month without being deported back to their country of origin). While it can be argued that such projects use the frameworks of the art world to foreground difficult ethical and political debates, it is also doubtful that the same projects have a lasting impact on the welfare of the labourers or refugees involved.

During this period, the artist Renzo Martens began to notice a colonial, extractivist tendency: art projects made in remote locations are only likely to create monetary value, and art-world status value, when displayed or exhibited within the specific value chain of biennials and contemporary art-world culture. Once artistic and economic value has been extracted remotely and changed into the literal currency of the art world (through its transmogrification into aesthetic art), that value also tends to then circulate within the art world itself. Those on the periphery of this system, whose subject matter, circumstances and often physical participation and labour go into the making of these projects, seldom see any financial or cultural returns. As a result, the value chains of the contemporary art world, no matter how decolonial its intentions, remain fundamentally rooted in the kind of extractivist plantation economics that historically allowed major industries to plunder natural resources and extract financial value from non-Western locations for little or no return.

Focusing on one such example – Unilever's extraction of palm oil from plantations in the Democratic Republic of the Congo to feed the growing market for the soaps and domestic cleaning products it manufactured – Martens began working with local inhabitants of ex-Unilever plantations so that they could make and sell their own art and, in doing so, begin to reverse the normative value chains of the global art-world system. Instead of the art world aestheticising the plight and conditions of ex-Unilever plantation workers as artworks to be consumed in museums and galleries, Martens effectively hacked into the usually closed circuit of commercial art exchange by enabling those ex-plantation workers to produce, exhibit and sell their own artworks within the mechanisms of the global international art market.

Martens had first begun to outline some of the uncomfortable relationships of exploitation within the current art-world system with the 2008 release of his film *Enjoy Poverty*.[16] Ostensibly recording his journeys and activities in Congo, Martens's film set out to establish that Congo's most lucrative global export is the image of poverty. Arguing that the poor being filmed generates more revenue than more traditional forms of exploitative plunder – of raw materials such as diamonds, gold and cocoa – Martens's point was that, as always, the poor whose images are being monetised gain little or nothing in return. To redress this imbalance, *Enjoy Poverty* traces Martens's attempts to persuade Congolese photographers to begin taking photos of war, famine and disaster, instead of weddings, funerals and social gatherings, as the international sale and circulation of such images would be exponentially more profitable.

Doomed to failure as a project, the real critical value of this film, for Martens, resided in its Trojan Horse-like impact on the art world itself. When shown as an artwork in White Cube settings across the Global North, *Enjoy Poverty* confronted conventional audiences with their complicity within these extractivist value chains. Instead of showing images which allowed those audiences to sympathise and empathise with the experience of people being exploited in the global south, or displaying symbolic reminders that the conditions of the exploited are frequently brought about by the mechanisms of global neoliberal occupation, the film confronted them with an uncomfortable fact. The display and consumption of such images, perhaps unavoidably within the spheres of neoliberal occupation, is itself part of a major profit-making industry. Martens's next move was to instigate a sustained examination of what he began to term 'reverse gentrification'.

IHA and the Congolese Plantation Workers Art League

Martens's film, along with the use of contemporary art as a tool to regenerate post-industrial cities, highlights a gap in the smooth surface of the global art system. This gap is the geographical and ideological divide between the conditions that exist within those peripheral locations that the art world loves to exploit, and the art world itself. There is a yawning chasm between places where exploitation, inequality and conflict actually occur and their symbolic relocations, as artworks, within the exhibitionary value chain of gentrification, spectacle and consumption – and this exploitative gap largely resembles the extractivist mechanisms of any other globalised industry, such as petrochemicals, fast fashion, mobile technology and so on, Martens set up The Institute of Human Activities as a mechanism by which this unequal division of artistic labour could be repurposed and reversed.[17] Observing that those who profit from the production of socially conscious contemporary art are rarely those who co-produce those works, Martens simply suggested that all co-participants should benefit equally from the value they produce. Like Tania Bruguera, whose thinking drove the formation of the Association of Arte Útil, Martens recognised that symbolic artworks do little or nothing to disrupt the value flows of a contemporary art world that is now adept at profiting from public acts of shock or effrontery. The Institute of Human Activities effectively allows Martens a means by which the systems and value chains of the existing global art industry can be hacked and reappropriated.

Based in Congo, and operating from a former Unilever plantation, the Institute of Human Activities generates artworks and sells them, diverting the profit to local recipients from the global circuits of the contemporary art system. This profit is then reinvested locally by providing training, resources and paid work to former Unilever plantation workers as artists. In turn, this has enabled former plantation workers – who organised themselves into the Cercle d'Art des Travailleurs de Plantation Congolaise (CATPC) in 2014 – to begin buying back land for farming.[18] It has also enabled CATPC members to supplement their income through the production of artworks that are regularly displayed, exhibited and bought by major museums and galleries around the world. Initially, this started as CATPC members began to make self-portraits and drawings which imagined their futures. This work then evolved into a series of sculptural self-portraits, made from Congolese river clay, which were scanned in 3D. The scans were then sent to Belgium, where they were made into chocolate moulds and recast. Using a recipe that included cocoa and palm oil from the artists' plantation, these small chocolate sculptures were then sold for a profit in museum and gallery gift shops. Again, the profits from this activity were returned to the CATPC and the plantation for further use.

As a next step, this method of using the hand-made, and of reactivating traditional making skills that had been taken from plantation workers during the period of colonial occupation, was then recombined with digital technologies to produce larger-scale sculpture. This resulted in the exhibition of CATPC chocolate sculptures in major museums and galleries such as the Van Abbemuseum (Eindhoven) in 2015, the National Museum of Art (Cardiff) in 2015, the Museum of Modern Art (Warsaw) in 2016 and SculptureCenter (New York) in 2017. In this way, and by using the materials of cocoa, palm oil and sugar cane, normally produced by plantation workers for global industry at below the living wage, CATPC members are able to reoccupy places within the value chain of contemporary art that are usually reserved for the upper and middle classes in locations far from where they live and work. In turn, the money they generate from sales can be used directly for the benefit of the community – replenishing the health of plantation soil, providing local food security and allowing CATPC members to address issues of climate change by returning to a more biodiverse ecology.

Resituating the White Cube

Martens went on to take this pattern of decentralisation away from distant colonial profiteering towards local Useful Art activism further with the building of the Lusanga International Research Centre for Art and Economic Inequality (LIRCAEI) on the former Leverville site, where Lever Brothers first opened a Congolese palm oil plantation in 1911.

The intention of LIRCAEI is to continue developing ways that the current art-world system, which has benefited from the corporate sponsorship of industries built upon the imposition of industrialised monoculture on the global south, might be fundamentally changed. Opened on a site of prime significance for the colonial history of the region, LIRCAEI is intentionally located at the geographic, economic and political crossroads of climate change, outdated extractivist business models and post-colonial economic urgency. At the centre of LIRCAEI is a classic White Cube art space, which was opened in 2017. As Renzo Martens argues:

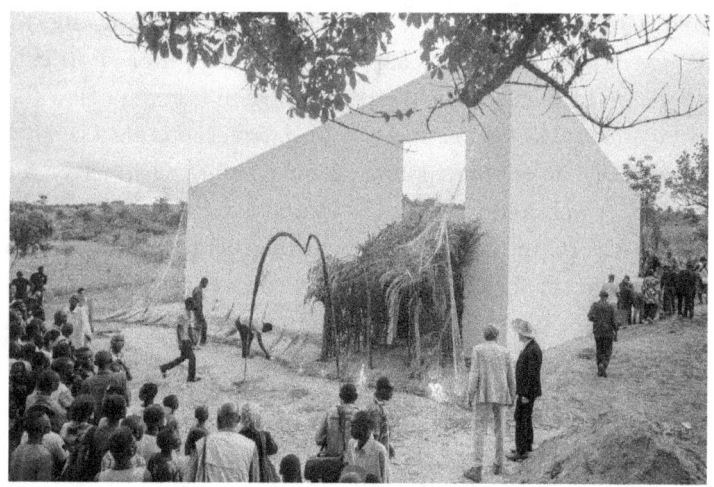

5.3 Congolese Plantation Workers Art League, 'The Repatriation of the White Cube', 2007. Image courtesy of Human Activities, © Thomas Nolf

There is a direct relation between white cubes and plantations: Profits extracted from plantations, through imposed monoculture, have financed the establishment of Tate Britain, of the Van Abbemuseum, the Museum Ludwig collection, and many more museums. The white cube and the plantation are two sides of the same coin. White cubes are places for dissent, critique and taste. They gather people, funds and ideas. Plantations, on the other hand, are places where monoculture is imposed on people, on plants and on landscapes. Often this is done through forced labour, by burning down the rainforest and with armed forces. These are places where profits are extracted from, where dissent is crushed by the military, and the police and where people flee and emigrate from.

The white cube has been separated for too long from the economic structures that sustain it. It must now be re-contextualized and put to the service of the people that financed it. The task is to reformulate what the white cube and the plantation are.[19]

Because of this, the LIRCAEI White Cube, which nestles incongruously within the former plantation site, also reminds us that it is our global peripheries which often fuel the condition of neoliberal occupation within which our major cultural institutions now lie. Additionally, it reminds us that conditions of neoliberal occupation can themselves be repurposed, through Useful Art, as active sites of value production on their own terms.

In 2023, The Congolese Plantation Workers Art League minted a series of 306 NFTs (non-fungible tokens), known as the Balot NFTs, which were launched for sale at Basel Art Fair. Sales of these NFTs were intended to enable the CATPC to continue buying back and replenishing land around the White Cube and to continue the process of planting trees and reintroducing biodiversity on the site of their former Unilever plantation. The NFTs allow CATPC to effectively use the most recent form of digital economic exchange, in this case blockchain, as an activist tool of 1:1 scale decolonisation.

The 'Balot' NFTs are themselves based on a 1931 sculpture, carved during an uprising of the Pende people against the systematic atrocities and rape they had endured from Belgian colonial officials acting on behalf of the Unilever plantation system. The Balot sculpture itself, which is now held in the Virginia Museum of Fine Arts in Richmond in the US, was based on the Belgian officer Maximilian Balot, who was beheaded during the uprising. In a series of six short films, 'Plantations and Museums', a background to the Balot NFT project is provided as we follow the journey of two CATPC members – Matthieu Kasiama and Cedart Tamasala – as they travel to the US in an attempt to track down the original Balot sculpture and its complex meanings.[20] They meet historians and writers,[21] as well as collector Herbert Weiss (who bought the Balot sculpture for $120 in 1971) and Richard Woodward (curator at the Virginia Museum of Fine Arts), and we witness a complex and shifting dialogue opening up around objecthood, ownership, display, function and art.

During these conversations, Kasiama and Tamasala guide us through a history in which plantations, slavery and bonded labour provided the raw materials that drove the Industrial Revolution and which, in turn, sparked the conversion of dirty money into cultural capital through the philanthropy of rich industrialists. As Western industrial and cultural colonialism spread across the world, objects were plundered from their original contexts. As history was rewritten from a Western perspective, collections of these stolen objects began to be housed in new civic museums, and a corresponding expert culture began to grow around the new meaning of these objects as artefacts. In doing so, the role and function of those objects fundamentally shifted – from one of everyday symbolic, religious and community use to one of ethnographic illustration.

By stating a clear ambition to exhibit the original Balot sculpture at the CATPC White Cube in Lusanga, Kasiama and Tamasala instigate a process of repatriation which is far more than the taking back of something which has been lost or stolen. Instead, the conversations they initiate interrogate the relationships between centre and periphery, between the local and the global and between centralised monoculture and grass-roots alternatives. By expressly wanting to be artists, by repurposing the plantation which is their home, and by embedding themselves within the flows of a neoliberal art-world value chain that would otherwise

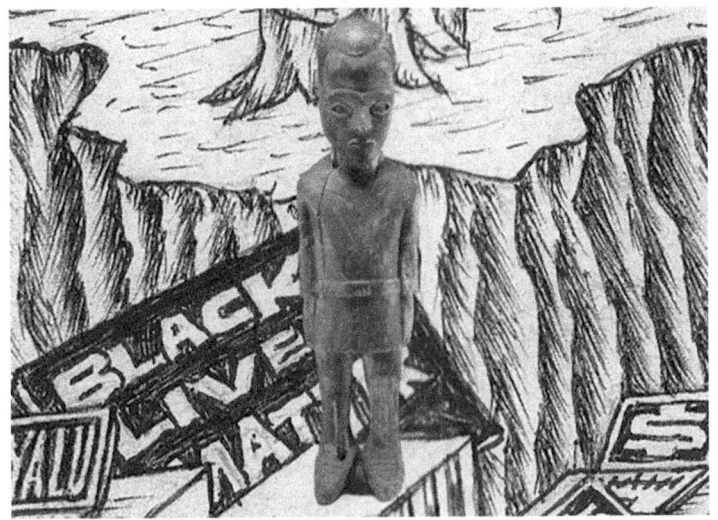

5.4 Congolese Plantation Workers Art League, Balot NFT 140, 2022

exclude them, Kasiama and Tamasala represent a community who are actively re-empowering themselves by returning useful-ness to art. However, as we know, this is a long and far from easy journey. As Simon Gikandi puts it, when asked why the art-world establishment seems to exclude and trivialise their ambitions to use art as a tool for social change:

> My suspicion is that the people who provide the critique, are working under the impression that you, as the labourers in the plantation, are not capable of or are not interested in art. You have to be strong and say: 'We are doing this for ourselves. And we are doing this for our community. We have a right to art.' Art doesn't just belong to the middle class in Kinshasa, or the Europeans in Brussels. When we see plantation workers producing art, that is radical as far as I'm concerned.[22]

These projects show how current art-world systems can be hijacked, hacked and repurposed as a means to reverse their flows and subvert their power structures. We can also see how it is possible for local communities to activate Useful Art as tool of ground-up re-empowerment and change. By creating spaces in which they can operate as equals within the contemporary culture industries, the CATPC are simultaneously disrupting the extractivist supply chains of that cultural economy and using the proceeds to reintroduce sustainable biodiversity, both environmental (via repurchase of plantation land) and artistic (insisting on new voices, spaces and economies). In recognition of the ongoing impact of these operations, Martens and the CATPC were invited to provide the Dutch entry for the 2024 Venice Biennale, directly linking the LIRCAEI White Cube to one of the global art system's most established and prestigious exhibitions.

However, repatriation and fair renumeration for labour represent only one side of the decolonial coin. The other is the question of how we escape our condition of neoliberal occupation, by learning to live otherwise. The manifold murmuration of voices, communities, ideas and cosmologies that arise from both peripheries and forgotten centres alike offer us new possibilities and models. The work of Renzo Martens and his collaborators represents ways in which the usual flows of neoliberal supply and value chains can be disrupted and reversed – by opening up wormholes and points of connection and access between the centres of neoliberal accumulation and their former sites of colonial value extraction. Our next example shows us a different strategy: Jonas Staal's 'New World Summit – Rojava' turns towards political representation and democracy.

Jonas Staal and the New World Summit – Rojava

In 2018, a new 'people's parliament' was officially opened in Rojava, in the west of Kurdistan, formerly the northern part of Syria. Initially, the people's parliament was commissioned in 2014 when Amina Osse, Chairman of the Committee of Foreign Affairs for The Democratic Self-Administration of Rojava (DSA), asked artist Jonas Staal and his 'New World Summit' organisation to build a public parliament for the region.

The DSA arose from the Rojavan Revolution of 2011. As the Syrian war forced Assad to redeploy most of his troops and resources to the south of the country, Kurdish revolutionaries seized the opportunity to reclaim their land. In open collaboration between the various peoples, ethnicities and religious groupings who called the region home, such as Arabs and Syriac Christians, the Democratic Self-Administration of Rojava was formed – declaring itself to be a self-governing, stateless and borderless nation that would organise itself along the principles of Democratic Confederalism. Since 2012 Staal, together with 'The New World Summit', have developed and held parliaments for more than thirty stateless political organisations, including Azawad, Somaliland, Tamil Eelam and the Basque Country and in cities such as Brussels and Berlin. However, the 'New World Summit – Rojava' provides the first 1:1 scale assembly point through which a newly formed 'stateless democracy' can govern itself.[23]

The physical architecture of 'New World Summit – Rojava', based in Derîk, Cezîre Canton (one of three cantons that makes up Rojava), takes the form of a sphere. In its centre lies a circular agora, or public gathering space, where non-hierarchical discussions and debates can take place. The Democratic

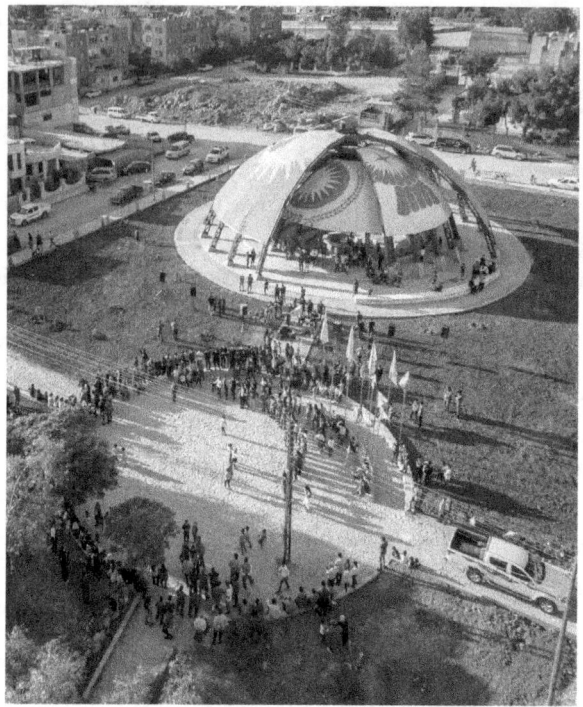

5.5 'New World Summit – Rojava', 2015–18. Democratic Self-Administration of Rojava and Studio Jonas Staal. Image courtesy of Jonas Staal

Self-Administration of Rojava (DSA) depends on a network of local and regional councils, who represent the decisions and interests of neighbourhood councils, and so this is a space for the coming together of multiple voices to constitute and operate shared governance. The roof of the people's parliament is made from six canvas sections, each of which is a snapshot taken from the flags of local organisations that make up the DSA. Together they add up to a prismatic kaleidoscope which is intended to symbolise the tolerance and multiplicity inherent in the DSA's nature. The roof of the people's parliament is itself held up by a series of pillars, each of which carries words or concepts, written in Kurdish, Arabic and Assyrian, that are central to the 'Social Contract' of the Rojava Revolution: gender equality, secularism, communalism, social ecology, self-defence and democratic confederalism. In Staal's words:

> The idea that the autonomy of art can be instrumentalized – or repurposed – in relation to larger social struggles has great potential. It is not a way of abandoning art, but rather an endeavor to understand the imaginative and morphological capacities of art differently; to see art not as a mere object of contemplation, but as a means to construct new notions of subjectivity. The assembly as an aesthetic and political practice is very much a part of that effort.[24]

'The New World Summit – Rojava' evolved into a people's parliament, a physical, public space that would be used for local demonstrations, cultural events and international conferences. At the same time, the parliament would act as both a symbol for a new world in the making and a concrete example of how that new world could be made.

Democratic confederalism and Useful Art

The self-administration of Rojava is based on the writings of the Kurdish revolutionary and former leader of the Kurdistan Workers' Party (PKK), Abdullah Öcalan. After his abduction and imprisonment by the Turkish government of Tayyip Erdoğan in 1999, Öcalan began to develop a series of ideas and proposals for developing forms of democratic confederalism, the kind of nationless self-governance which, since the declaration of the Democratic Self-Assembly of Rojava (DSA) in 2012, the Rojavan Revolution has sought to put into practice. While he was leader of the PKK, which was initially focused on the establishment of a Kurdish nation-state, Öcalan began to propose alternative forms of decentralised and borderless autonomy and self-determination which, he argues, would be capable of escaping the bureaucracy and authoritarianism of state socialism and global neoliberalism alike. Through bottom-up forms of self-governance, communal economy and gender equality, alongside a rejection of the existing nation-state model, Öcalan's proposal would ensure fairer and more democratic forms of participatory power-sharing across all levels of organisation and decision-making:

> Our idea of a democratic nation is not defined by flags and borders. Our idea of a democratic nation embraces a model based on democracy instead of a model based on state structures and ethnic origins. Turkey needs to define itself as a country which includes all ethnic groups. This would be a model based on human rights instead of religion or race. Our idea of a democratic nation embraces all ethnic groups and cultures.[25]

Seen in this light, the democratic confederalism of the DSA also provides a working model of what is often referred to as non-representational politics. Instead of a system in which formal elections are run to nominate candidates who stand for and represent party-political viewpoints, and who then act as representatives for their voting constituencies in centralised government forums, democratic confederalism works around continual forms of neighbourhood and local discussions. The results of these local discussions, which are not aligned to party policies, are then discussed and agreed at regional and national level.

Useful Art and the power of the local

This model offers a contrast to devolution of power to local governments, which is a more common way of decentralising power. Devolution usually operates along the lines of delegating fiscal responsibility over budgets that have been decided at a distance from those communities they will affect, and still requires that the imperatives and operational systems of centralised government are upheld. In Rojava and the work of Öcalan, we see a much more radical, locally determined and community-driven form of government, unshackled from the one-size-fits-all approach of centralised control and watered-down efforts to devolve power.

These locally constructed political alternatives show us the kinds of roles and functions that Useful Art can play in real-world social, economic and political change. We know that Useful Art provides a set of open-source toolkits and strategies by which local communities can again learn to reclaim forms of autonomy, agency and re-empowerment from within the condition of neoliberal occupation, and a means by which these toolkits can be reused by a growing network of activists and artists who wish to reimagine and remake themselves otherwise. At a time when globalisation relies upon the instrumentalising imposition of exchange value as the only means by which we communicate, organise and understand ourselves and each other, the 'New World Summit – Rojava' offers a clear blueprint for socially regenerating forms of local use value.

Useful Art, activated on a local scale, connects and enables users who are based at dispersed geographical and distinct political contexts (in this case the various neighbourhoods) to effect real-world change in a way that can be shared, repurposed and replayed by other activists, artists and communities. These alternative organisational strategies, such as democratic confederalism, form part of the toolkit of Useful Art, allowing local users to learn and share methods for destabilising and decentralising the instrumental logics of capitalism from within.

'The Museum as Parliament'

'The Museum as Parliament', which opened in the Van Abbemuseum in 2018, is a permanent installation that operates as a 1:1 Scale Useful Art reconstruction of the People's Parliament of Rojava. It offers a physical and institutional means by which the values of the Rojava Revolution can be explored, shared, propagated and disseminated. In return, it also offers the Van Abbemuseum, in collaboration with its many local, regional and international constituencies, a means by which new and experimental forms of public assembly can be activated and played out from within a European public museum. Working with the same themes and values, the architecture of the 'Museum as Parliament' closely resembles that of the 'New World Summit – Rojava'. A circular dome of kaleidoscopic flags covers a seated theatre in the round which hosts public meetings, artist talks, conferences, seminars, workshops and other activities that support local, national and international communities of users through the Van Abbemuseum's programming of events. Again, a series of pillars, supporting the dome, represent key values of democratic confederalism such as 'gender equality', 'social equality' and 'secularism', and its circular shape is intended to embody ideals of decentralised democratic representation.

'The Museum as Parliament' was initially programmed as a collaboration between the Rojavan diaspora of the Netherlands and Europe, the Van Abbemuseum, and the 'New World Summit' organisation.[26] Its intention was to introduce multiple users from

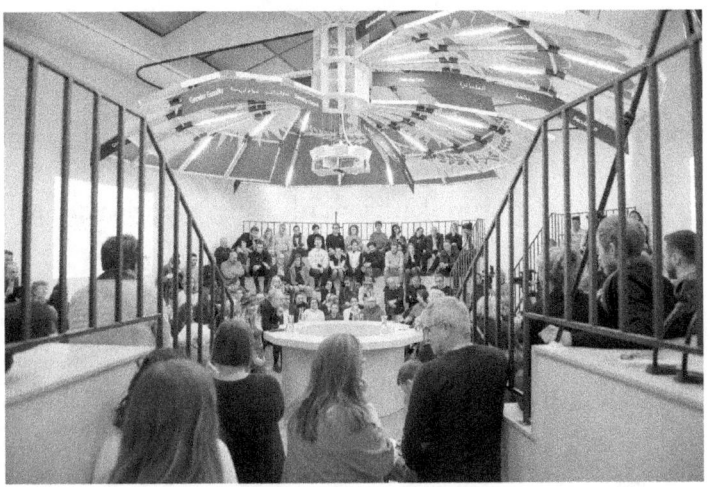

5.6 'Museum as Parliament', Democratic Self-Administration of Rojava and Studio Jonas Staal, Van Abbemuseum, Eindhoven, 2018–ongoing. Image courtesy of Jonas Stall

diverse and geographically distinct perspectives and origins to the toolkits of stateless democracy. The aim was to enable them to meet within a space where new forms of democracy can be imagined and to build new emancipatory alliances of stakeholders, activist groups and cultural workers. For example, 'The Museum as Parliament' space now hosts events such as the annual María Lugones Decolonial Summer School.[27] This is curated by sociologist and author Rolando Vázquez (Mexico/The Netherlands) and theorist Walter Mignolo (Argentina/the US) and uses informal conversations, organised conversations, workshops and lectures to examine the concept that there is no modernity without coloniality. Another offering has been 'True Counterpower', a series of workshops and training sessions organised by Serda

Demir and Iliada Charalambous. The initial aim of the sessions was to provide an open platform that would invite activist, social and art organisations alike to share their methodologies and approaches. True Counterpower also promotes alliances between those groups, and facilitates networks of anti-colonial and anti-capitalist solidarity, working towards fairer, participatory and ecological futures for us all.

These activities have brought together diverse groupings of activists using 'The Museum as Parliament' as a place to talk, teach, collaborate and share their activist toolkits with each other – from the Kurdish Women's Movement in Europe (TJKE) to the Sudanese Refugee Collective, Fossil Free Culture and Refugee Solidarity Network Germany. Here art is being used as a tool for activating decentralised political alternatives, often with vulnerable and marginalised groups at their centre, at a time when our traditional systems of European and global democracy seem increasingly open to threat and abuse.[28]

'The Museum as Parliament' has been a means for the Van Abbemuseum to test and exceed its own institutional limitations and expectations by purchasing a 'work' of Useful Art: 'New World Summit – Rojava' – or, more accurately, an option to rebuild and reactivate it. As major museums and galleries usually purchase objects which they can own, store and display as public spectacle, such a manoeuvre means that the Van Abbemuseum can experiment with participation in, rather than possession of, a 1:1 scale and non-representational political process as an activation of Useful Art.

Both 'The New World Summit – Rojava' and 'The Museum as Parliament' provide us with an example of how activist artists operating in the Global North can learn directly from the global south. My fourth and final example of Useful Art in process is the 'Speculative Library', which opened in 2023. This was part of an ongoing project, instigated by curator and Useful Art activist Barto Bartolomeus, which began at Yamaguchi Centre for Arts and Media (YCAM) in 2022. The reason for looking at the 'Speculative Library' is that it shows how the strategies and tactics of Useful Art can converge productively. The project is based within the context of a relatively wealthy and comfortable location in the Global North – the city of Yamaguchi, which sits in the Western Honshu district of Japan. As a consequence of this, the 'Speculative Library' offers an opportunity to see how the open-source playbook of Useful Art can be drawn upon to challenge traditional notions of what art was, or used to be, from within a situation where these traditional paradigms of aesthetic and useless art prevail. It also offers us a chance to see how the deployment of Useful Art tactics and strategies, which begins as an opportunity for local audiences to rethink how they might use a traditional gallery space, can provide a participatory context of constituent ownership and re-empowerment, one that can spread far beyond the walls of the repurposed institution in question.

Barto Bartolomeus and the 'Speculative Library'

YCAM opened in 2003 and was initially envisaged as a media- and technology-based arts centre, one which would house an exhibition space, cinema, library, several workshop spaces and restaurant. In the run-up to their twentieth anniversary, YCAM asked curator and Useful Art activist Leonhard Bartolomeus (or Barto for short) to lead a review of the institutional mecha- nisms, strategies and tactics through which YCAM connects with its local communities. As a long-term collaborator with ruangrupa and a former manager of the ruangrupa ekosistem Gudskul, Barto brought an extensive network of ideas, influences and collaborators to this review which, in turn, enabled him to situate the urgencies and needs of the local community within a global and operational context of Useful Art activism. As well as his established links with ruangrupa and Gudskul, Barto was also able to draw upon other interconnecting Useful Art networks to which he contributes, which include the Association of Arte Útil and the L'Internationale confederation of museums and galleries.

I first met Barto in Liverpool, UK when we attempted to formulate a collaboration between Liverpool John Moores University, Liverpool Biennial and Gudskul. Although this initial collaboration didn't take off, Barto reconnected with me, Alistair Hudson and Alessandra Saviotti of the Arte Útil team as part of an 'Alternative Educational' programme he instigated during the COVID-19 pandemic (which included the 'KURIKULAB: Moving Classroom' project with the Indonesian collective Serrum), connected with the YCAM twenty-year review.

What emerged from this review was what any reader of this book so far might expect. The review confirmed that it is impossible for an institution to break out of the historical paradigms of exhibitionary display and spectacle that currently underpin the workings of the global art world unless (A) the institution in question is prepared to begin looking at ways in which it can adjust the mechanisms of its own operating systems and (B) that institution also begins to open up to shared participation with local constituencies and communities.

Barto and the staff team at YCAM acted on this by formulating a series of key questions and activities which aimed to develop new forms of local participation and constituent response. Their

Useful Art and the power of the local

'Speculative Library' sought to engage with local communities by establishing an accessible platform, or shared space, to spark societal change through creativity, exploration, curiosity and play. Japan has a rich tradition of community arts engagement, and this exploration involved finding ways in which local residents could renegotiate their own and one another's expectations of what it might be like to visit a gallery and engage as spectators with objects of art. In turn, this necessitated the careful and convivial instigation of a long-term co-building process between audiences and staff at YCAM, in which the sedimented expectations of spectatorship could be slowly eroded and replaced with new co-authored expectations of active engagement, conviviality, friendship building and co-ownership.

Local diversity and global monoculture

Japan is an interesting context within which to launch such an intersectional and experimental Useful Art project. As the world's fourth richest nation (by GDP), it is considered to be part of the Global North, though it sits geographically as an archipelago within the Pacific rim. Over the past decades, Japan has become acutely aware of its ageing society and population decline, which especially affects rural areas. Like many countries of the global north it is also experiencing rising income inequality while struggling, on a governmental level, with issues around women's rights, sexual orientation and gender identity.[29]

Since COVID-19, issues around social isolation, loneliness, mental health and well-being have become a concern and, as one of the world's top ten emitters of greenhouse gases, debates around climate change and environmental issues are also beginning to play a more prominent role in social and media debate.

Reconfiguring YCAM as a site where such urgencies could be talked through openly, as a means to develop and effect forms of social change within the local community, posed its own challenges in a country which traditionally prides itself on social fortitude and obedient complicity with power. As a result of this, Barto and the team at YCAM began to develop a series of long-term strategies, which could initially be staged within an existing gallery and exhibition context, but which would also provide open access, reusable toolkits by which forms of community re-empowerment could be negotiated and activated. In this way, and by inviting local audiences to fundamentally rethink their relationship to art as we know it or knew it to be, YCAM began to open itself up to a new role and an ongoing process of institutional power-sharing with its constituents.

To prepare the ground, Barto and YCAM instigated an initial 'Code of Conduct', meant as a creative provocation, to those attending the 'Speculative Library' – a way of inviting spectators to consider becoming users while, at the same time, providing a playful framework within which those new users were able to imagine using and sharing the YCAM space otherwise.[30]

A range of activities and spaces for discussion, interaction and planning were implemented within the physical space of YCAM, and at the centre of these was a 'Meeting Dome'. Designed as a multi-purpose space and platform for creative interaction, the 'Meeting Dome' was inspired by ruangrupa's domestic-scale creative meeting places and the space designer, Team Clapton, who often build a shared space using the DIT (do-it-together) method. The 'Meeting Dome', a bamboo and fabric structure that also provided a separate zone within the large hall of YCAM, slowly became a place where people met, played music together, exchanged knowledge and skills, discussed

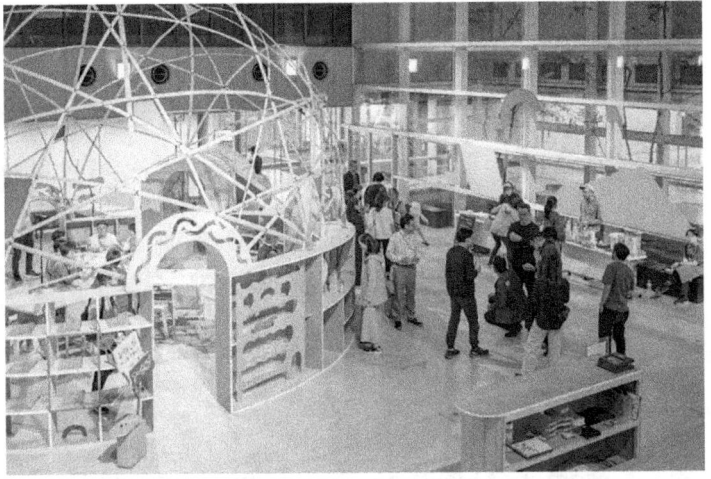

5.7 Yamaguchi Centre for Arts and Media (YCAM), 'Speculative Library Dome', 2023. Image courtesy of YCAM

ideas, gathered socially, pinned notes and drawings on the wall, held discussions with invited speakers and took part in workshops.

Some of the shelving areas that surrounded the 'Meeting Dome' where also locations for depositing and borrowing artworks from the 'Anywhere Art Appreciation' initiative led by Yamaguchi-based artist, Keijiro Suzuki. Leaning into, rather than mimicking, the kinds of ways that individuals might use a library (and YCAM shares the footprint of its building with the Yamaguchi City Library), 'Anywhere Art Appreciation' allowed 'Speculative Library' users to deposit and borrow small-scale artworks. Users could drop off their own work and see it within a gallery context. Their work might also be signed out and taken for a week to a home or a location. All artworks that were deposited for 'Anywhere Appreciation' were anonymised, so nobody knew if they were borrowing a work made by a major artist or a pupil from a local school – people borrowed and returned what they liked and could use to make their lives better. The rationale behind 'Anywhere Appreciation' was to build on the code of conduct of the 'Speculative Library', enabling users to be artists and to borrow works on trust. By depositing something in order to borrow something, discussions and conversations about sharing and alternatives to ownership began to take place. These conversations also helped to problematise and decentralise more normative structures and assumptions around art connoisseurship, spectatorship and monetary value.

'Memory Quest' and 'Re: Map Yamaguchi'

Some accompanying projects aimed to reconnect YCAM constituents to their location. These were 'Memory Quest' and 'Re: Map Yamaguchi'. Developed by the YCAM Interlab team, 'Memory Quest' is an interactive 3D VR game-like interface which allows users to walk through the streets of Yamaguchi while visiting the memories and stories of other users. Building around a game interface, YCAM engineers used the LiDAR scan available on iPhone Pro Max to create immersive environments within the virtual Yamaguchi. The users whose memories populated 'Memory Quest' also recorded short audio stories which, in turn, became accessible to other users who wandered through the virtual memory city via a simple joystick interface.

'Re: Map Yamaguchi' also encouraged users of the 'Speculative Library' to rethink, remake and share their relationships to the city. Drawing inspiration from mapping projects Barto had undertaken with ruangrupa, 'Re: Map Yamaguchi' literally presented a large-scale paper-based representation of the city which had most of the usual information associated with a city map – road names, district names, major buildings – removed. 'Speculative Library' users were then invited to add colour-coded stickers to the map – green for memories, yellow for ideas and red for trouble. For each sticker, users were required to write a short note or story. This simple analogue technology, coupled with the digital 'Memory Quest', encouraged participants and contributors to see their city and their environment differently and with a new sense of empowerment and ownership. Rather than seeing their local environment as a fixed set of geographical locations, defined and governed by private enterprise, housing markets and local council regulation, 'Memory Quest' and 'Re: Map Yamaguchi' reminded users that their city is also a complex aggregate of human interactions.

The 'Voice Library' and 'Asoberu Radio'

Building upon and away from these interactions with physical models of the city, the 'Voice Library' offered users an opportunity to contribute to a different kind of collectively built resource. Users of the 'Voice Library' can sit and record their response to one of fifteen questions that appear on a screen, and which explore relationships between the user, the City of Yamaguchi and YCAM. Once a user's voice recording is complete, a printout is generated which they can then correct or add to with a red pen. When complete, answers are collated into ring binders which provide both a record of the project and also an open-source archive which other users of the 'Speculative Library' can encounter, reuse and repurpose. In order to extend this imaginative network of stories, concerns and memories, the project 'Asoberu Radio', or 'Playable Radio', allowed users of

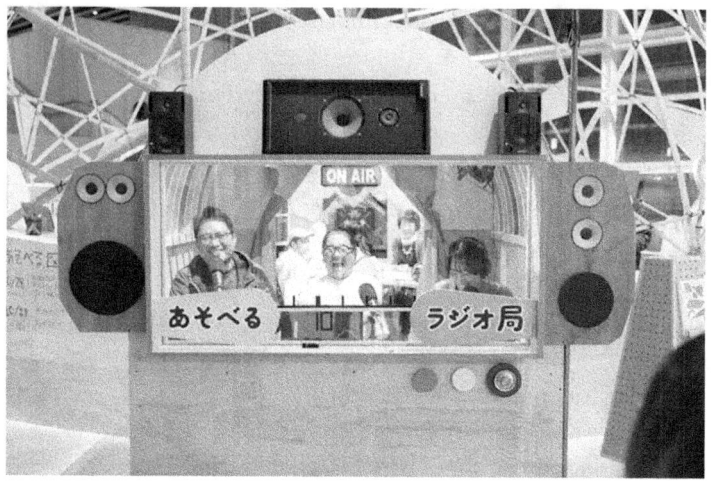

5.8 Yamaguchi Centre for Arts and Media (YCAM), 'Speculative Library Radio', 2023. Image courtesy of YCAM

the 'Speculative Library' to record conversations, create radio programmes and broadcast voices to those nearby via loudspeaker.

This was a pop-up extension of the 'YCAM GURUGURU Radio' podcast, which has been broadcast since 2022. The podcast's open-ended and constituent-led themes are based on the Indonesian term *guru-guru* (which loosely translates as 'an act of wandering' in English).[31] 'Asoberu Radio' was located in a small and intimate hut seating a maximum of three people, who were visible through a window while they recorded or spoke. These projects followed the belief held by both YCAM and ruangrupa that radio offers something uniquely valuable, based on the specificities and understandings of local users and their communities as opposed to the more uniform and globalising formats of social media. They hold that radio can trigger moments when users can talk and communicate about themselves, and with one another, in ways that are both more intimate and community-based.

'Thinking Together' and the Association of Arte Útil at YCAM

The activities and zones of the 'Speculative Library' also created both a context and a toolkit for an open meeting every fortnight, called the 'Let's Think Together Meeting', and an installation of the Association of Arte Útil's Archive. In the 'Thinking Together' meetings, which were divided into two parts, constituents and users had the opportunity to meet up and discuss ideas and experiences around Useful Art with an invited speaker. Constituents and users were organised into small groups who discussed questions or topics raised by the visiting speaker. The groups then fed back their responses in a larger discussion that was also joined by the guest or speaker. This encouraged the YCAM users to move beyond their usual role as passive receivers of expert knowledge. Instead, they could discuss, think, question and evaluate suggestions and ideas from speakers within the context of the 'Speculative Library' and how those ideas might be used to reboot the operating systems of YCAM itself.

The installation of the Association of Arte Útil's Archive was activated through a similar methodology to the 'Thinking Together' meetings. A presentation of fifty or so Japanese translations of Arte Útil projects was made permanently available during the 'Speculative Library' project. This was initially to encourage more active forms of usership among local constituents, and to prompt discussions about the possible reuse of such projects outside YCAM and within the context of Yamaguchi itself. Then, a series of Arte Útil workshops encouraged local users to produce their own Arte Útil solutions to local issues and problems. YCAM users were provided with blank Arte Útil 'Social Issue Cards' which enabled ideas to be noted down in a similar format to that appearing on the online Association of Arte Útil archive. Ideas were then discussed in small groups and presented informally to the larger group. Through this the project generated new 'Social Issue Cards' that could be added to the Arte Útil archive in the 'Speculative Library', which would then be available to a broad network of users and activists.

More locally, these group discussions and meetings encouraged users and constituents to think of how, when and why they might want to retake some control of their lives from the often anonymous bureaucracies of local and regional government. At the same time, it allowed YCAM and its users to rethink how they might productively interact together in ways that can't easily be measured in the more traditional context of the Japanese art world. As Barto himself suggests:

> To be honest, I did not want to fall into the trap of 'success' indicators such as visitor traffic or satisfaction surveys. What we did in Speculative Library is set up a model that could allow the user to play and explore the possibilities of using art as a tool. Using this model allows me to harvest the stories, ideas and also failures that happen on a daily basis. Then, the next step is to share this harvesting with others, something that looks like a playbook, where people could 'steal' the idea and adjust it to their own. I Imagine it's like an open-source code of playfulness. To see that happen, even for only one user, would be a 'success' for us.[32]

We have seen here how international networks and open-source playbooks of social change can be opened up, shared and activated in a specific local context. Whether that locality is a home in Jakarta, a disused shop in Kassel, a museum space in Eindhoven, a seminar in the Democratic Republic of Congo, a discussion in the People's Parliament in Rojava or a 'Social Issues' meeting in Yamaguchi, all begin to share, evaluate, use and repurpose Useful Art as a toolkit for real-world social change.

Conclusion: the revolution will be delicious

It's Saturday 15 June 2024 and I'm again sitting in the lecture theatre of the Van Abbemuseum in Eindhoven: the same place where Tania Bruguera announced her initiative 'the Association of Art Útil' during the Autonomy Symposium some thirteen years before. Charles Escher, Director of the Museum, is opening the exhibition 'Soils', which forms part of an ongoing research project between the Van Abbemuseum, the TarraWarra Museum of Art and the Indonesian collective Struggles for Sovereignty.[1] The title of the exhibition derives from the Palestinian mathematician, writer and radical educator Muni Fasheh's concept of four soils – earth soil, cultural soil, communal soil and affection-spiritual soil – which, he argues, we must nurture if we are to support life on our planet. The Soils project sets out to examine some of the most urgent social, political, economic and environmental issues which now confront us through the lens of one of the most common and commonly overlooked resources for which we all share responsibility – the soil beneath our feet and the ground on which we stand. Over the six years or so of its development, the 'Soils' collaboration has drawn upon multiple influences, learnings and cosmologies of thought. It suggests ways in which artists, communities and institutions can situate themselves through their physical and metaphorical understandings of soil as both specific location and connected resource.

One contributor to the 'Soils' project was Mexican farmers' collective Suumil Móokt'aan, which has used its skills and knowledge bases to evolve an intergenerational learning space. Central to the collective's teachings is the need to preserve the traditional way in which Mayan houses have been built over the centuries. Their landscape is changing already: over recent decades, the Yucatán peninsula has been subject to mass deforestation, the over-extraction of groundwater, and the building of the Mayan Train, a 1,000-mile railway linking the five states of Yucatán for the transport of cargo and tourism. Due to climate change, a series of hurricanes have devastated the region and destroyed local housing. In response to this, the Mexican government has offered subsidies to farmers to rebuild their houses on the condition that they are made of concrete and follow a prescribed and unitary design.

The Suumil Móokt'aan community does not want these houses. They are strongly opposed to this imposition of monoculture on their heritage and they see this push away from local tradition as a symptom of a shift to embed Yucatán within a global extractivist supply-chain economy. For them, the sharing and preservation of their traditions (and the refusal of concrete houses) is a form of resistance within the condition of neoliberal occupation.

By sharing the traditions of the Mayan Solar (a way of organising land for growing of crops, raising livestock and organising domestic activities) and the Mayan Milpa (a sustainable way of rotating crops on a small piece of land), Suumil Móokt'aan

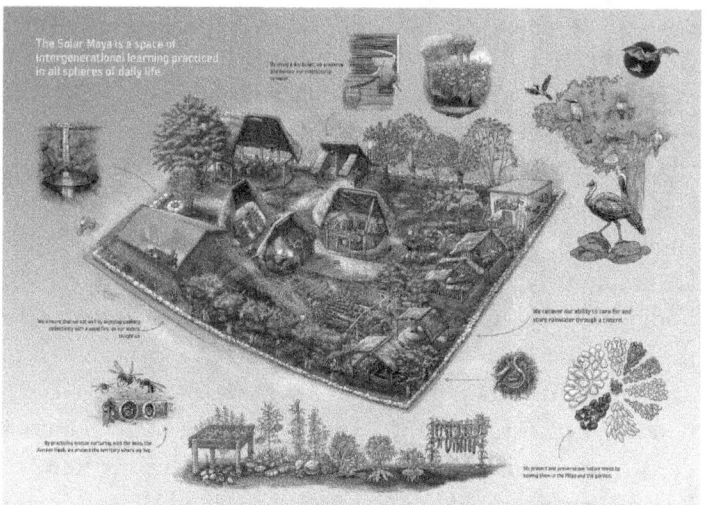

6.1 Suumil Móokt'aan,' Solar Maya diagram. Image courtesy of Suumil Móokt'aan and Alberto Guera

teaches and preserves Mayan traditions which are grounded in the rhythms of daily life, health care and food sovereignty. The collective does this by holding open classes on their farm, posting lessons and discussions on social media, hosting a website and accepting invitations to share their skills and knowledge with others wherever and whenever they can.

You may not be faced with challenges so stark as rehousing your family in the face of climate disasters while resisting neoliberal steamrollering of your landscapes, cultures and traditions. All the same, there are lessons here for aspiring practitioners of Useful Art, and anyone else who is interested. How can you 'dig where you stand' into the soil of your own communities and networks?

Conclusion: the revolution will be delicious

The uses of art

Over the course of this book, we have established that Useful Art can provide a toolkit for individuals and communities to use and share when initiating ground-up forms of activist change and micro-resistance.

We've discussed what 'art' might be, and what the qualities of Useful Art might be, if art is no longer a thing in a gallery to go and look at and there is no longer an inside or an outside to the art world. On one level (or indeed many levels, as you'll see below), the idea of a handbook for identifying Useful Art in the wild is an exercise in missing the point, but if we look beyond the visual at the activity of these artworks, we can find some shared aims, acts and features for those who find comfort in categories or simply want to know that their own instigations and activations are heading in the same direction as the Useful Art that has gone before.

Useful Art is more than simply making a statement about what might be art or not, or what art should or should not be. It is both a toolkit and invitation, a means by which we might use and share art in other ways, outside and beyond the usual borders and conventions of what we tend to think art should or should not be. Instead of trying to be artists, whether useful not, we should instead try to think of living artfully as an act of micro-resistance. Over the last five decades or so we have collectively lost a great deal, as individuals and communities, within the condition of neoliberal occupation. What advantages we have gained from globalisation, in terms of access to goods, travel and resources, have also been offset by precarious working conditions, debt and pending environmental disaster. In this often overwhelming context it is easy to feel as if we have been abandoned or let down by our existing democratic systems, to feel as if we have no longer have any agency within or community or over our personal lives. Useful Art allows us to regain some of this social agency or personal control as individuals and communities who want to make a real-world defence to their social, political and economic conditions.

Stealing gold from the gods can simply be using the means that are available to us in order to take back what has been lost to or stolen from us in terms of the local, the handed-down, the community-driven, the handmade, the shared and the enduring. In this sense Useful Art is about small individual and social acts of reclamation and preservation – the act of using our individual and shared creativity and resources to make a difference to our own and one another's lives. It is about digging where we stand, re-evaluating where we are right now – the air we breathe, the soil on which we stand, the food we cook and eat and the environment in which we live. It is about making small, incremental differences that, on a broader scale, add up to wider community change.

Of course, governments, politicians, economists and business gurus should sort out the mess in which they have landed us all. And Useful Art, as both a toolkit and means to activate individual and local change, should never be mixed up with the job of doing neoliberalism's dirty work for free. But holding hope for change, and finding creative ways in which we can reclaim what has been lost to the condition of neoliberal capture, is not the same as replicating the logics and mechanisms of global capitalism for free. Deregulation, the quasi-autonomy of local authorities and governments to control their own situation, as long as they replicate the business models and economic demands of the centre, is not the same thing as decentralisation, in which local communities begin to work with and use their own resources of creativity, skill, knowledge and hope. Useful Art is about sharing the skills, tools and means to make creative changes happen. It is about rethinking and redefining what we might need and what we value both in ourselves and with each other. It is about identifying the needs and resources that are necessary not only to imagine ourselves otherwise, but to become otherwise together. Useful Art is about the communal pooling of resources, knowledge bases and skills. It is a *lumbung* approach to how we might teach ourselves and our children the skills we need to live more collaborative, tolerant and creative lives together. It is about connecting our lives and communities in ways that will allow us to re-circuit how we might live together now, and what we might become together in the future.

The act of resistance is often aligned with the moil and toil of struggle, the hard labour of forcing change to happen at the top of our existing systems. But Useful Art offers us an opportunity to recalibrate resistance by aligning it with joy, hope, compassion, creativity and friendship. It offers new forms of solidarity, and new forms of shared identity, that can be gained from the process of pushing back against the influence of the global and the bland. Through preserving and remaking the local, by reskilling, by handmaking and repurposing, by recycling and upcycling, by thinking of how local resources can be better fostered and distributed, we can begin to participate in alternative forms of sharing and exchange that are helpful, hopeful and fun. It is up to us, as individuals and communities, to glean from our lost and disappearing knowledge bases, grow and evolve our resource bases, tend to our local ecologies and, above all, open ourselves to the lessons we can learn, reactivate and reuse from other people, other communities and other cosmologies of thought.

Useful Art in your community

If you would like to activate some Useful Art, a good first step might be to take some time to consider and map your own relationships to your local community and communities. This would also involve spending a little time thinking beyond our more standard notions of communities as strong groups of people who share a belief or an identity, and to think also about our communities of friendship, compassion, sharing and care, our families, friends and colleagues, those we can share knowledge with and with whom we can learn and grow.

1) What communities do you feel part of? Or would you like to feel part of?

Think about your local community or communities and jot down some responses and ideas on a piece of paper or on your phone. Is there one, or are there many? What makes a community, and which communities might you feel part of, and why? You might want to reflect on whether you gravitate towards the familiar, or whether you are interested in finding out how other people from other communities or walks of life do things differently. This might be the way they cook, or the foods they use, or the knowledge they have, or the way they teach or learn. In the same spirit, what skills, ideas, or knowledge do you have that could be shared? Think about spaces in which you could arrange to meet, local issues that could be best addressed together, or new identities that could be fostered and grown. What can be gleaned from and between the communities you feel a part of (or would like to feel a part of) that could be activated to make living together a more creative and artful process? Are there things that communities share, or which bring them together?

2) What skills have been lost to your community (adopted or original)?

After thinking about the community or communities in your area, and which of those communities you would like to feel part of, now begin to think about the skills that might have begun to disappear in your adopted or original community. Have some of the ways in which communities identify themselves and communicate amongst themselves been lost or taken? If so, how could they be taken back, and would this help to grow new senses of community in your locality? Thinking around a local urgency, such as the need to reclaim a space for building senses of community, can help you to identify some of the specific needs of your neighbourhood that may not be a priority for local councils or business. Think also of the kinds of skills that might be needed in order for positive change to happen. Are there historical, locally specific skills (or songs, or stories) that can be shared, developed or revived? What about traditions of making, crafting, cooking, growing, singing, dancing or playing? Perhaps you have skills from your original community that could be shared, developed or revived in your new location?

3) What needs to change in your local area or community?

Is there something that you feel could make a change or a difference in your local community? In the spirit of Useful Art, think about issues of inequality, lack of understanding, lack of provision or connection, not enough places to meet, not enough places for children to play safely. Have libraries or community centres closed down? Is there access to green space? Are there places to grow food or to learn how to grow food, share skills, learn how to cook? Exchange ideas about healthier living? Perhaps there is a lack of community care for older people, or a problem with loneliness. What is there for local people to learn or create or do beyond the skills that are needed for gaining employment within the condition of neoliberal occupation?

4) How could you use Useful Art to help make these changes?

Finally, take another look at what is there already around you – are there community resources available? These could be any scale or any type – you're not only thinking of financial or physical resources, either. It's just as important to have a think about care and emotional support as much as food welfare or adult education. This is also the part of the exercise where, if you haven't already, you can begin to join some of the earlier thoughts, ideas and observations that have cropped up while you are mapping or drawing your local community. Identify the local knowledge and skills that need to be preserved and passed on, and find other people to form a group with whom to instigate a project. Speak to neighbours, organise a meeting, look together on-line at examples of how other communities are using Useful Art as a tool for social change. Could you connect with others to form hubs of Useful Art – places for learning and sharing craft, for remaking and recycling, for education, gardening, cooking and so on? Perhaps you could find a way to exchange skills or services – swapping things in kind and avoiding financial transactions. Maybe you could help to extend knowledge of connected, useful things that are already happening but quietly, by setting up a website or helping a group or community with their social media. There are many examples to be found on-line of communities that have initiated local change of different kinds, if you want to look beyond the examples in this book for ideas and inspiration. When you're up and running, think about connecting with existing local and community initiatives, locally or on-line, to form wider networks of Useful Art and to help inspire others.

To go back to the Van Abbemuseum and the 'Soils' launch for a final visit, I would like to leave you with the words of the instigator and activist Valiana Aguilar, who spoke on behalf of Yucatán farmers' collective Suumil Móokt'aan. She expressed a sentiment that all activists and activators of Useful Art will support, from the Yucatán Peninsula to my favourite bakery in Anfield. Speaking about the need for revolution, the deep need for change at a local level to resist global neoliberal occupation, she gave us a timely reminder that the struggle will be worth it in the end. Summarising this resistance through preserving tradition, through making with care, through educating others and through growing, cooking and sharing food, she made an excellent point:

'The revolution will be delicious.'[2]

Postscript

It's Sunday 19 May 2024, and I'm waiting in a queue at Home-baked in Anfield again. The occasion is the last match of the 2023/24 Premier League season and, also, the final match over which the much-loved manager Jürgen Klopp will preside. It's a sunny day and a good-natured and celebratory atmosphere is punctuated by laughter and singing. We're in the presence of many film crews from around the world, all of whom are trawling like whales through plankton for appropriate TV and social media vox pops.

As I near the counter, I am thinking of Useful Art, 1:1 Scale Practice, social re-empowerment, community, micro-activism and, if I'm honest, how I might finish this book. I also notice that there are wildflower seed bombs on sale. Proceeds go to the National Wildflower Trust (set up in Liverpool), which ask purchasers to promise that they will spread flower seeds wherever there might be disused, overlooked or unattended soil. I buy a packet with my coffee and pie. As I do so, I hope that anybody who reads this book might decide to sow the wildflower seeds I have offered here. Instead of simply representing another chess piece in the 200-year battle over what is or is not art, I hope

Postscript

this book helps you see Useful Art, at least partially, as a set of possibilities and toolkits that might enable us to reach beyond and through our current social conditions and confines. If this is so, it also means that, as time goes on, we may need to rethink the potential of what art might be or become as a tool for community activism – and, also, to participate within this change as activist artists ourselves. But that's perhaps the next step of the journey – if, of course, you'd like to join in.

Notes

Introduction

1 'Homebaked Community Land Trust', www.homebaked.org.uk (accessed 9 August 2024).
2 Ibid.
3 Ibid.
4 Ibid.
5 Bruguera's project 'Immigrant Movement International' originated as a collaboration with the Queens Museum, New York in 2011.

Chapter 1

1 Claire Bishop, *Artificial Hells: Participatory Art and the Politics of Spectatorship* (London: Verso, 2012).
2 Morgan Quaintance, 'Teleology and the Turner Prize or, Utility, the New Conservatism', *e-flux Conversations* (2015). https://conversations.e-flux.com/t/teleology-and-the-turner-prize-or-utility-the-new-conservatism/2936 (accessed 23 July 2024).
3 Ibid.
4 Ibid.
5 Ibid.
6 Ibid.
7 Ibid.

Notes

8 Boris Groys, 'Self-Design and Aesthetic Responsibility', *e-Flux Journal* #07 (June 2009). www.e-flux.com/journal/07/61386/self-design-and-aesthetic-responsibility (accessed 23 July 2024).

9 Ibid.

10 Ibid.

11 There is no better historical overview of the contested term 'avant-garde' than that provided by Linda Nochlin, 'The Invention of the Avant-Garde: France, 1830–1880', in *The Politics of Vision: Essays on Nineteenth-Century Art and Society* (London: Thames & Hudson, 1991). Also, for an overview of the 'precariat' as a rising class see Guy Standing, *A Precariat Character: From Denizens to Citizens* (London: Bloomsbury Academic, 2014).

12 See for example, Shoshana Zuboff, *The Age of Surveillance Capitalism: The Fight for a Human Future at the New Frontier of Power* (London: Profile Books, 2019). Here, Zuboff argues that the excess information from every point and click we make, across all the digital-media platforms with which we personally interact, are being monetised and resold by companies, such as Google, as behavioural data which, in turn, inform machine intelligence to predict and pre-empt what our next online interests and options might be.

13 There are now an overwhelming number of research sources available on the subject of neoliberalism, which is partly my point here, but for a good 'foothold' on the subject see David Harvey, *A Brief History of Neoliberalism* (Oxford: Oxford University Press, 2005). Also David Harvey, *The Anti-Capitalist Chronicles*, eds Jordan T. Camp and Chris Caruso (London: Pluto Press, 2020). A good and popular sense of alternative to the monolith of neoliberalism is offered by Mark Fisher, *Capitalist Realism: Is There No Alternative?* (Winchester: O Books, 2009). Also, a sense of the ongoing urgency of some of these debates is also posthumously captured in the transcripts of Mark Fisher's previously unpublished lectures and manuscripts in Mark Fisher, *Postcapitalist Desire*, ed. Matt Colquhoun (London: Repeater, 2021).

14 There is no better encapsulation of the spirit of this era than that offered by Jon Savage, *England's Dreaming: The Sex Pistols and Punk Rock* (London: Faber, 2005). Thanks to the work of my long-term friend and colleague, my university, Liverpool John Moores, also holds the John Savage 'England's Dreaming' Archives, a collection of Savage's notes and ephemera from this era, collated mainly in his role as participant and music journalist – a journey through which offers a portal into a

Notes

world that offered do-it-yourself change and new forms of ground-up activism through punk.

15 I have to admit that I have based most of the 'history' of the next sections on my lived experience and memory, which offered both a context and political background to my growing involvement with the radical/activist potential of Useful Art. However, a series of three accessible, detailed and humorous books by Alwyn W. Turner that offer an insightful overview of this period from a largely UK perspective are: *Crisis? What Crisis? Britain in the 1970s* (London: Aurum, 2009); *Rejoice! Rejoice! Britain in the 1980s* (London: Aurum, 2010) and *A Classless Society: Britain in the 1990s* (London: Aurum, 2014).

16 See for example Stephen Rousseas, *The Political Economy of Reaganomics: A Critique* (London: Routledge, 2018).

17 See Edward J. Nell, *Free Market Conservatism: A Critique of Theory and Practice*, 1st ed. (Abingdon: Routledge, 2010), doi:10.4324/9780203858257

18 See for example Andy McSmith, *No Such Thing as Society* (London: Constable, 2010).

19 Mark Crispin Miller, *Cruel and Unusual: Bush/Cheney's New World Order* (New York: W. W. Norton, 2004).

20 See Gerard Goggin and Mark J. McLelland, *The Routledge Companion to Global Internet Histories* (New York: Routledge, 2017). For a good overview see also Brian McCullough, *How the Internet Happened: from Netscape to the iPhone* (New York: Liveright Publishing, 2018).

21 Francis Fukuyama, 'The End of History?', *National Interest* 16 (1989), pp. 3–18. www.jstor.org/stable/24027184 (accessed 4 July 2025). See also Francis Fukuyama, *The End of History and the Last Man* (London: Hamish Hamilton, 1992).

22 2 Hans Belting, 'Contemporary Art as Global Art: A Critical Estimate', in Hans Belting and Andrea Buddeseig (eds), *Contemporary Art and the Museum: A Global Perspective* (Ostfildern: Hatje Kantz, 2007), p. 2.

23 Julian Stallabrass, *Art Incorporated: The Story of Contemporary Art* (Oxford: Oxford University Press, 2004).

24 John Harris, *The Last Party* (London: Harper Perennial, 2010).

25 Nityanand Deckha, 'Britspace™? The Cool Britannia Effect and the Emergence of the Creative Quarter', *M/C journal* 5:2 (2002), https://doi.org/10.5204/mcj.1957

26 Chris Smith, *Creative Industries Mapping Documents 2001 – Introduction* (GOV.UK, 2001).

27 Harris, *Last Party*.

28 Sylvère Lortinger and Christian Marazzi (eds), *Autonomia: Post-Political Politics* (Los Angeles: SEMIOTEXT(E), 2007). See also Michael Hardt and Paulo Vrino, *Radical Thought in Italy: A Potential Politics: 7 (Theory Out of Bounds)* (Minneapolis: University of Minnesota Press, 1996).

29 Brian Holmes, 'Artistic Autonomy and the Communication Society', *Third Text* 18:6 (2004), 547–55, 552, https://doi.org/10.1080/0952882042000284952

30 Groys, 'Self-Design and Aesthetic Responsibility'.

31 Liam Gillick, 'The Good of Work', *e-Flux Journal* 16 (May 2010).

32 See Luc Boltanski and Eve Chiapello, *The New Spirit of Capitalism* (London: Verso, 2005).

33 Dave Beech, *Art and Postcapitalism: Aesthetic Labour, Automation and Value Production* (London: Pluto Press, 2019).

34 Tom Hayden (ed.), *The Zapatista Reader* (New York: Thunder's Monthly Press/National Books, 2002). See also Gloria Muñoz Ramírez, *The Fire and the Word: A History of the Zapatista Movement* (San Francisco: City Lights Books, 2008). See also Thomas Nail, *Returning to Revolution: Deleuze, Guattari and Zapatismo* (Edinburgh: Edinburgh University Press, 2015).

35 Subcomandante Marcos, 'The Fourth World War', *In Motion Magazine* (11 November 2001 (1999)). www.inmotionmagazine.com/auto/fourth.html (accessed 3 July 2025).

36 The G7 is an international governmental and political forum made up of the largest and most advanced IMF countries: the US, the UK, France, Germany, Italy, Japan and Canada. It was originally set up in 1973 in response to the decoupling of the dollar from the Gold Standard. The G20 was founded in 1999 in response to several world economic crises and consists of nineteen countries plus the European Union.

37 Marc James Léger, *Vanguardia: Socially Engaged Art and Theory* (Manchester: Manchester University Press, 2019). See also Marc James Léger, *Brave New Avant Garde: Essays on Contemporary Art and Politics* (Winchester: Zero, 2012).

38 John Byrne, 'The Yes Men: Art and the Culture of Corporate Capital', in Astria Suparak (ed.), *Keep It Slick: Infiltrating Capitalism with the Yes Men* (Pittsburgh, PA: Miller Gallery at Carnegie Mellon University, 2009), pp. 19–22. www.internationaleonline.org/contributions/brexit-new-nationalism-and-the-new-politics-of-migrancy (accessed 26 June 2025).

Notes

39 Bishop, *Artificial Hells*.

40 Brian Holmes, 'Escape the Overcode: Activist Art in the Control Society' (Amsterdam: Stedelijk Van Abbemuseum, 2009).

Chapter 2

1 Social growing is a term used by Tŷ Pawb to encourage a range of activities, based around community gardening, aimed at improving mental health and well-being and developing stronger social bonds between various local communities.

2 The Association of Arte Útil is an international initiative, instigated by the artist Tania Bruguera, which seeks to link up forms of activism and Useful Art across the globe. Tŷ Pawb hosts a branch of the association in its Useful Art Space. The online presence for the Association of Arte Útil can be found at www.arte-util.org (accessed 4 July 2025).

3 Private email correspondence with Jo Marsh, 27 July 2023.

4 Stephen Wright, *Toward a Lexicon of Usership*, eds Nick Aikens and Stephen Wright (The Hague: Van Abbemuseum, 2013), 3. www.museumarteutil.net (accessed 4 July 2025).

5 Ibid.

6 Ibid.

7 Subcomandante Marcos, 'The Fourth World War Has Begun', *Le Monde diplomatique* (1997). www.mondediplo.com/1997/09/marcos (accessed 4 July 2025).

8 Ibid.

9 Ibid. 4.

10 Alan Kaprow, 'The Real Experiment (1983)', in Jeff Kelly (ed.), *Essays on the Blurring of Art and Life* (London: University of California Press, 2003).

11 Stephen Wright, 'An Art Without Qualities: Raivo Puusemp's "Beyond Art – Dissolution of Rosendale, N.Y."', *n.e.w.s.* (9 November 2013; original emphasis. www. northeastwestsouth.net/art-without-qualities-raivo-puusemps-beyond-art-dissolution-rosendale-ny (accessed 29 July 2025).

12 Martin Heidegger, 'The Age of the World Picture', in *The Question Concerning Technology and Other Essays*, trans. William Lovitt (London: Harper & Row, 1977).

Notes

13 Jean Baudrillard, *Simulacra and Simulation*, trans. S. F. Glaser (Ann Arbor: University of Michigan Press, 1994).

14 For an excellent overview on how forms of participatory practice began to emerge from a hybridisation of public art and community art see Miwon Kwon, *One Place after Another: Site-Specific Art and Locational Identity* (Cambridge, MA: MIT Press, 2002).

15 Sharon Irish and Suzanne Lacy, *Suzanne Lacy: Spaces Between*, 1st ed. (Minneapolis: University of Minnesota Press, 2010).

16 Vivien Green Fryd, 'Suzanne Lacy's Three Weeks in May: Feminist Activist Performance Art as "Expanded Public Pedagogy"', *NWSA Journal* 19:1(2007), 23–38.

17 Suzanne Lacy, 'The Oakland Projects (1991–2001)', no. 29/07/2024. www.suzannelacy.com/the-oakland-projects (accessed 3 July 2025).

18 Ibid.

19 Nicholas Gamso, 'Revisiting Suzanne Lacy's Oakland Projects', *PAJ: A Journal of Performance and Art* 42:3 (126) (2020), 76–81, https:// doi.org/10.1162/pajj_a_00524

20 These included the development of the stand-alone website www.theoaklandprojects.wordpress.com (accessed 4 July 2025).

21 Jeanne van Heeswijck, 'Radicalising the Local/Jeanne Heeswijck Interviewed by Kotryna Valiukevičiūtė', (2013), www.leidiniu.archfondas.lt/ en/alf-03/interviews/jeanne-van-heeswijk (accessed 29 July 2024).

22 Zara Stanhope, 'The Challenge of Uninvited Guests: Social Art at the Blue House', *Humanities Research* 19:2 (2013), 117–33. For another insight into Heeswijck's working methods see also Jeanne van Heeswijk, '5.5 Freehouse: Radicalizing the Local', in Miodrag Mitrašinović and Vikas Mehta (eds), *Public Space Reader* (London: Routledge, 2021), 250–64.

23 Adrian Anagnost, 'Theaster Gates' Social Formations', *Nonsite (Atlanta, Ga.)*, 24 (2018).

24 Ethan W. Lasser, 'Scaling up: Theaster Gates, Jr, and His Toolkit', *Journal of Modern Craft* 6:1 (2013), 79–86, https://doi.org/10.275 2/174967813X13535106841368

25 Kathleen Reinhardt, 'Theaster Gates's Dorchester Projects in Chicago', *Journal of Urban History* 41:2 (2014), 193–206.

26 Theaster Gates, 'How to Revive a Neighborhood: with Imagination, Beauty and Art', *TED* (2015), www.ted.com/talks/theaster_gates_ how_to_revive_a_neighborhood_with_imagination_beauty_and_ art?subtitle=en (accessed 4 July 2025).

Notes

27 See for example Roman Krznaric, *The Good Ancestor: How to Think Long Term in a Short-Term World* (London: W. H. Allen, 2021).

28 Permaculture is a term derived from the sustainable growing of plants and animals. As such, permaculture refers to ways of working with, rather than against, nature and is often also used as a term to denote long-term, thoughtful and open-ended or generative processes of solution-seeking. Because of this, permaculture it is also often contrasted to short-term or means–end solutions which are often sought in isolation to their broader social, political and ecological contexts

29 'Wicked Problems' is a design term first coined by design theorist Horst Rittel, who was Professor of Design Methodology at the Ulm School of Design, Germany. In his article 'Dilemmas in a General Theory of Planning', Rittel describes Wicked Problems which are made up by so many interdependent factors they seem impossible to solve. Because of this, Wicked Problems require solutions based on a deep understanding of the stakeholders involved and also need innovative approaches that can be provided by design thinking. W. J. Rittel Horst and Melvin M. Webber, 'Dilemmas in a General Theory of Planning', *Policy Sciences* 4:2 (1973), 155–69, https://doi.org/10.1007/BF01405730

30 'Tŷ Pawb – Welcome to Lle Celf Ddefnyddiol/ the Useful Art Space', 2023. www.typawb.wales/usefulartspace (accessed 30 July 2024).

Chapter 3

1 The Autonomy Project was itself organised around a series of summer schools, which took place at the Van Abbemuseum, the Dutch Art Institute and Liverpool John Moores School of Art and Design in 2010, 2011 and 2012, respectively. The aim of these was to bring together postgraduate, PhD and early-career artists who were interested in developing and contesting ideas around autonomy from their perspective.

2 Sven Lütticken, *Art and Autonomy: A Critical Reader* (London: Afterall, 2022).

3 For example, 'The Autonomy Project' also contributed to some of the key questions that underpinned the development of a further project with L'Internationale Consortium of Museums and Galleries' 'The

Notes

Uses of Art: The Legacy of 1848 and 1989', which was subsequently launched in 2013.

4 WochenKlausur is an activist art collective founded in 1993. The name can be translated as 'weeks of closure' or, rather, 'enclosure'. WochenKlausur's working methodology is to develop concrete proposals that are intended to provide small but effective improvements to sociopolitical problems.

5 The fifty or so students who were involved in this project were from Taipei National University of the Arts and National Taiwan Normal University. The project initially began in 2010 when the students' new teacher, photographer Yao Jui-Chung, asked them what they would like to work on during the semester. Rather than making individual projects, the students, across two universities, asked to make a documentation of the 'mosquito halls'. Using film, photography and written accounts, the group's joint investigation resulted in the production of three publications which were intended to act as irrefutable evidence of government neglect and oversight.

6 For Boal, 'transverse democracy' lies somewhere between contemporary delegate democracy and direct democracy (as practised in ancient Greece).

7 Debt Collective's rolling Debt Abolition Page, and details of how the funds have been distributed to date across a number of Debt Abolition projects, can be found at www.debtcollective.org/what-we-do/debt-abolition (accessed 4 July 2025).

8 Or the 'Asociación de Arte Útil', to give it its Spanish title. The online Asociación de Arte Útil can be found at www.arte-util.org

9 The 'Arte Útil Summit 2016' took place at Middlesbrough Institute of Modern Art from 22 to 25 July 2016. See http://www.arte-util.org/studies/arte-util-summit-2016/ (accessed 30 July 2024).

10 Alessandra Saviotti and Gemma Medina Estupiñán, 'Usological Turn in Archiving, Curating and Educating: The Case of Arte Útil' (paper presented at the Arts, 2022). See also John Byrne and Alessandra Saviotti, 'Hacking Education: Arte Útil as an Educational Methodology to Foster Change in Curriculum Planning', *Art & the public sphere* 11:1 (2022), 99–114, https://doi.org/10.1386/aps_00072_1

11 Stephen Wright, *Toward a Lexicon of Usership*, eds Nick Aikens and Stephen Wright (The Hague: Van Abbemuseum, 2013). www.museumarteutil.net (accessed 4 July 2025).

12 Ibid. 39–41.

Notes

13 Ibid. 39–40.

14 Ibid.

15 Ibid. 41.

16 In 2012 L'Internationale Consortium of museums and galleries consisted of Moderna Galerija Ljubljana, Slovenia; the Museo Nacional Centro de Arte Reina Sofia, Madrid, Spain; the Museu d'art Contemporani de Barcelona, Barcelona, Spain; the Museum van Hedendgaagse Kunst Antwerpen, Antwerp, Belgium; SALT, Istanbul and Ankara, Turkey and the Van Abbemuseum Eindhoven, the Netherlands.

17 John Byrne, 'Migrancy', in *The Glossary of Common Knowledge Online* (2015). https://glossary.mg-lj.si/referential-fields/geopolitics/migrancy (accessed 31 July 2024).

18 John Byrne, 'Brexit, New Nationalism and the New Politics of Migrancy', *L'Internationale Online* (2017). www.internationaleonline.org/contributions/brexit-new-nationalism-and-the-new-politics-of-migrancy (accessed 31 July 2024).

19 John Byrne et al., *The Constituent Museum: Constellations of Knowledge, Politics and Mediation: A Generator of Social Change* (Amsterdam: Valiz, 2018).

20 'The Constituent Museum: Collecting Relations and the Transformational Potential of Arte Útil , 2018 to the Present', 2019. www.outset.org.uk/supported-projects/the-constituent-museum-collecting-relations-and-the-transformational-potential-of-arte-util/#:~:text=The%20Constituent%20Museum%20is%20a,%3A%20Collecting%3A%20the%20collection%20dematerialises (accessed 31 July 2024).

21 While Alistair Hudson stepped down from his role as director of the University of Manchester's Whitworth Art Gallery and Manchester Art Gallery at the end of 2022, the Whitworth stated a desire to continue with the overall ethos of a Useful and Constituent Museum. In 2022 Hudson was appointed artistic-scientific chairman of the Centre for Art and Media Karlsruhe (ZKM) in Baden-Württemberg, south-west Germany, where he also continues to develop ideas around Arte Útil, the Useful Museum and Constituent Museum practice.

22 Alistair Hudson, 'Post-Exhibitionary' (2022), https://glossary.mg-lj.si/referential-fields/constituencies-II/post-exhibitionary (accessed 31 July 2024).

23 Ibid.

Notes

Chapter 4

1 'Grizedale Arts – What We Do', Grizedale Arts, www.grizedale.org/about (accessed 31 July 2024).

2 *Grizedale Arts – Adding Complexity to Confusion*, ed. Jonathan Griffin (Lowick Green: Grizedale Books, 2009.

3 The Yangjiang Group is a Chinese collective founded in Guangdong Province in 2002. They are known for their multimedia and multidisciplinary approach to making collaborative artworks that seek to blur the boundaries between activism, social practice and art. For the Colosseum of the Consumed, the Yangjiang Group collaborated with Grizedale Arts to develop a public programme of events which combined installation, retail, public discussion and food-related performance.

4 Franco Berardi ('Bifo'), 'What is the Meaning of Autonomy Today?', *Transversal Texts* (2023). www.transversal.at/transversal/1203/berardi-aka-bifo/en (accessed 31 October 2024).

5 Ibid.

6 Ibid.

7 Ibid.

8 Ibid.

9 Franco Berardi ('Bifo'), *After the Future*, eds Gary Genosko and Nicholas Thoburn (Edinburgh: AK Press, 2011), 113–12.

10 Fredric Jameson, *Representing Capital: A Reading of Volume One* (London: Verso, 2011).

11 Ibid.19–20.

12 Jacques Rancière, 'Afterword/The Method of Equality: An Answer to Some Questions', in Gabriel Rockhill and Philip Watts (eds), *Jacques Rancière: History, Politics, Aesthetics* (Durham, NC: Duke University Press, 2009), pp. 273–88.

13 Ibid.

14 Ibid. 275.

15 Ibid.; original emphasis.

16 Ibid.

17 Ibid. 276.

18 Ibid. 277; original emphasis.

19 Ibid.

20 Jacques Rancière, 'Good Times or Pleasure at the Barriers', in Adrian Rifkin and Roger Thomas (eds), *Voices of the People: The Politics and*

Notes

Live of 'La Sociale' at the End of the Second Empire (London: Routledge & Kegan Paul, 1988), 50.

21 Franco Berardi, *The Uprising: On Poetry and Finance*, Sémiotext(e) intervention series; 14 (Los Angeles, CA: Sémiotexte, 2012).

22 Ibid. 63.

23 George Yúdice, 'Static Gallery's Architecture of Flows as Extradisciplinary Investigation', in Nick Aikens, Thomas Lange and Jorinde Seijdel (eds), *What's the Use? Constellations of Art, History, and Knowledge: A Critical Reader* (Amsterdam: Valiz, 2016), 266–84.

24 Néstor García Canclini, *Art Beyond Itself: Anthropology for a Society without a Story Line* (Durham, NC: Duke University Press, 2014).

25 Ibid. 280–1.

26 Ibid. See also Brian Holmes, 'Extradisciplinary Investigations: Towards a Critique of New Institutions' (2007), www.transversal.at/transversal/0106/holmes/en (accessed 31 July 2024).

27 Ibid. 271; my emphasis and insertion.

28 Ibid. 283.

29 Ibid. 271.

30 Ibid. 267.

31 Yúdice, 'Static Gallery's Architecture of Flows as Extradisciplinary Investigation'.

Chapter 5

1 'iNSTAR', www.instar.org/menu.php?t=1&m=m1&path=pag/instituto/instar-origen-en.html (accessed 31 July 2024).

2 'Documenta fifteen', 2022, www.documenta-fifteen.de/en (accessed 31 July 2024). Documenta, which takes place every five years in the German city of Kassel, is something I always describe as the World Cup of Contemporary Art. Usually, it's a curated exhibition of artworks and installations held across a number of established, pop-up and repurposed venues in the city of Kassel itself. However, for Documenta fifteen, a range of process-based artworks and initiatives by both individual artists and artist collectives was spread across a series of venues that included the Fridericianum (Kassel's largest museum and one of the oldest in Europe), disused factories, abandoned warehouses, vacant shops, repurposed hotels and marquees.

Notes

3 For a good explanation of the work of Tretyakov and its contemporary legacy see Soo Hwan Kim, 'Sergi Tretyakov Revisited: The Cases of Walter Benjamin and Hito Steyerl', *e-Flux*, 103 (2019). https://www.e-flux.com/journal/104/298121/sergei-tretyakov-revisited-the-cases-of-walter-benjamin-and-hito-steyerl (accessed 4 July 2025).

4 'AAU Documenta fifteen' (2022), https://documenta-fifteen.de/en/ (accessed 31 July 2024). The panel included: Nick Aikens (then a lead curator at Van Abbemuseum); Muhannad Al Ulaby (Syrian filmmaker and visual artist); Tania Bruguera (artivist and instigator of INSTAR and the Association of Arte Útil); Fernando García Dory (artist, cheesemaker, shepherd and instigator of the collaborative agency INLAND); Annie Fletcher (Director of the Irish Institute of Modern Art) and Stephen Wright (writer, cultural activist and Professor at the European School of Visual Arts).

5 '#iNSTAR @ documenta: Is There Such a Thing as a "Usological Turn"?', YouTube, 2022, www.youtube.com/watch?v=CPXg13RGHVs (accessed 31 July 2024).

6 Ibid.

7 '#iNSTAR @ documenta: Towards an Archeology of Arte Útil', YouTube, 2022, www.youtube.com/watch?v=Ase5kRz1tQk&t=190s (accessed 31 July 2024).

8 For example, as we saw in Chapter 4, the Italian philosopher and activist Franco Berardi has argued that, in an increasingly digital and networked economy, the labourer has become fractalised – an ever 'interchangeable producer of micro-fragments'.

9 For the young among us the established economy of the music industry was shaken some quarter of a century ago when open-source peer-to-peer – P2P – protocols, such as Napster, briefly allowed for free file sharing across the internet.

10 Dominique Lucien Garadudel et al. (eds), *The Collective Eye: In Conversation with ruangrupa – Thoughts on Collective Practice* (Berlin: DISTANZ, 2022), 16.

11 A. K. Kaiza, *Documenta Fifteen Handbook: English* (Berlin: Hatje Cantz, 2022).

12 Ibid.

13 'Gudskul – Studies on Contemporary Art and Collective Ecosystem', https://gudskul.art/en/collective-study-and-contemporary-art-ecosystem (accessed 2 July 2025).

14 'lumbung.space' (2022), www.lumbung.space (accessed 1 July 2024).

Notes

15 'Ferral Trade' (2023) (accessed 1 July 2024).

16 Anthony Downey and Els Roelandt, *Critique in Practice: Renzo Martens' Episode III (Enjoy Poverty)* (Berlin: Sternberg Press, 2019).

17 'The Institute of Human Activities', www.humanactivities.org/en (accessed 1 August 2024).

18 In English, the CATPC is translated as the 'Congolese Plantation Workers' Art League'. See 'CATPC – Cercle d'Art des Travailleurs de Plantation Congolaise', www.catpc.org/home (accessed 1 August 2024).

19 Renzo Martens, 'CATPC in Conversation with Renzo Martens', in Eva Barois De Caevel and Els Roelandt (eds), *CATPC Congolese Plantation Workers Art League* (Berlin: Sternberg Press, 2017), 164.

20 'IHA – Balot Videos', Institute of Human Activities, www.humanactivities.org/en/balot-videos (accessed 1 August 2024).

21 Pende historian Gize Sikitele, art historian Zoë Strother, writer and academic Ariella Aïsha Azoulay and writer and academic Simon Gikandi.

22 'IHA – Balot Videos', Video 4, 'The Museum'.

23 Jonas Staal, 'Works by Democratic Self-Administration of Rojava and Studio Jonas Staal: New World Summit Rojava (2015–2017)', in Daphne Büllesbach, Marta Cillero and Lukas Stolz (eds), *Shifting Baselines of Europe* (Bielefeld: Transcript, 2017), 193–9.

24 Maria Hlalvajova and Simon Sheikh, 'World Making as Commitment – Jonas Staal in Conversation with Maria Hlalvajova', in *Former West: Art and the Contemporary after 1989* (Cambridge, MA: MIT Press, 2017), 674–5.

25 Abdullah Öcalan, *War and Peace in Kurdistan: Perspectives for a Political Solution to the Kurdish Question* (Cologne: International Initiative, 2009), 39–40. www.freedom-for-ocalan.com (accessed 3 July 2025).

26 'The Museum as Parliament' is a collaboration between Jonas Staal, the 'New World Summit' organisation, the Democratic Federation of North-Syria, the Kurdish Cultural Foundation and the Van Abbemuseum, Eindhoven.

27 The María Lugones Decolonial Summer School is organised as a collaboration between University College Utrecht, Utrecht Summer School and Duke University.

28 See for example Simon Tormey, *The End of Representative Politics* (Cambridge: Polity Press, 2015).

29 At the time of writing same same-sex relationships are not recognised by the government of Japan.

Notes

30 The key elements to this project were: Utilise, Exchange, Generate, Harvest, Freedom of Expression, Equality and Critical Thinking.

31 'YCAM GURUGURU Radio', initiated by Keina Konno, co-curator of the project and also a member of the YCAM Education Team.

32 Personal email correspondence with Barto Bartolomeus, 8 August 2024.

Conclusion

1 The Soils exhibition marks the second of three iterations. The first was hosted in Australia, at the Tarawara Museum of Art in 2023, and the final iteration will take place in Yogyakarta, Indonesia in 2025. The title of the exhibition derives from the Palestinian mathematician, writer and radical educator Muni Fasheh's concept of four soils – earth soil, cultural soil, communal soil and affection-spiritual soil - which, he argues, we must nurture if we are to support life on our planet. See Teresa Cos Rebollo et al., *Soils* (Eindhoven: Van Abbemuseum, 2024), chrome-extension://efaidnbmnnnibpcajpcglclefindmkaj/https://internationaleonline.org/site/assets/files/73515/25756_clphn238_soils_catalogue_final_en_sp_smaller.pdf (accessed 29 July 2025).

2 Ibid.

Bibliography

'AAU Documenta fifteen' (2022), https://documenta-fifteen.de/en (accessed 31 July 2024).

Anagnost, Adrian. 'Theaster Gates' Social Formations.' *Nonsite (Atlanta, Ga.)* 24 (2018).

Baudrillard, Jean. *Simulacra and Simulation*, trans. S. F. Glaser. Ann Arbor: University of Michigan Press, 1994.

Beech, Dave. *Art and Postcapitalism: Aesthetic Labour, Automation and Value Production*. London: Pluto Press, 2019.

Belting, Hans. 'Contemporary Art as Global Art: A Critical Estimate.' In Hans Belting and Andrea Buddensieg (eds), *The Global Art World*. Stuttgart: Hatje Cantz, 2009, 38–73.

Berardi, Franco ('Bifo'). *After the Future*. Eds Gary Genosko and Nicholas Thoburn. Edinburgh: AK Press, 2011.

Berardi, Franco ('Bifo'). *The Uprising: On Poetry and Finance*. Semiotext(E) Intervention Series; 14. Los Angeles, CA: Semiotext(e), 2012.

Berardi, Franco ('Bifo'). 'What Is the Meaning of Autonomy Today?' *Transversal Texts*. (2023). www.transversal.at/transversal/1203/berardi-aka-bifo/en (accessed 31 October 2024).

Bishop, Claire. *Artificial Hells: Participatory Art and the Politics of Spectatorship*. London: Verso, 2012.

Boltanski, Luc and Eve Chiapello. *The New Spirit of Capitalism*. London: Verso, 2005.

Bookchin, Murray. 'The Meaning of Confederalism.' In Renée In der Maur and Jonas Staal (eds), *New World Academy Reader #5: Stateless Democracy*. Utrecht: BAK, 2015. www.jonasstaal.nl/site/assets/files/1180/nwa5_stateless_democracy.pdf (accessed 26 June 2025).

Bibliography

Burton, Johanna, Shannon Jackson and Dominic Willsdon. *Public Servants: Art and the Crisis of the Common Good*. Cambridge, MA: MIT Press, 2016.

Byrne, John. 'Migrancy.' *The Glossary of Common Knowledge Online* (2015). https://glossary.mg-lj.si/referential-fields/geopolitics/migrancy (accessed 31 July 2024).

———. Elinor Morgan, November Paynter, Aida Sánchez de Serdio Martín and Adela Železnik. *The Constituent Museum: Constellations of Knowledge, Politics and Mediation: A Generator of Social Change*. Amsterdam: Valiz, 2018.

———. 'Brexit, New Nationalism and the New Politics of Migrancy.' *L'Internationale Online* (2017). https://archive-2014-2024.internationaleonline. org/research/alter_institutionality/85_brexit_new_nationalism_and_ the_new_politics_of_migrancy (accessed 31 July 2024).

———. 'The Yes Men: Art and the Culture of Corporate Capital.' In Astria Suparak (ed.), *Keep It Slick: Infiltrating Capitalism with the Yes Men*. Chicago, IL: Carnegie Mellon University, 19–22.

www.internationaleonline.org/contributions/brexit-new-nationalism-and-the-new-politics-of-migrancy (accessed 26 June 2025).

———. and Alessandra Saviotti. 'Hacking Education: Arte Útil as an Educational Methodology to Foster Change in Curriculum Planning.' *Art & the public sphere* 11:1 (2022): 99–114. https://doi.org/10.1386/aps_00072_1

'CATPC - Cercle D'art Des Travailleurs De Plantation Congolaise.' www. catpc.org/home (accessed 1 August 2024).

'Decentralising Political Economies.' 2021. www.dpe.tools (accessed 9 August 2024).

Deckha, Nityanand. 'Britspace™?: The Cool Britannia Effect and the Emergence of the Creative Quarter.' *M/C journal* 5:2 (2002). https://doi.org/10.5204/mcj.1957.

'Documenta Fifteen.' 2022. www.documenta-fifteen.de/en (accessed 31 July 2024).

Downey, Anthony and Els Roelandt. *Critique in Practice: Renzo Martens' Episode III (Enjoy Poverty)*. Berlin: Sternberg Press, 2019.

'Ferral Trade.' 2023. https://feraltrade.org (accessed 1 July 2024).

Fisher, Mark. *Capitalist Realism: Is There No Alternative?* Winchester: O Books, 2009.

———. *Postcapitalist Desire*. Ed. Matt Colquhoun. London: Repeater, 2021.

Fryd, Vivien Green. 'Suzanne Lacy's Three Weeks in May: Feminist Activist Performance Art As "Expanded Public Pedagogy".' *NWSA Journal* (2007): 23–38.

Bibliography

Fukuyama, Francis. 'The End of History?' *National Interest* 16 (1989): 3–18. www.jstor.org/stable/24027184 (accessed 7 August 2024).

———. *The End of History and the Last Man*. London: Hamish Hamilton, 1992.

Gamso, Nicholas. 'Revisiting Suzanne Lacy's Oakland Projects.' *PAJ: A Journal of Performance and Art* 42:3 (126) (2020): 76–81. https://doi.org/10.1162/pajj_a_00524

Garadudel, Dominique Lucien, Heinz-Norbert Jocks, Emma Nilsson and Matthias Kliefoth (eds). *The Collective Eye: In Conversation with ruangrupa – Thoughts on Collective Practice*. Berlin: DISTANZ, 2022.

García Canclini, Néstor. *Art Beyond Itself: Anthropology for a Society without a Story Line*. Durham, NC: Duke University Press, 2014.

Gates, Theaster. 'How to Revive a Neighborhood: With Imagination, Beauty and Art.' *TED* (2015). www.ted.com/talks/theaster_gates_how_to_revive_a_neighborhood_with_imagination_beauty_and_art? (accessed 29 July 2004).

Gibson-Graham, J. K., Jenny Cameron and Stephen Healy. *Take Back the Economy: An Ethical Guide for Transforming Our Communities*. 1st ed. Minneapolis: University of Minnesota Press, 2013.

Gillick, Liam. 'The Good of Work.' *e-Flux Journal* 16 (May 2010). http://worker01.e-flux.com/pdf/article_142.pdf (accessed 16 July 2025).

Goggin, Gerard and Mark J. McLelland. *The Routledge Companion to Global Internet Histories*. New York: Routledge, 2017.

Green, Charles and Anthony Gardner. *Biennials, Triennials, and Documenta: The Exhibitions That Created Contemporary Art*. Chichester: Wiley Blackwell, 2016.

Grizedale Arts – Adding Complexity to Confusion, ed. Jonathan Griffin. Lowick Green: Grizedale Books, 2009.

'Grizedale Arts - What We Do.' Grizedale Arts. www.grizedale.org/about (accessed 31 July 2024).

Groys, Boris. 'Self-Design and Aesthetic Responsibility.' *e-Flux Journal* #07 (June 2009). www.e-flux.com/journal/07/61386/self-design-and-aesthetic-responsibility (accessed 23 July 2024).

'Gudskul – Studies on Contemporary Art and Collective Ecosystem.' https://gudskul.art/en/collective-study-and-contemporary-art-ecosystem (accessed 2 July 2025).

Hardt, M. and A. Negri. *Empire*. Cambridge, MA: Harvard University Press, 2000.

Hardt, Michael and Paulo Vrino. *Radical Thought in Italy: A Potential Politics: 7 (Theory Out of Bounds)*. Minneapolis: University of Minnesota Press, 1996.

Harris, John. *The Last Party*. London: Harper Perennial, 2010.

Bibliography

Harvey, David. *A Brief History of Neoliberalism*. Oxford: Oxford University Press, 2005.

——. *The Anti-Capitalist Chronicles*. Eds Jordan T. Camp and Chris Caruso. London: Pluto Press, 2020.

Hayden, Tom (ed.). *The Zapatista Reader*. New York: Thunder's Monthly Press/National Books, 2002.

Heidegger, Martin. 'The Age of the World Picture.' Trans. William Lovitt. In *The Question Concerning Technology and Other Essays*. London: Harper & Row, 1977, 115–54.

Hlalvajova, Maria and Simon Sheikh. 'World Making as Commitment – Jonas Staal in Conversation with Maria Hlalvajova.' In *Former West: Art and the Contemporary after 1989*. Cambridge, MA: MIT Press, 2017, 667–78.

Milena Hoegsberg and Cora Fisher (eds) *Living Labour*. Berlin: Sternberg Press, 2013.

Holmes, Brian. 'Artistic Autonomy and the Communication Society.' *Third Text* 18:6. (2004): 547–55. https://doi.org/10.1080/0952882042000284952

——. 'Escape the Overcode: Activist Art in the Control Society.' Amsterdam: Stedelijk Van Abbemuseum, 2009.

——. 'Extradisciplinary Investigations: Towards a Critique of New Institutions.' (2007). www.transversal.at/transversal/0106/holmes/en (accessed 31 July 2024).

'Homebaked Community Land Trust.' www.homebaked.org.uk (accessed 9 August 2024).

Horst, W. J. Rittel and Melvin M. Webber, 'Dilemmas in a General Theory of Planning', *Policy Sciences* 4:2 (1973), 155–69. https://doi.org/10.1007/BF01405730

Hudson, Alistair. 'Post-Exhibitionary.' (2022). https://glossary.mg-lj.si/referential-fields/constituencies-II/post-exhibitionary (accessed 31 July 2024).

'IHA - Balot Videos.' Institute of Human Activities. www.humanactivities.org/en/balot-videos (accessed 1 August 2024).

'instar.' www.instar.org/menu.php?t=1&m=m1&path=pag/instituto/instar-origen-en.html (accessed 31 July 2024).

'#instar @ Documenta: Is There Such a Thing as A "Usological Turn"?' YouTube, 2022. www.youtube.com/watch?v=CPXg13RGHVs (accessed 31 July 2024).

'#instar @ Documenta: Towards an Archeology of Arte Útil.' YouTube, 2022. www.youtube.com/watch?v=Ase5kRz1tQk&t=190s (accessed 31 July 2024).

Bibliography

Irish, Sharon and Suzanne Lacy. *Suzanne Lacy: Spaces Between*. 1st ed. Minneapolis: University of Minnesota Press, 2010.

Jackson, Shannon. *Back Stages: Essays across Art, Performance, and Public Life*. Evanston, IL: Northwestern University Press, 2022.

Jameson, Fredric. *Representing Capital: A Reading of Volume One*. London: Verso, 2011.

Kaiza, A. K. *Documenta Fifteen Handbook: English*. Berlin: Hatje Cantz, 2022.

Kaprow, Alan. 'The Real Experiment (1983).' In Jeff Kelly (ed.), *Essays on the Blurring of Art and Life*, 201–18. Oakland: University of California Press, 2003.

Kim, Soo Hwan. 'Sergi Tretyakov Revisited: The Cases of Walter Benjamin and Hito Steyerl.' *e-Flux* 103 (2019). www.e-flux.com/journal/104/298121/sergei-tretyakov-revisited-the-cases-of-walter-benjamin-and-hito-steyerl (accessed 24 July 2024).

Koch, Alexander. 'From Clay to Chocolate: Adding Feelings and Meanings to Resources.' In Eva Barois De Caevel and Els Roelandt (eds), *Catcp Congolese Plantation Workers Art League*. Berlin: Sternberg Press, 2017.

Krznaric, Roman. *The Good Ancestor: How to Think Long Term in a Short-Term World*. London: W. H. Allen, 2021.

Kwon, Miwon. *One Place after Another: Site-Specific Art and Locational Identity*. Cambridge, MA: MIT Press, 2002.

Lacy, Suzanne. 'The Oakland Projects (1991–2001).' No. 29/07/2024. www.suzannelacy.com/the-oakland-projects (accessed 3 July 2025).

Lasser, Ethan W. 'Scaling Up: Theaster Gates, Jr, and His Toolkit.' *Journal of Modern Craft* 6:1 (2013): 79–86. https://doi.org/10.2752/174967813X13535106841368

Léger, Marc James. *Brave New Avant Garde: Essays on Contemporary Art and Politics*. Winchester: Zero, 2012.

———. *Vanguardia: Socially Engaged Art and Theory*. Manchester: Manchester University Press, 2019.

Lortinger, Sylvère and Christian Marazzi (eds), *Autonomia: Post-Political Politics*. Los Angeles, CA: Semiotext(e), 2007.

'lumbung.Space.' 2022. www.lumbung.space (accessed 1 July 2024).

Lütticken, Sven. *Art and Autonomy: A Critical Reader*. London: Afterall, 2022.

Marcos, Subcomandante, 'The Fourth World War Has Begun.' *Le Monde diplomatique* (1997). www.mondediplo.com/1997/09/marcos (accessed 4 July 2025).

Bibliography

———. 'The Fourth World War.' *In Motion Magazine* (11 November 2001 (1999)). www.inmotionmagazine.com/auto/fourth.html (accessed 27 July 2024).

Martens, Renzo. 'CATPC in Conversation with Renzo Martens.' In Eva Barois De Caevel and Els Roelandt (eds), *CATPC – Congolese Plantation Workers Art League*. Berlin: Sternberg Press, 2017.

McCullough, Brian. *How the Internet Happened: From Netscape to the iphone.* New York: Liveright Publishing, 2018.

McSmith, Andy. *No Such Thing as Society.* London: Constable, 2010.

Miller, Mark Crispin. *Cruel and Unusual: Bush/Cheney's New World Order.* New York: W. W. Norton, 2004.

Muñoz Ramírez, Gloria. *The Fire and the Word: A History of the Zapatista Movement.* San Francisco: City Lights Books, 2008.

Nail, Thomas. *Returning to Revolution: Deleuze, Guattari and Zapatismo.* Edinburgh: Edinburgh University Press, 2015.

Nell, Edward J. *Free Market Conservatism: A Critique of Theory and Practice.* 1st ed. Abingdon: Routledge, 2010. doi:10.4324/9780203858257

Nochlin, Linda. 'The Invention of the Avant-Garde: France, 1830–1880.' In *The Politics of Vision: Essays on Nineteenth-Century Art and Society.* London: Thames & Hudson, 1991, 1–18.

Öcalan, Abdullah. *War and Peace in Kurdistan: Perspectives for a Political Solution to the Kurdish Question.* Cologne: International Initiative, 2009. www.freedom-for-ocalan.com (accessed 3 July 2025).

Öcalan, Abdullah. *The Political Thought of Abdullah Öcalan: Kurdistan, Women's Revolution and Democratic Confederalism.* London: Pluto Press, 2017.

Quaintance, Morgan. 'Teleology and the Turner Prize Or, Utility the New Conservatism.' *e-flux Conversations* (2015). https://conversations.e-flux.com/t/teleology-and-the-turner-prize-or-utility-the-new-conservatism/2936 (accessed 23 July 2024).

Raicovich, Laura. *Culture Strike: Art and Museums in an Age of Protest.* London: Verso, 2021.

Rancière, Jacques. 'Good Times or Pleasure at the Barriers.' In Adrian Rifkin and Roger Thomas (eds), *Voices of the People: The Politics and Live of 'La Sociale' at the End of the Second Empire.* London: Routledge & Kegan Paul, 1988, 45–94.

———. 'Afterword/The Method of Equality: An Answer to Some Questions.' In Gabriel Rockhill and Philip Watts (eds), *Jacques Rancière: History, Politics, Aesthetics.* Durham, NC: Duke University Press, 2009, 273–88.

Bibliography

Reinhardt, Kathleen. 'Theaster Gates's Dorchester Projects in Chicago.' *Journal of Urban History* 41:2 (2015): 193–206.

Rousseas, Stephen. *The Political Economy of Reaganomics: A Critique.* London: Routledge, 2018.

Savage, Jon. *England's Dreaming: The Sex Pistols and Punk Rock.* London: Faber, 2005.

Saviotti, Alessandra and Gemma Medina Estupiñán. 'Usological Turn in Archiving, Curating and Educating: The Case of Arte Útil.' Paper presented at the Arts, 2022.

Smith, Chris. *Creative Industries Mapping Documents 2001 – Introduction*: GOV. UK, 2001.

Stall, Jonas. 'Works by Democratic Self-Administration of Rojava and Studio Jonas Staal: New World Summit Rojava (2015–2017).' In Daphne Büllesbach, Marta Cillero and Lukas Stolz (eds), *Shifting Baselines of Europe.* Bielefeld: Transcript, 2017, 193–9.

Stallabrass, Julian. *Art Incorporated: The Story of Contemporary Art.* Oxford: Oxford University Press, 2004.

Standing, Guy. *A Precariat Character: From Denizens to Citizens.* London: Bloomsbury Academic, 2014.

Stanhope, Zara. 'The Challenge of Uninvited Guests: Social Art at the Blue House.' *Humanities Research* 19:2 (2013): 117–33.

'Tate Exchange.' 2016–21. www.tate.org.uk/tate-exchange (accessed 9 August 2024).

The Future Is Degrowth: A Guide to a World Beyond Capitalism. Eds Matthias Schmelzer, Andrea Vettera and Aaron Vansintjan. London: Verso, 2022.

'The Institute of Human Activities.' www.humanactivities.org/en (accessed 1 August 2024).

Tormey, Simon. *The End of Representative Politics.* Cambridge: Polity Press, 2015.

Turner, Alwyn W. *Crisis? What Crisis? Britain in the 1970s.* London: Aurum, 2009.

————. *Rejoice! Rejoice! Britain in the 1980s.* London: Aurum, 2010.

————. *A Classless Society: Britain in the 1990s.* London: Aurum, 2014.

'Tŷ Pawb – Welcome to Lle Celf Ddefnyddiol/the Useful Art Space.' 2023. www.typawb.wales/usefulartspace (accessed 30 July 2024).

van Heeswijk, Jeanne. '5.5 Freehouse: Radicalizing the Local.' In Miodrag Mitrasinovic and Vikas Mehta (eds), *Public Space Reader*, 250–64. London: Routledge, 2021, 250–64.

Bibliography

————. 'Radicalising the Local/Jeanne Heeswijck Interviewed By Kotryna Valiukevičiūtė.' 2013. www.leidiniu.archfondas.lt/en/alf–03/interviews/jeanne-van-heeswijk (accessed 29 July 2024).

Weiss, Rachel. *Making Art Global (Part 1): The Third Havana Biennial 1989.* London: Afterall in association with the Academy of Fine Arts Vienna and Van Abbemuseum, Eindhoven, 2011.

Work: Documents of Contemporary Art, ed. Friederike Sigler. Cambridge, MA: MIT Press, 2017.

Wright, Stephen. 'An Art Withhout Qualities: Raivo Puusemp's "Beyond Art – Dissolution of Rosendale, N.Y."' *n.e.w.s.* (9 November 2013). www.northeastwestsouth.net/art-without-qualities-raivo-puusemps-beyond-art-dissolution-rosendale-ny (accessed 29 July 2023).

————. *Toward a Lexicon of Usership.* Eds Nick Aikens and Stephen Wright. The Hague: Van Abbemuseum, 2013. www.museumarteutil.net.

Yúdice, George. *The Expediency of Culture: Uses of Culture in the Global Era.* Durham, NC: Duke University Press, 2003.

————. 'Static Gallery's Architecture of Flows as Extradisciplinary Investigation.' In Nick Aikens, Thomas Lange and Jorinde Seijdel (eds), *What's the Use? Constellations of Art, History, and Knowledge: A Critical Reader.* Amsterdam: Valiz, 2016, 266–84.

Zuboff, Shoshana. *The Age of Surveillance Capitalism: The Fight for a Human Future at the New Frontier of Power* (London: Profile Books, 2019).

Index

Index

Index

Index

EU authorised representative for GPSR:
Easy Access System Europe, Mustamäe tee 50,
10621 Tallinn, Estonia
gpsr.requests@easproject.com